EIGHTEENTH-CENTURY STUDIES

PRESENTED TO

ARTHUR M. WILSON

EIGHTEENTH CENTURY STUDIES

PRESENTED TO

ARTHUR M. WILSON

EDITED BY PETER GAY

THE UNIVERSITY PRESS OF NEW ENGLAND

HANOVER · NEW HAMPSHIRE

Frontispiece: ARTHUR M. WILSON
Photograph by Adrian N. Bouchard

Acknowledgment is made to
Jeanne M. Prosser and Jacqueline B. Sices
for their generous assistance in translating.
Special thanks are due
Mary T. Wilson for compiling
"The Writings of Arthur M. Wilson."

CONTENTS

Preface
John Sloan Dickey   vii
The Age of Personal Monarchy in England
Stephen B. Baxter   1
Polinière and the Teaching of
Experimental Physics at Paris: 1700–1730
Blake T. Hanna   13
The Role of England in Voltaire's Polemic against Pascal:
Apropos the Twenty-fifth *Philosophical Letter*
Roland Desné   41
Why Was the Enlightenment?
Peter Gay   59
Hume's Republic and the Universe of Newton
Richard Kuhns   73
Johnson and Foreign Visitors to London: Baretti and Others
James L. Clifford   97
Diderot and Legal Theories of Antiquity
Jacques Proust   117
The Crudeli Affair: Inquisition and Reason of State
Paolo Casini   131
"Sensibility," "Neoclassicism," or "Preromanticism?"
Roland Mortier   153
The Philosophes and Napoleon
Ernest John Knapton   165
The Writings of Arthur M. Wilson   187
Contributors   191
Index   193

PREFACE

IT NEEDS LITTLE SAYING THAT THE MAN IN WHOSE HONOR THIS VOL-
UME WAS CREATED IS EXTRAORDINARY BOTH IN ACADEMIC ACCOMPLISHMENT
AND IN HIS PERSON. SCHOLARS LIKE OTHER PROFESSIONALS ADMIRE A GREAT
PERFORMANCE AND LIKE OTHER MORTALS THEY USUALLY ARE GLAD FOR
THE PRESENCE OF A GOOD MAN AMONG THEM—SO LONG, THAT IS, AS THE
goodness is not oppressively conspicuous. On both counts Arthur Wilson
merits this remarkable tribute of his peers. I should also quickly add that I
use *peers* to include the host of former students whose debt to him is
acknowledged warmly by the several who have been privileged to help finance
this book. Much more should be said about Arthur's skill as a teacher, but
this is the point to say that without ever forgetting that a great teacher is
never just "one of the boys," Arthur Wilson, the teacher, never fails to treat
students as peers in the experience of learning. There are, of course, other
ways to win the plaudits of students but none, I think, is better calculated
to teach the student to become a learner.

Arthur has done about as well as any man does in giving that small but
capacious word *both* full scope in his life and career. He is proudly a product
of both Yankton College, South Dakota, and of Oxford, a combination that
presumably infused him with that extra measure of hybrid vigor he brings
to his work. Never one to lean too comfortably on the lazy side of leaving
well enough alone, he finished off his six earned degrees in 1933 with Harvard's Ph.D. He has taught in both high schools and universities; his professional credentials pass at a premium in both history and political science; he
is both one of our foremost scholars on the Enlightenment, a world-renowned
biographer of Diderot, and a college teacher who was not afraid of being
contemporary and relevant twenty years before those terms were debauched
in our groves by the passion of fashionableness.

For over a quarter of a century he was a pioneer in developing biog-
raphy as a humanistic department of the university world while at the same

time, from 1944 on, holding a joint appointment as professor of government. In 1946 we were partners in establishing and directing the Great Issues course at Dartmouth.

The story of Arthur Wilson's well-nigh forty years at Dartmouth is wonderfully reassuring to anyone who is willing to be disabused of the universality of such university "truths" as that there is something incompatible between being a fine teacher and a first-rate scholar, that committee service is mainly a justification for doing little else well, and perhaps above all that a distinguished academician cannot afford to be too much attached to an institution lest he be too little attached to his discipline. His example in these respects puts the entire academic community, as well as Dartmouth, in his debt beyond even the barest acknowledgment of these few words. Let it be quickly said, however, Arthur's work has not gone unnoticed. His writings twice, in 1938 and 1958, won him the Herbert Baxter Adams Prize of the American Historical Association. In 1953 he received the Modern Language Association's Oxford Award for his book, *Diderot: The Testing Years, 1713–1759.*

Finally, it is surely in order in this brief word of appreciation of the man and scholar to say that Arthur Wilson the scholar as well as Arthur the man is not single. Mazie Wilson is a historian in her own right as a student of human foodstuffs, and no less a judge than her husband will gladly testify that as collaborator and companion she truly knows her Diderot—as well as his *Diderot.*

On behalf of all who in so many ways are the beneficiaries of what the Wilsons are and do, I record abiding appreciation for the tribute this volume pays to Arthur Wilson, distinguished teacher-scholar and a gentleman in any realm, in any season.

John Sloan Dickey

EIGHTEENTH-CENTURY STUDIES

PRESENTED TO

ARTHUR M. WILSON

THE AGE OF PERSONAL
MONARCHY IN ENGLAND

BY STEPHEN B. BAXTER

SO MUCH ATTENTION IS PAID NOWADAYS TO "THE WINNING OF THE INITIATIVE BY THE HOUSE OF COMMONS" AND TO *Cabinet Government* THAT WE ARE IN SOME DANGER OF FORGETTING THAT ENGLAND'S ONE ATTEMPT AT REPUBLICAN FORMS WAS A DISMAL FAILURE. IT MAY BE TRUE THAT THE CONVENTION OF 1660 RESTORED THE LAW AND THAT THE CAVALIER Parliament restored the Church. But we must not neglect the fact that the Restoration, with a capital *R*, was the Restoration of the monarchy. From 1660 to 1810 or even 1837 we are faced with a period in English history that may be given various labels—we may call it the *ancien régime*, or the age of personal monarchy, or if we are administrative historians we may speak of the departmental system. But whatever term we select, one thing we do not have a right to do is to be influenced by Walter Bagehot's *The English Constitution*. It is very hard for us to get Bagehot out of our minds, to forget his division of the government into dignified and efficient segments with the monarchy neatly tucked into bed in the dignified part of the house. Yet in eighteenth-century history Bagehot has no place. And one wonders whether a great deal of room need be given to the outbursts of literary gentlemen of Whiggish persuasion. It is of course true that Horace Walpole in his *Memoires* called George II "the shadow of monarchy, like Banquo's ghost." [1] But then, Horace Walpole was not king. He was not even Sir Robert Walpole.

All of us are aware of the dangers of anachronism, as all of us are to a certain extent at least its prisoners. There is a risk that in attempting to achieve fairness we will overcompensate, and give the eighteenth-century monarchy all the authority attributed to that of Elizabeth I, whom Jean Bodin considered to be an absolute sovereign. This is not one of the most felicitous passages in *The Six Bookes of a Commonweale*.[2] Bodin's visit to England in 1581 was very brief and he did not fully comprehend what he saw. Neither in 1581 nor at any other time was Elizabeth I an absolute

---

[1] Horace Walpole, fourth earl of Orford, *Memoires of the last ten years of the Reign of George the Second*, 2 vols. (London, 1822), i, 327.

[2] Jean Bodin, *The Six Bookes of a Commonweale*, ed. Kenneth Douglas McRae, (Cambridge, Mass., 1962) 96–98.

sovereign. She was at least far more powerful than her successors, and I wish to make it clear that I am not claiming for William III or his successors the powers of *Gloriana*. The idea is absurd. Yet it would be far less absurd than to talk of phantoms and of Banquo's ghost. The truth is that the initiative won by the Commons and so brilliantly described by Professor Notestein in his Raleigh Lecture was not continuously maintained.[3] For the most part the kings of the period of personal monarchy could take the initiative if they wished to do so, and if they had a little skill.

If we stretch this term *personal monarchy* to its farthest limits and use it to cover the entire span 1603–1837, we find that for the great majority of the time England formed merely one parcel of a complex real estate holding; always the largest and most important parcel, to be sure, but by no means the only one. The early Stuarts did not derive much aid or comfort from their Scottish subjects. On the other hand George II, with a Civil List of £800,000, is said to have had a Hanoverian revenue of £500,000, so that the net income from the two governments may have been substantially equal. It is easy to forget that Anne and Oliver Cromwell, whom we should probably include at least for the years of the Protectorate, were the only two rulers between 1603 and 1837 to govern a unitary state. The other ten all had access to an independent army, an independent diplomatic corps, and an independent purse. The practical effects of this dual monarchy, its real meaning at any given moment, must still be worked out in detail. It is safe to say at this point that any analysis of the Stuart and Hanoverian monarchy or administration which omits the foreign position is too simple. For much of the period the capital of England was not Westminster or Whitehall, but rather a yacht in the middle of the North Sea.

A second factor of importance is the education given each of our twelve rulers. Princes as a class are not well trained; the extreme in this respect is the fantastic system of the Ottoman Empire, where the accession of an able or experienced man as Sultan had been made impossible before the end of the sixteenth century. If in England the atmosphere was less enervating the problem was still severe, and this makes it all the more important that so many of the English rulers of the seventeenth and eighteenth centuries were not born to the purple. James I, Oliver, William III, George I, and to a lesser extent George II were all outsiders in this respect.[4] If to these we add Charles

[3] Wallace Notestein, "The Winning of the Initiative by the House of Commons," in *Proceedings of the British Academy*, xi (1924–1925) 125–175.

[4] George II was the weakest of this group, at least in his later years. The comment of Horace Walpole quoted above refers to 1754 when the king was seventy-two and a coward. Earlier in life he had been a brave man, but when he said "I" he meant the Elector of Hanover. William III, however, always meant the King of England rather than the Prince of Orange or the stadholder of the United Provinces when he said "I" after 1689. Stephen B. Baxter, *William III* (London, 1966) 345–346.

II, who though *porphyrogenitus* matured in exile, we may say that exactly half the kings of England in this period escaped the toils of a court education. As we should expect, they are the stronger members of the group. Lacking practical experience, the court-educated Charles I, Anne, George IV, and William IV are the weakest of the twelve. Military experience appears to have been of especial importance. Oliver, William III, and George I are stronger men than the civilians James I and Charles II.

Both as a soldier and as the beneficiary of an exceptional education William III is well worth studying, and there are even better reasons for studying his system of government. His reign happens to be a crisis period. It would take many years for the real meaning of the Revolution of 1688 to be worked out, and in many ways the techniques, indeed the mere whims, of William III were to be of as much importance in the formation of a new order as were the techniques and whims of George Washington on a similar occasion. William set precedents which were followed, with awe, for a century and a half. His Grand Alliance of 1689 was resurrected by the younger Pitt in 1787, while his failure to give the English army its own commissariat was copied by his successors for an even longer period. In 1689 the Amsterdam firm of Machado and Pereira took care of the supply problem. By 1854 Machado and Pereira had gone out of business, as Lord Raglan discovered to his dismay, but nothing new had taken their place. Even in 1898 the hats worn by the Boers in the South African war were the same broad-brimmed felts, pinned up on one side, that figure in several of the king's portraits.

Luckily William III left behind him an unusually voluminous set of records. Eleven volumes of his letters have been published already, and others remain in manuscript. Letters about him are almost more common than those written to him, since William was an international figure from the moment of his birth. Our greatest good fortune, however, lies in the fact that William III was presiding over a dual monarchy. One or the other of his governments always had to be run through the mails; when William was with the army all the governments were operated at long distance. This explains our wealth of source material, as it explains the frequent presence of foreign ambassadors in camp or at het Loo during the summer months, rather than in London; but it involved a large secretariat. A Dutch, a Scottish, an English, and often an Irish Secretary, each with his files and several clerks, accompanied the king wherever he went. Obviously no one living in England could hope to be a "prime minister" under such a system. William was careful to send reports of what he was doing and copies of formal documents to London, but the thread of affairs remained in his own hands throughout his lifetime. Even in 1701, when he was politically weak and physically exhausted, he concluded the Second Grand Alliance on the continent; and while he was doing so he made the decision to dissolve Parliament over the bitter opposition of his ministers. No "prime minister" is to be found in this reign save the king himself. Carmarthen from 1690 to 1693, Somers in the middle years of the reign, and Rochester in 1700–1701 come the closest of any to holding the position of first minister, or simply minister; but none of the three had the king's entire confidence even in such matters as patronage. No one of them could make or break a first lord of the treasury, or spend a shilling beyond his own salary, or write a line of the speech from the throne. This last was, from the examples of which we have record, written by the king in French and then translated for stylistic purposes by some subordinate official or another. Although William III spoke English he did so imperfectly and he would never agree to write in that language. As it happened the speech from the throne in 1692 was tactless, and in later years the English translations of the draft were polished by the Cabinet Council before being sent to the printer. But the legislative program of the government was that of the king and not that of any single minister or group of them.

If there was no prime minister, there was indeed a Cabinet Council. As Professor J. H. Plumb and Miss Jennifer Carter have demonstrated, the one essential for a Cabinet Council meeting down to 1717 was the physical presence of the sovereign.[5] Sessions held in the king's absence were called meetings of the Committee, and William III controlled both the agenda and the composition of the board. Indeed he controlled its very existence, for in the summer of 1694 there was no Cabinet Council, and it is easy to see that no body could have much self-confidence when the threat of suppression was so immediate. The composition of the Cabinet Council varied from year to year. The heir to the throne—in this reign George of Denmark attended to represent the Princess Anne—had a right to attend Cabinets but not Committees. Others with a right to attend in ordinary circumstances were the Archbishop of Canterbury, the Lord Chancellor, Lord President, Lord Chamberlain, Lord Privy Seal, the two Secretaries of State and the First Lord of the Treasury, but the position of each was insecure. Thus Charles Montagu was First Lord of the Treasury for half a year in 1697 before he entered the Cabinet Council, while the duke of Leeds was forbidden to attend Cabinets for his last four years as Lord President.

After the king's rudeness in the speech from the throne in 1692, one can discern the gradual development of a negative veto on the part of the ministers. The formation of policy remained in the hands of the king. But the ministers, who had the task of coating the pill, could tell him what

---

[5] J. H. Plumb, "The Organization of the Cabinet in the Reign of Queen Anne," in *Transactions of the Royal Historical Society*, 5th series, vii (1957), 137–157. Jennifer Carter, "Cabinet Records of the Reign of William III," in *English Historical Review*, lxxviii 1963), 95–114.

medicine would go down with Parliament and what would not. In 1695, for example, the problem of the coin became acute. Would there be a recoinage at par or would there be a devaluation? William wanted a recoinage at par, and when he broached the topic at a Cabinet Council meeting on 16 October 1695 he made this clear.[6] On the central issue he had his way. But he also wanted to act by proclamation rather than by statute, citing as precedents the recoinage of Henry VII and that of Mary I. At a later Committee meeting of 10 November two of the lords, Shrewsbury and Devonshire, took fright and the rest then agreed that Parliament should be consulted.[7] William, therefore, turned the whole matter over to Parliament in his Speech of 22 November. By conceding the form the king got what he really wanted, a recoinage at par.

After peace was concluded in 1697 the authority of the king declined still further, to a point at which a Secretary of State could write in 1699 of the ministers:

> If they cannot do every thing that the King may think a gratification to him, yet I believe he may depend upon it they will keep the government upon its present basis, which is no small consideration; but then they must be at liberty not to meddle with things they see reason to despair of; . . .[8]

Thus in 1699 the beaten Whigs did preserve the dynasty and get through the supply bill; and they did follow the king's commands on the Partition Treaty. But they did not exert themselves to obtain the king's other proposals, the adoption of the Gregorian calendar and a union with Scotland. Nor did they prevent the resumption of the Irish forfeitures, though here they did try. The Tory ministry of 1700–1701 was even worse. Lord Dartmouth relates that

> Lord Rochester had an assuming manner, both in his behaviour and discourse, that was extremely disagreeable. Lord Jersey told me, he was with him once in the king's closet, where he took the liberty to tell the king, that princes must not only hear good advice, but must take it. After he was gone, the king stamped about the room, and repeated the word "must," several times; at last, turning to lord Jersey, said, "If I had ordered him to have been thrown out of the window, he *must* have gone; I do not see how he could have hindered it." [9]

[6] Trumbull Cabinet Memoranda, Berkshire County Record Office, Reading.
[7] *Ibid.*
[8] James Vernon to the duke of Shrewsbury, 16 December 1699. G. P. R. James, ed., *Letters Illustrative of the Reign of William III from 1696 to 1708 Addressed to the Duke of Shewsbury* . . . , 3 vols. (London, 1841) ii, 394.
[9] Gilbert Burnet, *Bishop Burnet's History of his own Time,* ed. Martin Joseph Routh, 2d ed. enlarged, 6 vols. (Oxford, 1833) iv, 518 n.

In the end William changed the ministry, though he did not order its defenestration. By firing the Tories he momentarily recovered much of the authority lost since 1692. But Anne was unable to continue in this path and when George I left the Cabinet Council in 1717 he threw much of the game away.

The Cabinet Council met on Sunday mornings after church and the Privy Council on Thursdays, a schedule determined by the arrival of the foreign mails. Thus for at least five full days out of the seven William III worked alone. If it would be untrue to suggest that the king assigned an importance of five to his sessions with individual heads of departments and an importance of two to his sessions with groups of them, it is simply the case that this was the way in which he divided his time. Hence the use of the term "departmental system," to denote these meetings between the king and one particular servant. It was the departmental system rather than the Cabinet Council or the Privy Council that made the wheels of government go round; and the departmental system was still in effect during the reign of George III.

It is notorious that William III kept the conduct of foreign affairs to himself throughout his reign. The first outline of the Grand Alliance of 1689 was actually sent off to Vienna two full weeks before the Prince of Orange was elected king. In 1690 when he went to Ireland, William thought so little of his English diplomats that he made the Spanish ambassador, Don Pedro Ronquillo, a member of Mary's Cabinet Council and, in effect, Foreign Secretary. The king's control over the Treasury was almost equally strong, since he attended Treasury meetings once a week while he was in England and corresponded with it directly whenever he was on the Continent. His attendance at treasury board meetings gave William the opportunity to hear any dissenting opinions of the junior treasury lords and also to influence decisionmaking before the stage of a minute was reached. Anne, interestingly enough, also attended treasury meetings when in 1710–1711 she made use of a commission, but George I did not. Here again his lack of English and his failure to undertake detailed administrative functions probably weakened the authority of the first Hanoverian. To a formal minute he could say little more than *yes* or *no*. William III was far more active. He was the chief administrative officer as well as commander in chief of the forces, running the army himself with the aid of the Secretary at War and the paymaster. This was another of the burdens which he took up before the formality of his election as king. At first he did not pay equal attention to the navy and attempted to delegate that task to a Secretary of State, Lord Nottingham, by analogy with his previous Dutch administrative system. The English Admiralty would not tolerate such treatment. In the end William was obliged to take over the day to day administration of the navy, a process that was complete by about 1696 as John Ehrman has already pointed out.[10] In church appointments the king's influence was probably far less significant, although it seems clear that the queen would have preferred the appointment of Compton as archbishop of Canterbury in 1690 rather than Tillotson who actually received the post. Particularly at the end of the reign the king paid a good deal of attention to Ireland, and here he was prepared to fight his English ministers in order to secure the general welfare. John Methuen, the Irish Lord Chancellor and one of a committee of three Lords Justices who were then executing the post of Lord Lieutenant, left behind him a fascinating series of letters to his fellow Lords Justices that has come to light at Blenheim. In April of 1698 he wrote from England that

> My Lord Chancellor (Somers) alone seems not to be perswaded to govern our Affairs with the King, the rest of the Ministers seem no great Friends to us and to a great Degree Enemies to Ireland. All the hopes that Offer are that the King looks on the intentions of the Ministers toward Ireland to be very wrong, and contrary to his own Interest directly, & seems capable to take reşolutions in his Closset and declare them in the Cabinet Council in such manner as to prevent contradiction. . . .[11]

It should not be assumed that the Cabinet Council or its individual members had a monopoly of access to the sovereign at this period or even at a much later one. Every peer, his wife, his daughters, and probably also his sons had *entrée* at Court. Every member of the House of Commons could in practice obtain an interview, though a stranger at Court would have to undergo the humiliation of finding someone to introduce him; and the game was not always worth the candle, for William could be "disgustingly dry" at a first meeting. In addition to casual meetings the king systematically took the advice of men who held either no public position or else an apparently irrelevant one. The most important of these men held the position of a Harry Hopkins and were often extremely influential; an American might call them "coordinators of information," an Englishman "King's Remembrancers." The function of Lord Portland, for example, was to remind the king of what he had to do in relation to the government of the United Provinces, although there was also an official Dutch secretary with a staff of clerks. Portland was permitted to read the extremely detailed correspondence between William and the Grand Pensionary Heinsius, discussed the formation of policy in that field with the king, and jogged the royal elbow whenever William needed to be reminded about an approaching deadline. He acted in the same capacity as coordinator of information for Scotland

10 John Ehrman, *The Navy in the War of William III, 1689–1697* (Cambridge, 1953) 608.
11 John Methuen to Lord Galway 14 April 1698. Blenheim Palace Archives, Sunderland Letter Book 3.

until 1699. Down until the end of 1697 the King's Remembrancer for Ireland was the man who happened to hold the office of Lord Chamberlain. When Sunderland retired at Christmastime it became necessary to find a new channel by which the Irish Government could reach the king's ear, and in time the earl of Albemarle was given the task. Albemarle was already the coordinator for the business of the army on the Continent, for negotiations with the Swiss cantons, and since the end of 1695 for the government of the Dutch Republic. John Methuen described the Irish arrangement as follows in a letter to his fellow Lords Justices at Dublin:

> To setle our Correspondence I spoke to the King about My Lord Albemarle having first his leave, I find the King and My Lord Albemarle both enter into the matter very warmly, that is that Mr. Secretary Vernon shall be appointed for Your Lordsps to Correspond with in all things. But that in all matters of importance we shall give a private account to My Lord Albemarle from whom we shall be sure to receive the King's particular commands from Mr Vernon.[12]

This means, of course, that the Remembrancers constituted a special rank in the administrative hierarchy between the king and Heinsius, between the king and the governments of Scotland and Ireland, and at least at times between the king and the English ministers themselves. In 1698 and 1699 Lord Somers, as he complained bitterly, could not get William to discuss business with him though he appeared to the public to be at the head of the administration. Historically the position of Portland and Albemarle, of Shrewsbury and Sunderland, is that of "Favourite," an irresponsible minister. Like so many of the administrative techniques of William III, it was continental in origin, though there are also several well known English parallels. Like so many of his techniques it was also a bit old-fashioned, although the last important English example is that of Lord Bute as minister "behind the curtain" at the beginning of the reign of George III.

It was impossible for the Remembrances to engross the king, just as it was impossible for the Cabinet Council to engross him. On certain matters Heinsius was instructed to report on separate slips of paper inserted into the letters which he was required to send William twice a week. Portland and later Albemarle knew perfectly well that there should be two letters a week, which they had a right to read. But the King could remove the separate slip of paper from a letter before handing it over, and thus preserve his secrets even from the Favourite of the moment. He never confided his whole mind to any of them and never permitted them the wide freedom of action that

[12] John Methuen to the Irish Lords Justices 23 April 1698. Blenheim Palace Archives, Sunderland Letter Book 3.

his predecessors had accorded to Burghley or to the first duke of Buckingham.

On the whole, therefore, one may say that in the last two centuries of personal government, in the age between Bodin and Bagehot, the business method of an individual sovereign was not entirely insignificant. The way in which one ruler handled his work load, or indeed the topics which one ruler considered to make up his work load, need not bind his successor except in very broad outline. Those departments which a king wished to manage himself, most notably the army and the conduct of foreign policy, were the last to "go out of court" and they did not do so completely until well into the nineteenth century. When a king wished to operate the Treasury himself, as William and to a certain extent Anne did, the fact that Charles II and James II had not done so was of no importance. The departmental system operated alongside the Cabinet Council, which did not acquire control of its own agenda until George III fell ill. Obviously much depended on the vigor, ability, and previous experience of the man who was king. James I, William III, and George I all had unusual opportunities in that they were experienced men when they achieved the throne, men who had something to add to discussions and who had a right to their own opinions. They did not need to go through the administrative apprenticeship of a Charles I or a George III. All three, as men of achievement, had to be respected at least at the beginning of their reigns. If none of them had the administrative genius of a Frederick William I of Prussia, it must also be remembered that many of the German kings' servants needed their salaries. Germany was much less wealthy than England, and many English administrators as well as every member of the English Parliament was a person of independent means. An Englishman could always afford to argue or, if needs be, resign as Shrewsbury did in 1690 over a question of principle, while not every German could.

No one would argue that the power of the monarchy was not in decline in this period, or that that of the ministers and of Parliament was not on the rise. Obviously the royal authority was in decline even during the reign of William III. But the process was not a simple one nor was it to be completed in a day. If the Revolution of 1688 meant the ultimate end of divine right monarchy and the ultimate supremacy of Parliament, the English kings of the eighteenth century were still to occupy a great office and they were still to have influence in many fields. The problem must be studied in much greater detail, ruler by ruler, before we have anything approaching a satisfactory answer. But we may, I hope, disagree with Lord Rochester's bitter comment that William III took the crown of England and made of it something "little better than a night-cap." [13] On closer inspection the night-cap looks suspiciously like a crown.

[13] Burnet, iv, 25 n.

POLINIÈRE AND THE TEACHING OF EXPERIMENTAL PHYSICS AT PARIS: 1700-1730

BY BLAKE T. HANNA

THE COLLECTION OF ESSAYS ENTITLED *Enseignement et diffusion des sciences en France au XVIIIe siècle*, EDITED BY RENÉ TATON,[1] LEAVES LITTLE DOUBT THAT AT THE BEGINNING OF THE EIGHTEENTH CENTURY, THE TEACHING OF PHYSICS IN FRANCE WAS LARGELY A SPECULATIVE MATTER. IT WAS NOT UNTIL THE PUBLICATION IN 1702 OF GUILLAUME DAGOUMER'S *Philosophia ad usum scholae accommodata* [2] that the emphasis in the teaching of philosophy at the University of Paris shifted from scholasticism to Cartesianism, and the teaching of physics, which occupied most of the second year of philosophy, remained profoundly attached to the aims and methods of philosophical speculation. The theories of various philosophers concerning matters pertaining to physics were advanced, discussed, and either accepted or refuted on purely rational grounds.[3] Little intervened in the way of experimentation until 1752, when a chair of experimental physics was founded in the *collège de Navarre*.[4] Its first occupant was the renowned abbé Nollet, pupil of Réaumur and author of the often reedited *Leçons de physique expérimentale*.[5]

In the rival Jesuit colleges, the teaching of physics developed even more slowly. Few textbooks were in use at the turn of the century and the physics course was entirely dictated in Latin to students who devoted three or four hours a day during one entire academic year to writing it painstakingly in their notebooks. Although demonstrations were apparently held in the physics class at Paris's *Louis-le-Grand* as early as 1711, the development of such teaching methods was greatly hampered by the conservatism of Jesuit provincial authorities whom we find in 1706, 1731, and 1751 recalling to the doctrines of Aristotle certain of their colleagues whose physics courses had strayed into greener Cartesian fields.[6] It must be remembered against the

[1] (Paris, 1964).
[2] (Paris, 1702–1704), 4 vols.
[3] Taton, 146.
[4] *Ibid.*, 147–148, 622–624.
[5] (Paris, 1743–1748), 6 vols.
[6] Taton, 35–36, 39–40, 44–46.

background of these exhortations that as early as 1740, Pierre Sigorgne of the *collège du Plessis* had introduced the theories of Newton into the classrooms of the University of Paris, whose administration had ceased wasting its time in promoting the cause of medieval scholasticism.[7]

Such then was the development of the teaching of physics in the early eighteenth century. And yet, some fifty years before the establishment of the first chair of experimental physics in the university, a remarkable precursor of Nollet by the name of Pierre Polinière was already conducting demonstrations in the physics classes of the colleges of both the university and the Jesuits. Conducted at a time when the philosophical pendulum was reaching its Cartesian extreme, Polinière's experiments anticipated by forty years the introduction of empirical doctrines into the teaching of physics at Paris.

Polinière was born in Coulonce, near Vire in Normandy, on September 8, 1671. He studied the humanities at the University of Caen and philosophy at the University of Paris, where he learned mathematics under the celebrated Pierre Varignon, professor at the *collège Mazarin*. His insatiable taste for the sciences led him to study not only mathematics, but physics, natural history, geography, and chemistry. He terminated his studies at the Faculty of Medicine. Married in 1707 to Marguerite Asselin of Vire, he had two daughters and two sons, one of whom, Julien-Pierre, became a doctor of medicine like his father. It was apparently toward 1703 or 1704 at the *collège d'Harcourt* in Paris that he began the physics demonstrations that he was to continue for over thirty years. Methodical and unassuming, he seems to have had a gift for translating the theories of others into easily grasped experiments which he explained with a simplicity and a clarity that were ideally suited to the young minds he was called upon to teach. In 1722, he was given the opportunity of performing his experiments before the king. Fontenelle, secretary of the Academy of Sciences, named him tutor to his nephew. Quiet, frugal, even-tempered, and obliging, he was noted for the single-mindedness with which he applied himself to his work. He died suddenly at his summer home in Coulonce on February 9, 1734, at the age of 63.[8]

The manual in which Polinière published the experiments he had been conducting in the classroom is entitled: *Expériences de physique*. The second volume contains a note which specifies that the book was derived from the work in the classroom, rather than the contrary.[9] He began compiling it in 1700 or 1701, according to a notice published at the beginning of volume

---

[7] *Ibid.*, 142, 159, 627.

[8] Louis Moréri, *Le Grand Dictionnaire historique* (Paris, 1759), VIII, 431; *Biographie universelle, ancienne et moderne* (Paris, 1811–1862), XXXV, 192–193; Pierre Polinière, *Expériences de physique* (Paris, 1741), I, fol. aiij; II, fol. c–cij v°.

[9] Polinière, II, fol. c v°.

two in the fifth edition,[10] which goes on to relate that the privilege to publish the first edition was obtained on March 27, 1703. It was to be six years,
however, before this first edition finally saw the light of day. Out of print in
less than a year, a privilege covering a second edition was obtained on August
27, 1710, but once again, the new edition was not to be published for another
eight years. Needless to say, this deliberateness on the part of Polinière made
his work the easy victim of plagiarists, and the author's skirmishes with them
are described in some detail in the above-mentioned notice.

All told, the manual went through five editions.[11] It dominated the field
for thirty years until it was supplanted in 1743 by Nollet's *Leçons de
physique expérimentale,* a far more detailed work counting six volumes to
Polinière's two.

The views of Polinière concerning experimental physics are set forth in
the notice at the beginning of his first volume:

> If the conclusions that are drawn concerning the properties of a
> substance are not based on experimentation, they can only be con-
> sidered as uncertain conjectures or even as pure imagination. For as
> there is an indefinite number of possible things and as different
> causes can produce similar effects, it is possible to attribute effects
> to causes other than those which produced them. In order to choose
> among the possible causes those which do indeed produce the effects
> under consideration, we must base our conclusions only on the an-
> swers that Nature gives us through experimentation: the only means
> we have of questioning her and of learning from her own lips what
> she really is like.[12]

Armed with this conviction, Polinière set about assembling the equipment
necessary to observe the various phenomena of nature. Invited by several
eminent professors of philosophy in Paris to duplicate his experiments before
their classes, he obtained such success that he was urged to make his work
known to the public through the manual that we are about to examine.[13]

---

10 *Ibid.,* II, "Avertissement concernant les anciennes éditions de ce livre".

11 1ère éd: Paris, 1709, VIII—508 p.; 2e éd: Paris, 1718, VIII—553 p.; 3e éd: Paris,
1728, XII—606 p.; 4e éd: Paris, 1734, 2 vols.; 5e éd: Paris, 1741, 2 vols.

12 "... si les raisonnemens qu'on fait sur les propriétés des corps ne sont appuyés
sur l'Expérience, ils ne peuvent passer que pour des conjectures incertaines, pour ne pas dire
de pures imaginations. Car y ayant une infinité de choses possibles, & différentes causes
pouvant produire de semblables effets, il peut souvent arriver qu'on attribue des effets à
d'autres causes qu'à celles qui les produisent. Pour choisir donc parmi ces causes possibles,
celles qui produisent véritablement les effets qui sont le sujet de nos méditations, nous ne
devons fonder nos jugemens que sur les réponses que la Nature nous fait dans les Expériences
qui sont la seule voie par laquelle nous pouvons l'intérroger & apprendre d'elle-même ce
qu'elle est." Polinière, 5e éd: I, "Avertissement sur ces expériences."

13 *Ibid.,* I, Préface.

The edition we are dealing with is the final one, published in 1741, into which Polinière had introduced a number of changes and additions, necessitating the engraving of two new plates and the publication of the work in two volumes, the contents having become too abundant to be contained in one volume that would be easily portable.[14] The illustrations accompanying the experiments are contained in nineteen plates, eleven at the end of the first volume and eight at the end of the second, bound in such a manner as to unfold beyond the right margin of the book, making it possible to consult them without turning any pages while reading the text. The second volume contains a detailed alphabetical index.

Now let us examine the experiments themselves. Space limitations will necessitate eliminating certain experiments which repeat conclusions arrived at through other experiments, as well as certain experiments which require elaborate equipment whose description is beyond the scope of the present article. Like most of his contemporaries, Polinière did not consider chemistry as being an autonomous science, and his manual includes a series of chemical experiments which will also be omitted as they are not relevant to the subject under discussion.

The first thirty pages of volume one contain descriptions of the simple machines. The most striking feature of these descriptions is the almost complete lack of mathematics. Polinière is concerned only with the principle behind the machines he is describing, and he never actually evaluates the moments of force involved: the forces and the distances over which they are brought to bear. The nearest he comes to dealing with the mathematical side of the question is to observe that the weight at one end of a lever is to the force that moves it as the distance between the force and the fulcrum is to the distance between the weight and the fulcrum. But even here he devotes little time to solving the proportions thus expressed, nor does he go so far as to deal mathematically with the work performed by any of the other simple machines.

This attitude is characteristic of the teaching of philosophy in France in the early eighteenth century. Physics was considered an outgrowth of metaphysics, while mathematics was treated as a specialized form of logic. Apart from the fact that both logic and metaphysics fell under the heading of philosophy, little connection was seen to exist between the two sciences, and it did not occur to these instructors to point out to their students that the mathematics they learned during their first year of philosophy might be applied to the physics they were studying during the second year. On the contrary, the study of physics, and even that of experimental physics as introduced into the curriculum by Polinière, was treated in a theoretical manner, with little attempt being made to study it quantitatively.

[14] Polinière, I, "Avertissement sur cette nouvelle édition".

The first seven experiments concern hydraulics. In the first one, Poli-nière demonstrates centrifugal force by whirling a wineglass around his head at the end of a string without spilling any of the water he has put into it. He correctly explains this effect by showing how the forces compose themselves into a vector tangent to the circle at any given point. (I, 31–33.) [15] He goes on to draw from this experiment a number of conclusions based on the vortex theories expressed by Descartes in his *Principes de philos-ophie* [16] concerning the propagation of light and the movement of the planets in their orbits. These theories were largely refuted by later scientists.

The second experiment demonstrates how liquids of different densities, colored so as to be readily identifiable and then shaken together in a glass tube, will sort themselves out in layers when left to stand for a time. Poli-nière offers no explanation as to why this occurs, although he does point out that the liquids arrange themselves according to weight. He also explains that the ancients felt that this experiment proved that earth, water, air, and fire arranged themselves in concentric spheres in the order named. He refutes this conclusion by pointing out that no experiment has ever demonstrated that a sphere of fire exists and the ancients furthermore erred in formulating hypotheses based in part on the weight of air when they did not know whether the air weighed anything or not. (I, 38–41.)

The third experiment concerns the specific gravity of fluids. By sub-merging a weighted float in a wineglass of water, Polinière demonstrates Archimedes' principle stating that a floating body displaces a volume of water equal to its own weight. By substituting vinegar for the water, he demonstrates how the specific gravity of a liquid can be read directly on a cardboard scale sealed in a glass float. By pouring first mercury and then water into a U-shaped tube, he demonstrates how the specific gravity of the mercury can be calculated by comparing the height of the two liquids in the two arms of the tube. (I, 41–48.)

Using a wineglass of water, scales, and a series of weights made of different metals, Polinière's fourth experiment demonstrates the rest of Archimedes' principle: that a submerged body displaces its own volume of water. By measuring the loss of weight incurred, Polinière shows how the specific gravity of such a body can be calculated, frequently revealing the substance the body is made of. This calculation is done, as is usually the case with Polinière, by solving a proportion. (I, 48–52.)

The fifth experiment deals with the incompressibility of a liquid which results in its hydraulically exploitable property of transmitting pressures undiminished throughout its volume. Floating one beaker inside another one

[15] The volume and page numbers after each experiment refer to the 1741 edition of Polinière's *Expériences de physique.*

[16] Part III, art. 55, 63, 140; part IV, art. 19, 20. Polinière, I, 34, 37.

partially filled with water, Polinière demonstrates by adding water to the larger beaker how boats may be raised or lowered in a set of locks. He also shows by means of a diagram, but does not demonstrate, that the pressure exerted by a mass of water of a given height and base area is the same, whatever may be the shape of its container. (I, 52–58.)

The sixth experiment shows how a weight resting on four deflated balloons can be raised by blowing into a tube connected to the necks of the balloons. Polinière does not know why this occurs, but his hypothesis is imaginatively close to the mark. He considers the air as being made of an infinite number of small wedges. The experimenter raises the load by introducing more of these little wedges into the balloons through the tube. If we make allowance for the rather picturesque terms in which Polinière couches his explanation, the only fundamental error he commits is that of considering air as an incompressible fluid, rather than a compressible gas. (I, 58–64.)

The next experiment is performed by putting an empty bottle with a very small neck into a beaker of water. The bottle is weighted so it will sink. Polinière observes that the air remains in the bottle despite the fact that it is lighter than the water. When the bottle is filled with wine, however, it slowly mixes with the surrounding water. The effect is due to surface tension, but Polinière explains it once again in terms of little wedges. The water, being denser than the air, is composed of larger wedges that cannot work their way into the wedges of air. In the case of the wine, however, the wedges are the same size as those of the water and the two can intermingle freely. (I, 64–69.)

The second group of experiments deals with air pressure. Experiment eight describes the building of a mercury barometer and explains why the height of the column of mercury varies with the elevation. The ninth experiment explains how the barometer reacts to changes in the weather. The tenth experiment explains why the onset of bad weather is accompanied by a change in the atmospheric pressure. The discussion of the meteorological questions involved in these three experiments occupies nearly forty pages. (I, 70–108.)

Experiments eleven and twelve deal with the heavy weight of air each person carries about with him. Polinière calculates it at 19,500 pounds, but explains correctly that we do not feel it, since it is counter-balanced by internal pressure. He also explains why old people with rheumatism, et cetera, are walking barometers. He thinks that the body's fluids circulate because of air pressure and concludes that the changes in pressure that accompany bad weather hinder the circulation of the blood and the humors. It may not be the right explanation, but it is apparently as good a one as anyone has come up with since. (I, 108–115.)

Experiment thireen demonstrates the action of the syphon. (I, 115–

122.) Experiment fourteen demonstrates capillary action. Polinière fills a container with mercury and observes that the mercury does not rise to the same height in a narrow J-tube connected to it. But when he replaces the mercury with water, he notes that it rises higher in the J-tube. He also demonstrates capillary action by using a strip of cloth and a loaf of bread. He plunges them into a container of water and notes that the water rises higher in the bread and in the cloth than the level of the liquid in the container. Polinière only half understands capillary action. He shows that he comprehends the role played by adhesion between the fluid and the walls of the tube when he remarks that the water wets the tube while the mercury does not. What he does not grasp, however, is the countering effect of cohesion between the molecules of the liquid, because he makes no connection between this experiment and number seven, dealing with surface tension. As we have seen in discussing number seven, he does not understand surface tension in the first place. As far as capillary action is concerned, he suspects that the principle of the syphon is somehow involved, because the action is more rapid in the case of water if the strips of cloth are dampened and wrung out first. This is why he places this experiment after number thirteen, rather than after number seven. (I, 122–126.)

In experiment fifteen, Polinière fills a glass with water, puts a playing card on top of it, tips the whole thing upside down and takes his hand away without spilling the water. He explains how air pressure keeps the water in the glass. (I, 127–131.) In experiment eighteen, he demonstrates how various pumps work. The experiment includes a detailed description of an early eighteenth-century fire engine. (I, 141–158.) There follows a four-page discussion of the elasticity of various substances. Polinière feels that the various solids must be like a loosely built brick wall with air in the spaces between the bricks. The closer together the bricks are, the denser the material is and the less space there is between the bricks for air which acts as a cushion, making the substance more elastic. (I, 158–162.) This is one of the experiments in which Polinière demonstrates that he does not understand molecular movement.

In experiment twenty-one, he uses a thermometer to demonstrate that heat causes a liquid to expand. The explanation he offers bears further witness to his ignorance of molecular movement and of the fact that heat is a form of energy. He considers it rather as some sort of rarefied substance—"*matière subtile*"—the particles of which insinuate themselves among the particles of liquid in the thermometer, forcing them apart. (I, 173–175.)

In experiment twenty-three, he demonstrates that solids expand when they are heated and contract when they are cold. He puts colored water into a bottle with a tube cemented into its neck. When he pours hot water on the bottle, it expands, causing the level of the liquid in the tube to fall.

When he plunges the heated bottle into some cold water, it contracts, causing the level of the water to rise. (I, 178–181.)

In experiment twenty-four, he proves that heated gases expand by blowing up a sealed bottle in a fire. (I, 182–185.) The experiment must have been greeted with considerable enthusiasm by Polinière's young students, who were doubtless impressed by its dramatic outcome. Experiment twenty-five demonstrates the force of compressed air by shooting a lead pellet out of an air gun with enough force to pierce a pine board. (I, 185–192.) Here again, his experiment must have encountered an enthusiastic reception on the part of those who witnessed it. The following experiment is a similar one conducted with a fountain actuated by compressed air which emits a jet of water strong enough to support a lead ball. (I, 192–195.)

In experiment twenty-nine, Polinière uses a flask with a long tube joined to the neck. He heats the flask causing the air to expand and then plunges the end of the tube into a beaker of water. As the flask cools and the air contracts, it is replaced by water, which rises in the tube. In his explanation, Polinière presents this experiment as a demonstration of how sap rises in trees, indicating once again that he does not understand capillary action. His explanation of how sap flows is that during the day, the sun shines on the plant, expanding the air in its cells. During the night, this air contracts and sap rises from the roots to take its place. He then goes on to explain how plants grow, by stating that during the winter, the air in the plant cells contracts. When spring comes, the heat of the sun expands it and the day-night cycle he has just described sets in, causing the sap to rise. However, he points out, the channels the sap runs through have one-way valves in them which prevent the sap from returning to the roots. With each cycle, therefore, space must be found for more sap and the only solution is for the upper part of the plant to expand (that is, to grow) and to produce leaves to make room for all the sap. (I, 206–209.) Nothing is more typical of the role played by physics in early eighteenth-century thinking than this purely mechanical explanation of a complex botanical phenomenon.

In experiment thirty, Polinière heats a little flask to expand the air therein and applies it to his hand. As the air cools and contracts, the flesh of his hand expands into the neck of the flask, indicating the presence of air under atmospheric pressure within the body's tissues. He goes on to explain that doctors frequently use this principle to suck the infected matter out of abscesses, et cetera, indicating that there is air disolved in the blood, lymph, and other body fluids. All this is well and good, but Polinière's considered opinion as a doctor of medicine is that such treatment is not indicated in cases of cerebral hemorrhage. The reaction of a stroke victim to a blood-letting of this sort is one of pain, not of relief. He characterizes the treatment as cruelty on the part of the doctor and a form of torture that the patient has not deserved. (I, 209–212.) His views on the subject are remarkably modern for an era when medical treatment in nine cases out of ten boiled down to removing blood from a patient already weakened by sickness.

Experiment thirty-one utilizes a complex system of tubes and bottles to prove that water driven by air pressure will spurt up into a bottle from which part of the air has been evacuated. (I, 212–214.) Number thirty-two demonstrates the same thing in a simpler and more dramatic fashion. Polinière cements a glass tube into the neck of a pint bottle in such a manner that it reaches to the bottom and protrudes from the top. When he sucks on the tube and then plunges it upside-down into a beaker of water, some of the water rises into the bottle to replace the air he has evacuated. And conversely, when he puts a little water into the bottom of the bottle and then blows into the tube, the water spurts out all over the floor when he stops, demonstrating precisely what he sought to demonstrate in experiment thirty-one, but doing so in a vastly more entertaining manner. (I, 214–217.)

Experiment thirty-three is similar, except that it resorts to heating and cooling the air, rather than to blowing or sucking. Polinière, however, goes on to develop a hypothesis concerning the origin of the winds that is based on this experiment. He feels they come from various cavities in the earth filled with air and water. The heat in the center of the earth causes the air in these cavities to expand, creating the winds which he feels come out of holes in the ground that communicate with the cavities. (I, 218–223.)

Between experiments thirty-four and thirty-five is a detailed description of a vacuum pump for use in the laboratory. (I, 226–233.) This particular pump is a stirrup pump actuated by foot power, in order to leave the hands free to conduct the experiments. Experiment thirty-five is a simple experiment which consists in making a stroke with the pump and then releasing the stirrup, watching the piston rise again of its own accord, actuated by the pressure of the outside air. (I, 233–235.) The next experiment demonstrates how, when a bell jar has been placed on the vacuum pump and the air exhausted from within it, it becomes impossible to separate it from the pump, due to the surrounding air pressure. (I, 236–239.)

Experiment thirty-seven consists in placing various flat-sided bottles or glass plates on the vacuum pump and watching them break under the weight of the outside air pressure as the pump is actuated beneath them. (I, 239–243.) Boys of the age Polinière dealt with are fundamentally interested in breakage of this sort, and using it to demonstrate a valid physical principle was a telling pedagogical blow struck by their teacher.

Experiment thirty-eight consists in placing a mercury barometer under a bell jar and watching the mercury fall as the air is evacuated. This experiment allowed the students to deduce that it was the air pressure that supported the column of mercury in the first place. (I, 243–246.)

Experiment thirty-nine is an ingenious and striking demonstration of the weight of the air around us. Polinière uses two flat, highly polished pieces of marble, one of which has a hook on one side of it. He shows that by dampening the polished surfaces and wringing or sliding them together, the surfaces are in such intimate contact that there is no room for air between them and the air pressure on the outside surfaces makes it extremely difficult to pull them apart. But how do we know that it is the outside air pressure that keeps them from coming apart? This is proved by hanging the blocks thus joined inside a bell jar by the hook mentioned. When the air has been evacuated from the bell jar, the blocks suddenly come apart. Polinière then goes on to demonstrate the same phenomenon through the use of a pair of Magdeburg hemispheres. When the latter are joined with a leather gasket and the air evacuated from within, two teams can engage in a tug of war without pulling the hemispheres apart. (I, 247–253.)

In experiment forty, Polinière puts a shriveled, overripe apple under a bell jar and starts to evacuate the air. As he does so, the skin of the apple smoothes out and eventually the fruit explodes. He then repeats the experiment with a deflated balloon to demonstrate what happened to the apple. Among his observations concerning the experiment with the apple is his unjustified conclusion that seeds grow because the heat of the sun expands the air inside them. (I, 254–256.)

Experiment forty-one gives an idea of the pressure of the air on the surface of the earth. Polinière puts a bladder one fourth full of air into a can with a twelve-pound lead weight on top of it inside a bell jar. As he pumps the air out of the jar, the expanding bladder lifts the weight. (I, 257–259.)

In number forty-three, Polinière puts a small animal under the bell jar and evacuates the air until the animal loses consciousness. Opening the valve, he watches the animal revive as the air returns. He explains that if the air is not readmitted promptly, the animal will die. He then goes on to provide his students with a detailed, anatomically sound explanation of the respiratory system, one of the fringe benefits of having a doctor of medicine for a physics professor. (I, 261–265.)

Experiment forty-four is another delightful demonstration of the simple faith of the early eighteenth century which tended to explain every natural phenomenon in terms of an elementary principle of physics. Polinière successively places a glass of beer, a glass of alcohol, a glass of hot water, and an egg with a hole in it under a bell jar from which he evacuates the air. He observes that the beer foams, the alcohol and the water boil, while the contents of the egg emerge from the hole, and his conclusion in each case is that each one of these substances contains a certain quantity of air which expands as the pressure is reduced. He is right in the case of the egg, since the shell contains an air pocket which expands, pushing everything else out of the hole. His further conclusion—that it must be the heat of the hen's body that expands the air, pushing the baby chick out of its shell—does not, however, appear to be justified. He is not far from the truth in the case of the beer as well, as the beverage contains carbon dioxide. When the pressure is reduced, the gas expands, causing foam as it comes out of solution. In the case of the alcohol and the hot water, however, he is confronted with a different situation. By reducing the pressure, he has simply reduced the boiling point of the liquids. Air is not involved. (I, 265–271.)

In experiment forty-six, Polinière notes that a candle or a glowing coal placed under a bell jar goes out when the air is exhausted. More exactly, he perceives that it is extinguished sooner or later in any case, but that it goes out more rapidly if the air is exhausted. His explanation is that the heat of the candle causes the air to expand. Since it cannot get out of the bell jar, its pressure increases. This is, of course, a contradiction in terms. The increase in pressure, he goes on to say, hinders the movement which is responsible for fire and flame itself, as well as hindering the circulation of air which is necessary to excite the fire. This, he feels, explains why the fire goes out in any case. The reason why it goes out more quickly when the air is exhausted from the bell jar, according to Polinière, is that there is no longer any air there to excite the fire. (I, 276–286.) This explanation illustrates once again the early eighteenth-century tendency to offer a physical explanation for chemical or biological phenomena. Here, Polinière confuses physics and chemistry, because he does not understand the role played by oxygen in combustion.

In experiment forty-seven, Polinière sets up a scale under a bell jar with a piece of lead and a piece of wax in balance on it. When he exhausts the air from beneath the bell jar, the two are out of balance, since the wax, with its larger volume, was being supported to a greater extent than the lead by the air it displaced. (I, 286–288.)

Experiment forty-eight uses a tall bottle having a complicated apparatus inside it that is arranged so that when the air is pumped out of it, a feather and a gold coin will drop, reaching the bottom simultaneously. This permits Polinière to demonstrate the resistance of the air to a falling body, since the feather falls more slowly than the coin when the air is let back into the bottle. (I, 289–292.)

Number forty-nine uses two identical syringes with their points plunged into glasses of liquid. One of them is in the open air and the other is in a bell jar that has the air pumped out of it. By actuating the plunger of each syringe, Polinière proves that it is the pressure of the air that fills syringes, since the one in the bell jar will not work in a vacuum. (I, 292–296.)

In his conclusion to the section dealing with the action of the air, Polinière points out that the tremendous force of atmospheric pressure was unknown to the ancients. He attributes to divine omniscience the fact that every living creature is not crushed by this pressure and the fact that it can even be put to work on man's behalf. (I, 304–305.)

The next section contains three experiments dealing with the transmission of sound. In number fifty-two, he shows how the air transmits sound by placing an alarm clock inside a bell jar and noting how the sound diminishes as the air is exhausted therefrom, then increases as the air is readmitted. The explanation given is the appropriate one. (I, 306–309.) Experiment fifty-three, performed with a megaphone, demonstrates how the latter appears to magnify the voice by concentrating in one direction the vibrations it sets up in the air. That the sound is transmitted by air vibrations is made apparent by placing the hand within the open end, where these vibrations can be felt. Polinière also demonstrates that the apparatus works in reverse by placing his ear at the mouthpiece, whereupon he can hear previously inaudible sounds. The experiment is accompanied by several pages in which Polinière explains with the aid of diagrams how echoes occur. (I, 309–319.)

Experiment fifty-four illustrates a principle that Polinière believes he is the first to demonstrate. He drops a silver coin on a table to hear it ring. Then he coats the coin with mercury and drops it again, whereupon it emits a dull thud. He goes on to remark that every different alloy has a different ring when made into a coin of the same size. His explanation is a complex one which speaks of little wedges of one metal introducing themselves into the pores of another, but on the whole, he appears to have grasped the fact that identical volumes of different metals having different densities also have different periods of vibration, a phenomenon which the ear perceives as a difference in pitch. (I, 319–324.)

The rest of the experiments described in volume one concern magnetism. The section opens with a three-page introduction concerning the origins, the properties, and the uses of the magnet. (I, 325–327.) Experiment fifty-five is done with a shaker full of iron filings, a magnet, and a piece of cardboard. Polinière puts the magnet on the cardboard and shakes iron filings over it. The latter arrange themselves in a pattern that indicates the lines of force around the magnet. The experiment illustrates remarkably well the role played by the experimental sciences in the development of knowledge. Polinière has never heard of electricity, yet he is able to describe with perfect accuracy the manner in which it functions by observing the results of this experiment. His hypothesis is that it must be some sort of invisible matter which can flow through metal more easily than it can through air. He sees, moreover, the relationship between magnetism and the earth's gravity and is aware of the fact that this mysterious and invisible magnetic "substance" is responsible for the movement and the arrangement of the different parts of the universe. (I, 328–335.)

Experiment fifty-six demonstrates that lines of magnetic force sur-
round the earth. Suspending a bar magnet by a string, he demonstrates that
it lines itself up in a north-south direction, and that it realigns itself when
disturbed. Here again, Polinière explains this phenomenon in a manner which
shows that he understands perfectly the lines of magnetic force surrounding
the earth, except for the fact that he considers this force as some form of
matter, rather than of energy. (I, 336–340.)

Experiment fifty-seven demonstrates that like magnetic poles repel each
other, whereas opposite poles attract. In his manual, Polinière describes how
this occurs, but he cannot explain why. In this case, he superimposes two
magnets, one atop the other, and shows how the top one swivels about to
face in the opposite direction. (I, 340–343.)

Experiment sixty-one demonstrates how an unmagnetized iron rod can
be magnetized by holding it parallel to the earth's magnetic field. By turning
it end for end and striking one end against the ground, its polarity can even
be reversed. Here again, Polinière can only describe *what* happens; he cannot
explain *why*, except in terms that depict magnetism as some invisible form
of matter that comes out of the earth and travels through the iron rod. He
suspects that the rod has submicroscopic canals running through it and that
these canals are lined with something like hair that allows this magnetic
current to travel in one direction only. He suspects that striking the end of
the rod against the ground changes the direction of the hairs. He presents
these views, however, purely as a hypothesis. A note informs us that the
source of this experiment is John Keill's *Introductiones ad veram Physicam
et veram Astronomiam.*[17] (I, 364–366.)

Experiment sixty-two shows how lines of magnetic force pass through a
piece of cardboard. By placing a compass on a table and moving a magnet
about beneath the table, he shows that these lines of force will also pass
through wood. Polinière feels this is because the wood and cardboard have
pores in them for the magnetic substance to pass through. (I, 367–369.)

Experiment sixty-three repeats experiment fifty-six, but this time
Polinière uses a needle floating on a dish of water, rather than a magnet
suspended by a string. Polinière errs in remarking that the needle floats because there are little particles of air trapped beneath it. As we have seen in
earlier experiments, he does not understand surface tension. (I, 370–376.)

Number sixty-four repeats the above experiment but with a compass
needle at the bottom of a glass of water this time. Polinière is hard put to
explain why it behaves just as it would in the air. Believing magnetism to
be a form of matter and being familiar with the laws governing the impenetrability of matter, he expects the magnetism to displace the water. As it
apparently does not, he concludes that it actually does, but that his eye is

17 (Lugdunum Batavorum, 1725), lect 8, p. 85. Polinière, I, 366.

not sharp enough to see it. (I, 377–378.) This experiment is significant because it shows that when the empirical method fails him, he falls back on rationalism.

Experiment sixty-five has two parts. First, he continues the foregoing series of experiments by placing fire between the magnet and the needle to show that it does not disturb the lines of magnetic force any more than the water did. He cautions the reader, however, not to get the magnet too close to the fire or it will lose its magnetism. The second half of this experiment consists in magnetizing the point of a knife and picking up a wire ring with it. Blowing on the ring causes it to revolve, using the knife point as a pivot. Apparently unrelated, these two experiments appear to Polinière to be demonstrations of the same principle: the speed at which the magnetic "substance" moves. It moves so rapidly, according to Polinière, that it does not disturb the flame when it passes through, nor does it allow time for the ring to fall. (I, 379–382.)

Once again, this experiment is typical of the theory prevalent in the eighteenth century which considered electricity as some sort of invisible fluid that ran through tiny channels in such substances as iron. As a legacy of this theory, we still speak of an electric "current" and say that it "flows" through a conductor, while electricity itself is referred to colloquially as "juice." But apart from his misconceptions concerning the nature of magnetism, Polinière's observations are remarkably accurate. Electrical energy does indeed move at high speed: 186,000 miles per second, while heat will indeed destroy a magnet by exciting the molecules therein. But as we saw in experiment eighteen, Polinière does not understand molecular action.

Experiment sixty-six demonstrates how a sword blade can be magnetized by rubbing the same pole of a magnet along it in the same direction several times. Polinière explains that rubbing it in the opposite direction an equal number of times demagnetizes it. He thinks this is because the sword blade is full of little tubes lined with iron hairs, and he believes the magnet makes all the hairs line up in one direction, offering an unimpeded path to the magnetic "substance" flowing through the tubes. Rubbing the blade the other way lines up the hairs in the wrong direction, impeding the passage of the magnetic force in the same way as stroking a cat the wrong way is more difficult than doing it the right way. (I, 383–391.)

The last experiment in volume one illustrates the declination of the compass needle. Polinière sets up a compass, lining north and south up with the geographic poles, and he notes that the needle deviates six or seven degrees from true north and that it gradually shifts position. He does not explain how he determines where true north is in the first place, and the only hypothesis he can offer to explain the declination of the needle is that it must be influenced by iron mines being formed in the vicinity while other iron mines somewhere else nearby are being destroyed. This hypothesis strikes us as being the result of sheer desperation, rather than that of rational reflection. (I, 394–398.)

Volume two opens with a discussion of static electricity wherein Polinière remarks that such substances as amber can be made to behave like magnets by rubbing them. He describes a number of experiments designed to demonstrate this effect. One of them consists in attaching a hollow glass globe to a potter's wheel and making it rotate rapidly while rubbing it with a piece of cloth. When it is brought to a halt, it behaves like a magnet, attracting threads and cloth fibers to it and sparking in the darkness. He points out that nobody yet understands these phenomena, but he suggests they may be caused by the friction of the cloth against the globe generating heat which dilates and agitates the surrounding air. When the friction stops, the air condenses around the globe, carrying with it any light object floating in it. (II, 1–5.)

Next comes a preface to the section on chemistry, which Polinière defines as "the art of separating the different substances that a body is composed of in order to choose those which are useful." [18] He then relates how chemistry developed out of alchemy and how useful it is to the practice of medicine. (II, 6–13.)

There follows a twelve-page introduction which sets forth the basic principles of chemistry, describes the apparatus necessary to conduct chemical experiments, and tells how it is used. Polinière distinguishes four elements of which all matter is composed: salt, sulphur or oil, water, and earth.[19] Everything else is a compound made of these four elements. The salts are water-soluble and consist of two sorts: acid salts and alkali salts. The acid salts are composed of oblong crystals pointed at both ends, which is what makes them taste sour, he thinks. The alkali salts, which taste bitter, are composed of rough, porous crystals. Acids and alkalis are aqueous solutions of these salts. Acids attack metals and boil when mixed with alkalis, while alkalis cause fermentation and boil when mixed with acid. A third category of salts called compound salts—*sel composé*—can be prepared by mixing the first two. These have a salty taste and will not boil when mixed with acids or alkalis. Saltpeter and vitriol belong to this category.

Sulphur or oil is a viscous, inflammable substance, according to Polinière. It is their oil content that makes things inflammable. Oils are composed of interlocking, branched particles, he thinks, while water's fluidity is due to its being composed of oblong, highly polished particles with rounded ends which slip past one another with little friction. The shape of these particles

18 ". . . l'art de séparer les matières différentes qui composent les corps, pour choisir celles qui sont utiles." Polinière, II, 6.

19 *Ibid.*, II, 14.

enables them to insinuate themselves between the salt crystals, dissolving them.

Earth is the residue left when the salt, the sulphur, and the water have been removed from a compound. Polinière feels it serves only as a binder for the other three elements. Compounds differ one from another according to the elements they contain, the proportional amounts of each element and the way in which they are combined. In order to separate a compound into its elements, fire is necessary. (II, 14–20.)

Among other conclusions arrived at as a result of the chemical experiments conducted by Polinière is that fermentation results from the internal movement of the elements that compose a compound. The rarefied substance —*matière subtile*—works its way through the compound detaching and agitating the salt crystals, whose sharp edges divide and break up the rest of the compound, causing fermentation. Polinière believes that there is a rarefied substance which flows through various compounds and which causes the fluidity of liquids. This rarefied substance floats the sharp acid particles through the pores in the alkali crystals, which are much larger. Heat results from this movement. Eventually all of the sharp acid crystals lodge in the pores of the alkali crystals just big enough to admit them and the reaction ceases. (II, 41–44.)

Polinière also considers lightning as a chemical reaction, caused by the mixing of rarefied oils and acids in the middle airs. The resulting burst of flame, seen as lightning, heats and violently expands the surrounding air, which is heard as a thunderclap. The lightning zigzags because it detours around clouds. (II, 74–78.)

The section on anatomical experiments opens with a seven-page preface (II, 134–140) in which Polinière briefly describes the different parts of the body and the manner in which they function. He enumerates the medical discoveries of the seventeenth century and pinpoints the errors of the physicians of antiquity. It is interesting to note that he singles out the head as being the place where the soul resides and from which it controls the rest of the body.[20] He also marvels at the fact that insects start as eggs, turn into worms, and finally become winged animals, whereas snails, et cetera, are hermaphrodites. Such biological gymnastics, he informs us, are but another proof of the remarkable talents of the Creator, as is the infinite variety of animals and insects, the intricate and beautiful structure of a multitude of shellfish, et cetera.[21]

Next comes a nine-page introduction in which Polinière describes the instruments used in dissection, defines the anatomical terms he plans to use, and describes the way the various bodily organs function. (II, 141–149.)

[20] *Ibid.*, II, 135.
[21] *Ibid.*, II, 137–138.

Experiment thirteen consists in tying a live dog down to a table so it is immobilized and then slicing its abdomen open, singling out the chyle ducts and cutting them open to see how fats are transferred from the intestine to the blood stream. These manipulations are apparently not done without inflicting a certain degree of discomfort upon the dog involved, since four pages later, after having tied off one of the dog's veins in two places, slit it open along its entire length, pumped milk into the opening, and then made an incision in one of the arteries near the heart, Polinière remarks that the latter did not have very much blood in it after all because the dog was dead. The detachment with which he views the subject of his experiment reflects the Cartesian conviction that animals are fundamentally machines. (II, 150–157.)

In experiment fourteen, another dog is tied down, while Polinière opens its thigh and exposes the crural artery and vein. Tying each one off, he perceives that the artery swells up while the vein collapses between the ligature and the heart, showing which way the blood circulates. He then describes how the sweat glands work, leaving the dog tied down to the dissecting board with its heart still beating. (II, 158–164.) This oversight is rectified in experiment fifteen, during which Polinière cuts open the dog's neck, ties off the jugular vein, and makes an incision into it on the side nearest the heart. Into this incision he pours half a cup of vinegar, whereupon the animal "squirms and thrashes extraordinarily, appears to suffer much and dies in right little time." [22] He attributes the animal's demise to the coagulation of the blood due to the addition of the vinegar and remarks that upon dissecting the animal after this experiment, he has frequently found its heart and associated blood vessels to be full of blood of the consistency of salve. (II, 165–168.) Polinière's experiments, let us remember, were performed every year in each one of the ten teaching colleges of the University of Paris, as well as in the Jesuits' *Louis-le-Grand*. His systematic immolation of dogs in the interest of science may well explain why so little mention is made in the early eighteenth century of stray animals roaming the streets of Paris.

In experiment sixteen, he focusses his attention on such animals as toads and frogs, from which he removes the heart, noting that it continues to beat for about an hour after being removed from the body, which itself appears to remain alive for a similar period. He also cuts up a number of worms, snakes, eels, et cetera, and notes that the two halves apparently continue to lead a separate existence. He thinks this is because they breathe through the skin throughout their entire length and thus can function as two halves as easily as one whole. He admits frankly, however, that the toads and frogs have him mystified, for the experiment apparently refutes the

---

22 ". . . s'agite & se meut extraordinairement, paroît souffrir beaucoup, & meurt dans fort peu de temps." *Ibid.*, II, 165.

widely held belief that the brain produces animal spirits which are transmitted through the nerves to the heart. He wisely reserves judgment pending further experimentation, which he feels can only result in great advantage for "the progress of physics, the preservation and restoration of health, and even the better to contemplate the admirable designs of the Supreme Being who acts in us, around us and far from us in the vastness of the universe." [23]

The last group of experiments deals with color and light. There are thirty of them. In his introduction, he points out that no one can have an idea of what color is who has never had the use of sight, just as no one who was born deaf can understand sound. "Each one of us judges these different things solely by the impressions they make on the organs that are destined to receive them." [24] This is a sensualist theory which smacks of the philosophy of John Locke, and it indicates the degree to which Polinière, despite his Cartesian background, kept his mind open to the other philosophical theories developing around him.

Experiments eighteen and nineteen consist in mixing various dyes together to produce different colors. These colors, says Polinière, are produced by light reflecting off the surface of different objects in different manners or, in the case of liquids, by passing through them in different ways. (II, 179–191.)

Experiment twenty demonstrates the refraction of light rays as they pass from a medium of one density into a medium of another density, as, for example, an oar appears broken where it enters the water. Polinière demonstrates this very accurately, using a wine glass full of water with a coin in it and a protractor to measure the angle made by the ray of light. He points out that dawn and twilight are caused by this phenomenon. (II, 192–199.)

Experiment twenty-one demonstrates that prisms separate sunlight into the colors of the rainbow. The explanation offered by Polinière is that furnished by Newton's *Opticks* in the French translation published in 1720; [25] that light is composed of different rays, exciting the optic nerve in different manners, producing the impression of different colors, that these rays are reflected in different manners, and that they are refracted in different manners.[26] This experiment is therefore one of the ones added to later editions

[23] ". . . le progrès de la Physique, pour la conservation & pour le rétablissement de la santé, & même pour mieux contempler les desseins admirables de l'Etre suprême qui agit en nous, autour de nous, & loin de nous dans les espaces immenses de l'Univers." *Ibid.*, II, 172.

[24] "Chacun ne juge de ces différentes choses que par les impressions qu'elles font sur les organes propres à les recevoir." *Ibid.*, II, 178.

[25] *Traité d'optique sur les réflexions, réfractions, inflexions et couleurs de la lumière, par M. le Chev. Newton.* Amsterdam, 1720.

[26] Polinière, II, 203.

of the book, and it demonstrates the evolution of Polinière's thought under the influence of Newton as the latter's writings became better known in France. (II, 200–204.)

Experiments twenty-two, twenty-three, and twenty-four demonstrate that the different colors of the spectrum are refracted at different angles, twenty-two by using one prism, twenty-three by using two prisms, and twenty-four by using a prism and a mirror. In the latter experiment, for example, Polinière admits sunlight into a darkened room through a slit and passes it through a prism placed on top of a mirror. He notes that the violet is bent more sharply than the red as it passes through the prism and that the other colors are ranged in between. He further proves that the sunlight is indeed composed of all these colors by focussing the spectrum thus created through a magnifying glass on to a piece of paper, where it appears once more as white light. Since sunlight has all the colors in it, he explains, the color one sees is in the light, rather than in the colored object. The reason different things appear to be differently colored is that they reflect certain colors of the spectrum back to the eye of the viewer but do not reflect others. (II, 205–218.)

In experiment twenty-five, Polinière explains how the rainbow is created from sunlight reflected back to the eye of the beholder by a multitude of drops of water. (II, 218–222.) In his description, he points out that reproducing natural phenomena in the laboratory using techniques understood by the experimenter is the best way to learn how such phenomena are produced.[27]

In experiment twenty-six, Polinière demonstrates how the sun's rays can be focussed through a lens, or even a bottle of water, in such a way as to set fire to tinder or to a handful of sulphur matches. He also notes that black spots, such as print, on a piece of paper burst into flame more readily than the surrounding white paper, since black absorbs the light whereas white reflects it back to the eye. In the title of this experiment, he makes the statement that "the light of the Sun is a fire diffused through the air, similar to an ordinary fire."[28] In his explanation, however, he does not expand upon this fascinating theory, addressing himself rather to a detailed explanation of how the rays of the sun, which are considered as being parallel, can be made to converge in passing through a lens or a bottle of water. (II, 222–227.)

Experiment twenty-seven does the same thing with a candle placed at the focal point of a lens which concentrates its light at a considerable distance. (II, 228–233.) Number twenty-eight demonstrates that convex

---

27 *Ibid.*, II, 220.

28 "La lumière du Soleil est un feu répandu dans l'air, semblable à notre feu ordinaire." *Ibid.*, II, 222.

lenses magnify objects, whereas concave ones make them look smaller. (II, 233–236.) Experiment twenty-nine uses an apparatus much like a present-day camera to show that an object brought to focus by a lens is upside-down. In each of these two experiments, Polinière draws detailed diagrams to show the path of the rays of light from the object through the lens to the image. In order to show that the eye works the same way, Polinière uses a sheep's eye obtained from a slaughterhouse. He cuts a little window in the back of the eye, covers it with oiled paper and shows that the image of a candle flame is indeed formed on the paper upside-down. In the same experiment, he explains how to look at an object, first with both eyes, then with the right eye alone and then with the left eye alone. He thereby demonstrates that the right eye and both eyes see the object in the same place, while the left eye sees it in a different place. He apparently does not know what causes this phenomenon, which is due to the dominance of the left lobe of the brain over the right lobe, nor is he aware of the fact that the situation is reversed in left-handed people. (II, 236–245.)

Experiment thirty-one uses two lenses, one convex and the other concave, to show how glasses can be of help to nearsighted and farsighted people. Being a doctor, Polinière is aware that the vision of nearsighted people often improves with age and he explains how the changing shape of the eyeball brings this about. (II, 250–253.)

Experiment thirty-four shows that the planets rotate on their axes and revolve about the sun. Polinière describes how the mountains on the moon appear through a telescope, how their shadows lengthen and shorten, according to the elevation of the sun, and he supposes that the various other visible features are oceans, forests, and cultivated fields. Turning his attention to the sun, he explains how the eye may be protected from damage by using a smoked-glass eyepiece or by projecting the sun's image on a sheet of paper. He then describes how the telescope shows sunspots moving across the sun's disk. He believes them to be either rocks or foam floating in a luminous liquid and remarks that they take about thirteen days to cross the sun's disk and take another thirteen days or so to reappear from behind the sun, leading to the assumption that the sun has a twenty-seven-day period of rotation.

He observes that Mercury and Venus go through the same phases as the moon. He notes that Mars's orbit is outside that of the earth and says there is a large spot on it that changes shape as the planet changes its position with respect to the earth. He gives Mars's period of rotation as 24 h 40′ and its year as 686 earth days. He describes Jupiter as looking like Mars and notes the existence of its belts and the spot on it that passes from horizon to horizon. He also notes the existence of four satellites and gives Jupiter's year as eleven earth years, plus 313 days. He notes Saturn's rings and five satellites and gives its period of revolution around the sun as twenty-nine years and 155 days. (II, 271–283.) All of the data he supplies are reasonably close to twentieth-century figures, with the exception of the number of satellites belonging to Jupiter (twelve) and to Saturn (ten).

This experiment is followed by several pages of miscellaneous data concerning astronomy. For example, he identifies the Milky Way as a multitude of stars which he thinks are all suns and moons like our own, but farther away. He marvels, in fact, at the number of additional stars revealed by the telescope and offers several examples showing the difference between the number of stars in a given constellation that are visible to the naked eye and the number visible through a telescope. He also notes the existence of binary systems, both those whose light waxes and wanes as the position of the two components changes with relation to the earth and those which appear and disappear periodically, being composed of one luminous and one invisible member. He does not, however, suspect that two stars are involved in such systems.

Finally, he explains how the exact location of different places on earth can be calculated with a telescope and a precise chronometer, used to time the exact moment when a satellite of Jupiter goes into eclipse, as viewed from two different places. The difference in time permits calculating the difference in longitude between the places where the observations were made. (II, 284–288.)

Experiment thirty-five shows how a microscope works. Polinière explains in great detail, with the aid of diagrams, how the optical system of such an instrument behaves. (II, 289–295.) In experiment thirty-six, he demonstrates the circulation of the blood by looking at the tail of a tadpole through his microscope. (II, 295–300.)

In experiment thirty-seven, he describes some of the things to be seen with a microscope: the wing of a butterfly, the pollen in flowers, et cetera. He also describes the manner in which a multitude of little animals appear as if by magic in some water with a flower, a little hay, or a bit of bark in it left in the sun for several hours on a warm day. Far from believing in spontaneous generation, however, he feels that the little animals "come from other little invisible animals that fly through the air, laying their eggs in the plants, in the water, et cetera." [29] This part of the text is posterior to 1729, since it contains references to articles published in the *Mercure de France* that year.[30] (II, 300–311.)

Experiment thirty-eight explains how the eye of a fly forms a myriad of

29 "On prétend que les petits animaux ainsi vûs . . . viennent d'autres petits animaux imperceptibles qui voltigent dans l'air. Ces petits animaux . . . déposent leurs oeufs sur les Plantes, dans les eaux, etc." *Ibid.*, II, 303–304.

30 *Ibid.*, II, 306, 307.

images of the object viewed. (II, 311–316.) Number thirty-nine shows how the image of an object placed between two mirrors is multiplied an infinite number of times. (II, 316–318.) In experiment twenty-six, Polinière demonstrates how the sun's rays, focused through a magnifying glass, can be used to set things afire. In number forty, he shows how the same thing can be done with a parabolic reflector. Indeed, he points out that such a solar furnace will melt lead and tin. (II, 319–324.)

Experiment forty-one explains how a *camera obscura* works. (II, 325–330.) Experiment forty-two describes the construction of a magic lantern to project transparencies. Polinière's version uses pictures painted on glass with transparent paint, which are projected on a sheet with a lens mounted in a box. As a projection lamp, he uses either sunlight or a lamp with a parabolic mirror behind it. (II, 331–336.)

In experiment forty-five, Polinière comes to the conclusion that light is perceived as a subjective reaction due to the pressure exerted by some rarefied substance or other that is in motion. He is led to this conclusion by seeing sparks produced by static electricity in the dark. (II, 347–355.)

In experiment forty-seven, Polinière describes how certain minerals fluoresce in the dark after having been exposed to sunlight. He thinks that certain minerals are porous and soak up particles of light in much the same way as a sponge absorbs water. (II, 362–368.) In the last experiment, he describes how phosphorous glows in the dark. He feels this is due to a chemical reaction between some acid or other and a sulphurous material contained in the phosphorous. He further believes that the reaction is similar to displays of the Aurora Borealis he saw on the nights of October 19, 1726 and March 14, 1727. He also remarks on the phosphorescence of rotten wood, of certain fish, and of light emitted by glow-worms and by the static electricity obtained by stroking a cat's fur. (II, 369–376.)

The second volume closes with a number of general observations concerning experimental physics. Polinière feels that the experiments he has described offer visible proof of a divine being who has created the universe and who presides over its destinies. "Physics, when properly treated," he points out, "becomes a sort of demonstrative theology with a persuasive force that is irresistible to the most obstinate unbeliever." [31]

Physics did not come into its own, he thinks, until experimentation was added to reasoning. He rejoices that the science of physics has made more progress in the past one hundred years than it did in the previous two thousand, and he gives voice to a sort of breathless optimism at living in a time that is so favorable to the advancement of knowledge that almost any dis-

[31] "La Physique, bien traitée, devient une Théologie démonstrative d'une force insurmontable à l'incrédulité la plus opiniâtre." *Ibid.*, II, 379.

covery becomes possible and that no mystery is so obscure that the physicist cannot hope one day to penetrate it. (II, 376–382.)

What conclusions can we draw from a reading of Polinière's manual? First of all, his grasp of mechanics was quite sound. He understood simple machines and moments of force, centrifugal force, Archimedes' principle, specific gravity, the incompressibility of liquids, air pressure and the things it could accomplish, air resistance, gravity, the earth's magnetic field, the impenetrability of matter, the relationship between light and color, as well as parabolic reflectors, and he could adapt these optical devices to solar furnaces, magic lanterns, opaque projectors, telescopes, and microscopes.

On the other hand, he was completely ignorant of surface tension, molecular movement, and the difference as well as the relationship between matter and energy. Neither did he understand combustion, the fact that gases could be dissolved in liquids, static electricity, or the electrical nature of brain waves. He thought heat and fire were forms of matter and that static electricity was a form of heat.

The knowledge he possessed and the gaps therein produced a number of odd conclusions born of an incomplete grasp of his subject. For example, he knew how capillary action occurred from observing it, but he could not explain it satisfactorily because he did not understand surface tension. This being the case, he reduced plant growth to a question of hydraulics. He was familiar with medicine, biology, anatomy, the circulation of the blood, the respiratory system, et cetera, but he felt that baby chicks were born because they were forced out of the egg by the heat of the mother hen's body expanding the sack of air in the shell. He also felt that plant germination was due to the sun's heat expanding the air in the seed. Not understanding molecular movement, he described compressed air in terms of little wedges. He knew that heat expanded solids, liquids, and gases, but he imagined it was because little particles of the substance he thought heat to be insinuated themselves among the little particles of the solid, the liquid, or the gas. He knew air to be a fluid, but he did not understand the origin of the winds because he did not understand the nature of heat. He knew that air transmitted sound and he was familiar with the periodic vibrations of solids, the relation between the latter and the sounds they produced, as well as with Huygen's findings concerning the elasticity of solids. But being unfamiliar with molecular movement, simple harmonic motion, et cetera, he lacked the common denominator between these various phenomena that would have allowed him to explain them.

He was strongly influenced by Descartes's vortex theories and the latter's attitude toward animals, but he kept abreast of the work of later authorities such as Huygens, Newton, and Keill. His views toward medicine were admirably modern and humane; he understood the laws governing reproduction and thus did not waste time on the theory of spontaneous generation shared by so many of his less-learned contemporaries. Perhaps this is why he showed no tendency to embark upon the atheistic route followed by a number of later eighteenth-century thinkers. On the contrary, his work shows a strong religious bias.

His approach to physics was theoretical rather than quantitative. He was interested only in the principles involved and made little attempt to measure the phenomena he observed or to evaluate them quantitatively in any way. Perhaps it was just as well, for his demonstrations must have come as a dazzling revelation to the young minds he was called upon to deal with, unencumbered as they were with exacting calculations.

Indeed, this aspect of his work is of considerable interest to us today, for his dramatically exploding bottles, flying projectiles, jets of water, and rainbows projected on the wall must have done much to relieve the monotony of hours spent by students copying Latin into their philosophy notebooks under the dictation of less pedagogically resourceful colleagues. A forerunner in his own field of experimental physics, he was also an innovator in the teaching field. Instrumental in the training of hundreds of students, his methods were startlingly modern in an age that is commonly thought of as pedagogically sterile.

But the oustanding feature of his work was the manner in which he manipulated the empirical method. He felt that experimenting with natural phenomena was the logical complement to thinking about it, that empiricism was the counterpart of rationalism. He was, in fact, a rationalist by training who evolved toward empiricism. The manner in which he conducted his experiments was rigorously empirical, yet nothing betrays his Cartesian origins more surely than the manner in which he lapses into rationalism in experiment sixty-four of volume one, as he seeks to explain why the earth's magnetic force can travel through water without displacing it.

This is why he is of interest to us today. He represents the transition from rationalism to empiricism in the classrooms of the Paris colleges and he shows the manner in which it came about: through a conviction that reproducing natural phenomena in the laboratory would help his students to understand them better. His influence in this respect must have been considerable, particularly in view of his remarkably modern teaching techniques. Paris was then, as it is now, France's major center of learning, and Polinière's demonstrations were carried out each year, between 1703 and 1733, in all of the major colleges of the city. For thirty years, therefore, he was in a position which allowed him to influence all of the philosophy students who were being educated in the capital. His was indeed a strategic position, more strategic by far than the position he would have occupied had he been only a classroom teacher in one particular college. It permitted him to channel the thinking of an entire generation of France's most influential men by orienting it toward the empirical school. There is little doubt that he played a major role in the remarkably rapid evolution of philosophy teaching in the Paris schools, from scholasticism through rationalism to empiricism in a scant generation's time.

THE ROLE OF ENGLAND IN VOLTAIRE'S POLEMIC AGAINST PASCAL: APROPOS THE TWENTY-FIFTH *PHILOSOPHICAL LETTER*

BY ROLAND DESNÉ

THE TWENTY-FIFTH *Philosophical Letter* "ON THE *Pensées* OF MR. PAS-
CAL" IS MADE UP OF 57 REMARKS, OCCUPYING 99 PAGES OF THE 387 IN THE
JORE EDITION,[1] THAT IS TO SAY MORE THAN A QUARTER OF THE WORK. IT
IS, IN TERMS OF LENGTH, THE MOST IMPORTANT *Philosophical Letter*.

IT ALSO SEEMS TO BE THE MOST IMPORTANT IN CONTENT, SINCE,
according to Voltaire's own testimony in his *Correspondence*, it is supposed,
more than the other letters, to have brought repression upon him.[2]

The problem—or the paradox—is that this letter does not deal with
England; it does not discuss an aspect of the life, the beliefs, or the thought
of the English. It concerns a French philosopher, Pascal. Is there a connection
between the letters on the English and the letter on Pascal? Is it by chance—
or because of internal necessity—that Voltaire ends his plea for England by
an indictment of Pascal? These questions have often been asked in Voltaire
criticism. It does not seem useless to ask them again, if only to attempt to
circumscribe a set of problems.

A first problem, the most obvious, is, what connection can be established
between the twenty-fifth letter and the twenty-four that precede it? A
problem of creation: how and why in composing his book did Voltaire include this letter on Pascal in the collection of his letters on England? A
problem of theme: what are the links that connect his remarks on Pascal's
Pensées with the reflections found in the other letters?

Which leads us to a second problem: if we ask whether Pascal is not
out of place in the *English Letters*, are we not asking whether Pascal was
not present, in some manner, in the England that Voltaire knew? In other
words, to study the role of England in the remarks on Pascal compels one
to ask questions on the role of Pascal in contemporary England.

1 *Lettres philosophiques par M. de Voltaire*, (Amsterdam, chez E. Lucas, au livre d'or
[Rouen, Jore, 1734]). This edition served as the basic text for Gustave Lanson's critical
edition (reedited by André M. Rousseau, S.T.F.M., Paris, 1964).

2 See, for instance, letters to Cideville (May 8, 1734), to the duchesse d'Aiguillon
(around May 23, 1734). (Correspondence, vol. III, in *Complete Works*, ed. Besterman,
[Toronto-Geneva, 1969]; D 736, p. 15; D 746, p. 25.)

Roland Desné

From this point of view, might not the argument against Pascal be envisaged as one aspect of a participation in a vast current of ideas, a rationalistic and antireligious current common to England and France in these first years of the eighteenth century? That would be a third problem: one might suppose that Voltaire relied on the English example the better to discredit Pascal; by discrediting Pascal, he reinforced the Anglo-French current of free thinking.

In this perspective, a fourth and last problem appears: can we not find in the "anti-Pascal"[3] the affirmation of a view of man, the illustration of a moral conception that could find its full meaning only in the living example of the mores and thought of the English?

I

As for the connection between the twenty-fifth letter and the preceding twenty-four, it seems self-evident that we should see nothing more in it than a chance proximity. For Lanson *The English Letters* ended, "to tell the truth," with the twenty-fourth letter.[4] For the editor of "Blackwell's French Texts," Voltaire merely amused himself in adding to his reflections on England a piece of anti-Pascalian polemics: "This was an innocent and even defensible amusement."[5] Why therefore try to establish a serious connection between this attack and the description of England? The proof that such a connection does not exist could even be given in the stages of composition of Voltaire's book.

Voltaire, indeed, had been preparing a work on the English nation since his journey. On the spot he took notes, probably wrote several letters, and on his return to France undertook the main work of composition. His text was by then ready for the most part and underwent only a few corrections and changes in 1732. When, around December 15, 1732, Voltaire told Formont that he was about to send him "a manuscript copy of all [his] letters to Thiériot on the religion, the government, the philosophy and the poetry of the English,"[6] there was no mention at all of Pascal. A few months later, he told Thiériot: "I am sending you the letter on the Academies *which is the last one.*"[7]

So, on the one hand Voltaire was preparing a book on England; on the other hand the idea occurred to him to combat Pascal. It is difficult to tell exactly when this project took precise shape in his mind. We note that in the

---

[3] We mean by this all the remarks which make up the twenty-fifth Letter of 1734, in accordance with Voltaire's own words: "Limit yourself, I beg of you, to the letters and the anti-Pascal" (to Thiériot, July 14, 1733; Correspondence, II, 360).

[4] G. Lanson, *Voltaire* (Paris, 1906), 49.

[5] Voltaire, *Lettres philosophiques,* ed. F. A. Taylor (Oxford, 1965), p. 183.

[6] *Ed. cit.,* II, 260.

[7] Around April 1, 1733. *Ibid.,* 312.

44

Essai sur la Poésie épique (1728) Pascal, criticized by a disparager of Homer, is classified among the "overly philosophical minds who have stifled all feeling in themselves." [8] We note that during the summer of 1732, Voltaire actually worked on a refutation of Pascal: *Le Mercure de France* published on September 15 an epistle dated August 15 in which one can read:

> I examine with care the shapeless writings . . .
> of the famous Pascal—that bigoted satirist . . .
> I denounce his extreme severity.
> He teaches men to hate themselves.
> I would teach them self-esteem [9]

This new work was almost completed in June 1733. It was then that Voltaire expressed the wish to attach his remarks on Pascal to the letters on England already being printed. Formont whose opinion he asked advised him against following out this project.[10] Voltaire held firm and insited that Thiériot, in charge of the publication in England, add the letter on Pascal to the other twenty-four. But this Thiériot did not do.[11] No doubt it was too late to add an English translation of this "anti-Pascal" to the *Letters Concerning the English Nation*, which came out in August 1733. But the French version published in London in 1734 did not include the letter on Pascal either.

It was Voltaire who decided to include this letter in the edition published in Rouen by Jore, in that same year, 1734. As a consequence, as everyone knows, the title of the book was changed: *Lettres Philosophiques* instead of *Lettres écrites de Londres sur les anglais et autres sujets*.

This being so we may surmise that the connection established by Voltaire between the English letters and the twenty-fifth letter was a connection of interest, and nothing more: the author might have added the remarks on Pascal as an epilogue to reveal the philosophical meaning of his commentaries on England.[12]

---

[8] *Oeuvres*, ed. Moland, VIII, 319. Pomeau notes that Voltaire read Pascal as early as 1735 (*La Religion de Voltaire*, 2d edition [Paris, 1969], p. 97), and he thinks that the indication given by the first sentence of the twenty-fifth letter ("the critical observations I made long ago") would date the first version of these remarks from before 1726.

[9] Quoted by Lanson, *Lettres philosophiques*, II, 227. It is therefore difficult to agree with Pomeau (see note 8) when he asserts that Voltaire, having made a first draft of his remarks before 1726, "reworked and completed them in 1733." It was during the summer of 1732 that the refutation of Pascal was developed and organized.

[10] To Formont (around June 1, 1733); to Cideville (July 14), II, 343 and 358.

[11] And yet Voltaire's letter was urgent (to Thiériot, July 14, 1733; *ibid.*, 359–360).

[12] In his letter to Cideville (July 14, 1733), Voltaire, the better to convince his correspondent perhaps, limited himself to a technical argument ("the book was too short") and to a tactical argument ("if I displease the Jansenist fools, I shall have these scoundrelly Reverend Fathers on my side"). That same day he put forward to Thiériot an *ad hominem*

Roland Desné

This might explain why the references to England in this last letter are so scarce. Indeed, from the thematic point of view, it is clear that those who consider the link between the remarks on Pascal and the other *Philosophical Letters* to be merely artificial, can find support in the small number of precise references—either explicit or implicit—to English data. Here is their inventory as they arise in the remarks:

Rem. III   According to Lanson (see note 8, p. 229), Voltaire, discussing original sin, seems "imbued with the ideas" of the Anglican theologian King.

Rem. VI   (l. 204–212) [13]: The text quoted by Voltaire ("from one of my friends who lives abroad") is that of a letter from the English merchant Falkener.

(l. 225–226): Voltaire invites his reader to consider the human condition in terms that seem to echo a passage in Shaftesbury's *Characteristics* (see note 16 in Lanson, p. 231).

Rem. VII   (l. 242–247): The remark on the expectation of a Messiah by the Jews may have been suggested to Voltaire by Bayle or by Houtteville, but also by reading English newspapers (see note 20 in Lanson, p. 231).

Rem. XI   (l. 332): These "merchants [who] are supposed to have gone to the Indies out of charity" are, obviously, English merchants.

The whole of this *XIth Remark*, Lanson observes, expresses the "moral philosophy of English deism" (see note 30, p. 231–232) and he compares the Voltairian point of view with a passage from Shaftesbury.

Rem. XV   (l. 419–420): Lanson cites the *Discourse on the Grounds and Reasons of the Christian Religion* by Collins, about the argument drawn from the likeness between pagan oracles and biblical prophets, indicating however that: "there is no particular relation between Voltaire's text or thought and Collins's" (note 38, p. 232).

Rem. XXIII   (l. 521–526): Concerning the exercise of the faculty of thought, Voltaire answers Pascal as an adept of Locke's sensualism, although Locke is not named.

Rem. XXXI   (l. 672–674): "An Englishman named Flamsteed . . ."

Rem. XXXIV   (l. 707): Another reference to an English scientist: Newton.

argument (this "little book . . . must bring you further profits"); but he also added: "This will make it a reasonably long book without this last letter being in anyway inapropos."

[13] The line indications correspond to the numbers in the Lanson edition.

46

Rem. XXXVIII   (l. 760–762) : On the number of suicides in London.
Rem. L   (l. 902) : Voltaire mentions the name of Marlborough.

Thus, out of fifty-seven remarks only ten contain a direct or indirect allusion to English affairs or people; and in only five do English names occur, London being quoted twice.

These indications are indeed few in number. (Although, as we shall see, other points of similarity with English texts can be suggested.) They are few in number, but they are interesting. They might permit us to date certain remarks (the first?) that Voltaire wrote against Pascal from his stay in London. But this hypothesis must be proposed with caution: Voltaire may have added these few references to London, Newton, Marlborough, et cetera, afterwards, as if to confront Pascal from the point of view of an Englishman or of a Frenchman residing in England. In that case it would be a reading of Pascal through English glasses.

Do these half-dozen more or less explicit references to England constitute a mere device of presentation, allowing the author to give a kind of coherence, or a semblance of unity, to his collection of *Philosophical Letters?* Then this device would mask the purely national quality of the debate with Pascal: Voltaire, a Frenchman, settling accounts with another Frenchman for the benefit of French readers' meditation and culture. Which amounts to our wondering what Pascal could be to the English.

II

If Pascal is also an author that the English of that time can comment on or discuss, then looking at Pascal through English glasses is no longer merely a device. It is taking a stand in a debate.

We now know that Pascal's presence was a reality in England. He was known, he was read. Above all he was made use of. Pascal's success in England is obviously an aspect—or a consequence—of the relations between Jansenists and Anglicans. On this point all necessary information has been gathered in Miss Ruth Clark's book, *Strangers and Sojourners at Port-Royal.*[14]

We must recall that the Anglicans' sympathy with the Jansenists could have three different reasons: both had a common enemy, the Jesuits; the Anglicans, in order to break out of the relative isolation of the Church of England, placed their hope in Jansenism to draw closer to the Gallican Clergy—indeed throughout the seventeenth century there were plans for agreement between the two churches; finally, as a doctrine Jansenism was not devoid of analogies with Calvinism, which was related to Anglican Protestantism.

[14] (Cambridge, 1932). See also Pierre Janelle, "Pascal et l'Angleterre," in *Pascal présent 1662–1962* (Clermont-Ferrand, 1963).

Roland Desné

In these circumstances, it is not surprising that Pascal should have been translated in England very early: an English edition of *Les Provinciales* can be found as early as 1657. The *Pensées* did not enjoy so immediate a reaction. It was not until 1688 that they were published in a first translation by a certain Joseph Walker of whom nothing is known. From our present point of view the quality of the translation is not important. On the other hand it is most important to know that this translation contained, as a preface, a dedicatory letter to Sir Robert Boyle, patron of the Boyle lectures and champion of the fight against irreligion. This indeed was the beginning of the deistic offensive and the counteroffensive of the theologians. *Monsieur Pascal's Thoughts* made a direct contribution to the defense of Gallican orthodoxy. Moreover, in his preface, John Walker did not hesitate to compare Boyle with Pascal: "He was called, like you, a Christian philosopher and mathematician. You too devoted your entire life and your wealth to laborious research into the remotest corners of nature, for the Glory of God and religion, and for the welfare of mankind." [15]

Sixteen years later, in 1704, we find another edition of the *Pensées* in a translation by Basil Kennett, better than the first one. This translation had a second edition in 1727, a third probably around 1730; it was published again in 1741, 1749, and 1751.

This success of the *Pensées* in England, concerning which we have only limited evidence, ought to be the subject of a systematic study.[16] Examination of English periodicals and exploration of the private libraries of the period would no doubt bring further items for evaluation. It is enough, however, to recall this success, to note that the *Pensées* were republished in English at the very time of Voltaire's stay in England, in order to understand that Pascal in the 1720s and 1730s appeared as a common adversary to the French philosopher and his free-thinking English friends.[17]

To be convinced of this, one need only read the foreword—added to the 1727 edition—in which the story of Pascal's life by Gilberte Perier was presented: "The extraordinary Humility and Devotion of M. Pascal gives

[15] Not being able to consult the original, we have quoted here the translation by Pierre Janelle in his excellent study (p. 162). *Retranslated*.

[16] On a few echoes of Pascal in England, see L. Charlanne: *L'Influence française en Angleterre, le théâtre et la critique* (Paris, 1906), 112–113, and Pierre Janelle, who notes that *The Spectator* speaks twice of the *Pensées*, in 1711 and 1714. In the issue of July 15, 1711, Budgell, a cousin and collaborator of Addison's, discussed Pascal's idea on *distraction* in connection with hunting.

[17] Although he considers that the twenty-fifth letter "was linked to the rest of the book only by its polemical intent," A. Bellessort pertinently remarked: "I would not be surprised that the idea to add it came to Voltaire from the irritation he must have felt when he came up against Pascal's reputation among the English" (*Essai sur Voltaire* [Paris, 1925], 76).

a more sensible Mortification to the libertines of the Age than if one was to let loose upon them a dozen of missionaries." [18] By fighting Pascal, Voltaire expressed an active solidarity with English unbelievers. Had not Collins suggested an "anti-Pascal" when he reminded the reader in his *Scheme of Literal Prophecy*: "The celebrated Pascal says: *The most convincing of the proofs of Jesus-Christ are the prophecies . . .*"? [19] Voltaire knew he was not alone in the path which he had chosen: "It is not . . . Lord Shaftesbury, nor Mr. Collins, nor Mr. Toland, et cetera, who have carried the torch of discord in their native country: it is theologians, for the most part, who, first animated by the ambition of being leaders of their sect, have soon afterward desired to be heads of parties." [20]

III

Thus it appears that Voltaire's argument against Pascal is a contribution to the Anglo-French movement of rationalist thought.

Voltaire espoused the cause of deism against the apologists who were at work on both sides of the Channel. This passage from the thirteenth letter leaves no doubt on this point: ". . . Theologians have a bad habit of complaining that God is outraged when someone has simply failed to be of their opinion. They are too much like the bad poets who accused Boileau of speaking offensively of the King, because he was making fun of them." [21] We find something of an echo of this remark at the beginning of the letter on Pascal: "In fact, I think that all these books that people have been writing lately as proofs of the Christian religion are more likely to shock than to edify." [22] Was Voltaire here thinking in particular of the apologia by Abbé Houtteville? It is possible.[23] But the remark is quite in the spirit of deistic attacks against the English theologians.[24]

---

[18] Cited by Ruth Clark, 114.

[19] *The Scheme of Literal Prophecy* (London, 1726), 331. Cited by René Pomeau, 173, note 56.

[20] *Thirteenth Letter*, "On Mr. Locke," (ed. Lanson), I, 175–176.

[21] *Ibid.*, 170. This attack is aimed at certain "pious" Englishmen who fought against Locke. But when Voltaire wrote: "The superstitious are in society what cowards are in an army: they are seized by, and they spread, panic terror," it is evident that these "superstitious" are to be found in France as well as in England.

[22] *Ibid.*, II, 185.

[23] See note 2 in Lanson's edition, 228.

[24] See for instance how Tindal, in *A Defence of the Rights of the Christian Church* (London, 1709) 8, derides his adversary, Wotton, supported by the Anglican hierarchy: ". . . the papists can't but be pleas'd to see a Book which pulls up Popery by the roots, attack'd on such principles as overthrow the Protestant religion." See also how Collins attacks Whiston in the preface to his *Discourse of the Grounds and Reasons of the Christian Religion* (London, 1724). Let us note finally that in the year in which Voltaire was working on his "anti-Pascal," there appeared, through the efforts of Thémiseul de Sainte-Hyacinthe,

Our twenty-fifth letter is in the main stream of English freethinking. Voltaire adopts moreover all its different possible tones, from Locke's moderate tone in *The Reasonableness of Christianity*:

> "Christianity teaches nothing but simplicity, humanity, charity; to wish to reduce it to metaphysics is to make of it a source of error"; [25]

to the aggressive and insolent manner of an Anthony Collins or a John Toland:

> "The point is to prove that the religion of Jesus-Christ is the true one, and that those of Mahomet, the pagans, and all the rest are false." [26]

> "Scripture, then, speaks in accordance with this vulgar prejudice. . . ." [27]

> "Did all the pagans believe in the false miracles with which they were inundated, only because they had seen true ones?" [28]

Other examples could be given. The question here posed to researchers is that of the specific influence of the English deists on Voltaire. Voltaire seems in fact not to have used recognizable passages from the works of deists like Tindal, Woolston, Collins, or Toland. But, for that matter, Lanson does not reject the idea of a kinship between Voltaire and English deists: [29] we may remark with him that certain themes were very widespread at the time and wonder whether identifying possible references is not a vain or futile undertaking.

Failing to find such references, Norman Torrey, in the only comprehensive study devoted up to now to the relations between Voltaire and the English deists, thought he could go beyond Lanson's nuanced point of view and conclude that English influence, in this case, was exercised only at a much later date than that of the stay in England and of the *Philosophical Letters*. "There is no evidence in the note-book . . . that he had ever heard of Toland, Collins, or Woolston, or of the main deistic controversy. The evidence

---

the *Mémoires concernant la théologie et la morale* (Amsterdam, 1732), which contain the translation of a "Lettre anglaise de M. Thomas Chubb à un de ses amis": to those who accused him of promoting incredulity, Chubb retorted that *"representing religion as my adversaries represent it* is opening the way to incredulity" (pp. 181–182; author's italics).

[25] *Remark I*, Lanson's edition, II, 186.

[26] *Remark II, ibid.*, 187.

[27] *Remark XXXI, ibid.*, 212.

[28] *Remark XLI, ibid.*, 218.

[29] For instance, "it can only be presumed that Collins must have had some influence on the formation of Voltaire's critique of the Scriptures" (*ibid.*, 232). We have noted, above, Lanson's judgment on *Remark XI*.

from the *Philosophical Letters* is likewise mainly negative. Among the bolder deists, Collins and Toland are only mentioned, and merely named as philosophers." [30] This remark was taken up again and stressed by G. Bonno in his great study on English influence in France between 1713 and 1734.[31] This thesis does not seem totally convincing. On the one hand one must not ask from the notebooks more than they can supply: the two notebooks which may draw our attention here, the "Leningrad" one which covers the years 1726–1729 and the "Cambridge" one begun in 1726–1727 and used for several years, take up only nineteen and forty-two pages respectively in the Besterman edition. How might we find within a few dozen pages the trace of conversations and readings that engaged Voltaire's mind for six or seven years? If nothing could be found in these notebooks that had some relation to English deism, one should not draw from this the conclusion that Voltaire was indifferent or ignorant. If nothing could be found . . . but in fact, more than one deistic echo can be found. For instance: "How very few are wise enough to admire the daily birth of light and the new creation of all things wich born every day with light. . . ." [32] Or again: "Ignorant divines suported by more ignorant men are the founders of all religions, men of wit, founders of heresies, men of understanding laugh at both." [33] And this "Relligio, an [?custom] invented by craftsmen who are wonded by it." [34] Such remarks seem to be precise enough and, all told, numerous enough for us to assert, against Messrs. Torrey and Bonno, that Voltaire's attention was oriented toward the deists' works long before the final composition of the *Philosophical Letters*.[35] One may wonder especially that historians who were so well informed about English actualities could have put forward the idea that Voltaire, in his thirteenth letter, might have cited the names of Collins and

[30] Norman Torrey, *Voltaire and the English Deists* (New Haven, Conn., 1930), 50.

[31] G. Bonno, *La Culture et la civilisation britannique devant l'opinion française de la Paix d'Utrecht aux "Lettres philosophiques"* (Transactions of the American Philosophical Society, vol. 38, I, [Philadelphia, 1948]). "Before 1735, the attention of French writers was not attracted to that kind of work" (p. 109). "It was only later . . . around 1738, that Voltaire had his *first encounter* with the English deistic literature." (*Ibid.*, italics by me, R. D.) The exaggeration is obvious here.

[32] Carnet de Léningrad (ed. Besterman), *The Complete Works of Voltaire* (Geneva-Toronto, 1968) *Notebooks*, I, 55. This "English" remark curiously anticipates the description of a morning walk at Ferney, reproduced by R. Pomeau, 416–417.

[33] Carnet de Léningrad, *ed. cit.*, 62.

[34] Carnet de Cambridge, *ibid.*, 74. In the same notebook we also find: "No one contests the essential point of religion, which is to do good; we contest unintelligible dogmas" (71).

[35] Another proof of this will be found in the "outline of a Letter on the English" reproduced by Lanson (II, 256–267) in which Voltaire wrote: "I have seen four very learned treatises against the reality of Jesus Christ's Miracles [Woolston's discourses, R. D.], printed here with impunity, at the same time when a poor bookseller was pilloried for publishing a translation of *La Religieuse en chemise*" (*ibid.*, 264).

Toland as those of philosophers merely and not as deists. Collins's works show clearly enough, and often in their very titles, that such a distinction is idle and that for him philosophy consists precisely in the exercise of free-thinking. As for Toland, whose *Collection of Several Pieces* appeared in that very year, 1726, in London: he was looked upon, by every one, as a deter-mined adversary of Christianity.[36]

From his readings as much as from his conversations, Voltaire was perfectly well informed about the controversies between the English deists and their adversaries.[37] Although we need not look for a literal source for each of the arguments put forward against Pascal, English freethinking from Locke and Shaftesbury to Collins and Toland can be considered as the foster home of anti-Pascal criticism.[38] Voltaire was prepared moreover to benefit in that respect from his sojourn in England by the activity of French rationalists like Fontenelle, Bayle, and the authors of the first clandestine manuscripts. The themes upon which the reader of the twenty-fifth letter is invited to ponder are unquestionably those which English freethinkers had introduced to the general public. It is not difficult to draw up a list of them:

—the impossibility of proving the truth of Christianity (*Rem. V*).

[36] He defines himself, in his epitaph, as "veritatis propugnator, libertatis assertor" (*A Collection of Several Pieces of Mr. John Toland*, 2 vols. [London, 1726], vol. I, p. LXXX-VIII). It is enough to read at the beginning of this book the "Memoirs of the Life and Writings of John Toland" (pp. III–XCII), the obituary in the *Freeholders Journal* (cited p. XC) as well as "An Elegy on the Late Ingenious Mr. Toland" (pp. XIV–XV) to elimi-nate all doubt about this philosopher's place and reputation in England.

[37] And no doubt, thanks to Bolingbroke, even before he left for England. As André Rousseau observes, in a supplementary note to the Lanson edition (313, note 8), the rela-tionship between Bolingbroke and Voltaire should be restudied.

[38] To search for a precise English source for the various arguments put forward by Voltaire can seem to be, as we have already said, a futile undertaking. But a more attentive and more systematic study of the English philosophical output in the twenties and thirties would certainly stimulate various comparisons. Lanson felt for instance, concerning *Remark XV* that there was "no particular relation between Voltaire's text or thought and Collins's" (*ed. cit.*, 232). He could have noted however, concerning *Remark XIII*, that the argument and the quotation from Luc XXI are in *The Scheme of Literal Prophecy* (London, 1726), 157. If it is true that the remark on the expectation of a deliverer by the Jews (*Rem. VII* and *XII*) is "everywhere" (see Lanson, 231, note 20), it is also in the very first page of the first chapter in Collins's *Scheme* (13–14). When Voltaire, attacking the miracles (*Rem. XLI*) wrote: "The first man who was ever ill, believed, without any difficulty, in the first charlatan," he summed up, in a short sentence, commentaries he could have found about the woman cured of her bleeding, or about the man blind from birth in the second and third *Discourses on the Miracles* . . . by Woolston (London, 1728), A Second Discourse . . . 12–13; A Fourth Discourse . . . 11–14. Woolston felt that by his healing of the blind man, Jesus had not been equalled "by any *quack doctor*" and that he was "a juggling Im-postor" (a Fourth Discourse, 11 and 14). Woolston had said plainly that Jesus was a charla-tan. Voltaire was content to suggest it.

—the distinction between philosophy and religion (*Rem. II*), along with a variant: the distinction between morality and religion (*Rem. XLII*).

—the critique of original sin, and variations on the theme of natural morality (*Rem. III, IV, VI, XI, XIII,* etc.).

—the critique of the spirituality of the soul and of dualism (*Rem. IV, LVI*).

—the critique of predestination (*Rem. V*).

—the critique of the prophecies of the Old Testament (*Rem. VII, XII, XIII, XIV, XV*).

—the critique of the Hebraic tradition (*Rem. VIII, IX*).

—the contradictions in the Gospels (*Rem. VII*), and their corollary, their obscurity (*Rem. XVIII*) or their puerility (*Rem. XXXI*).

—the critique of the argument drawn from the Christian martyrs (*Rem. XXIX* and especially *XXXIII*).

—the critique of miracles (*Rem. XLI*).

We could take this inventory set down in the order of the remarks on Pascal, and, starting from the elements thus given by Voltaire, reconstruct an almost complete demonstration, in the manner of a deist debating against the argumentation of Anglican or Catholic apologists. Yet, unlike the anti-religious polemicists or the theologians who opposed them, Voltaire does not set up his arguments in a didactic order: he does not make a coherent demonstration. His refutation of Pascal follows a much more sinuous, seemingly disorganized, and whimsical path. In reality this supple and insinuating progress is in a way an application of Pascal's method at Pascal's expense. Here Voltaire conducts his plea in accordance with the *esprit de finesse,* unlike most of the deist authors who tended to indulge too heavily in the *esprit de géométrie*.[39]

One can therefore understand that these remarks on Pascal are in no way out of place in the series of *Lettres anglaises*. One must also observe that the space occupied by this polemic against Pascal is not excessive in quantity in relation to the proportions of the work. The twenty-fifth letter, as we said before, accounts for ninety-nine pages of the original edition, and the first seven letters (on the Quakers, the Church of England, the Presbyterians, the Socinians) account for sixty-three pages. That is to say, if we consider only Voltaire's text, not counting the quotations from Pascal, the *Philosophical Letters* open and close with two sets of reflections on religion of almost equal length. The first seven letters present a picture of tolerance in England, and it is a colorful and reassuring one; the twenty-fifth letter suggests the price of this tolerance: bringing "fanatics" like Pascal back to

[39] Note that, at the same period, in France, this "esprit de géométrie" was carried to extremes—and for the expression of atheism by the curé Meslier.

reason. In Pascal, Voltaire thus sees an obstacle to an enlightened religious attitude. He also sees the obstacle to a new moral attitude.

IV

We find again in the letter on Pascal—and almost in each remark— the two guiding ideas underlying the philosophy in the other letters as a whole. On the one hand, human nature must be taken as it is; on the other hand, the world must be taken as it is.

To take human nature as it is means not to condemn concrete mankind in the name of an abstract conception of man. Voltaire considers Pascal from the empiricist point of view, which is also Locke's: he refuses to get involved with the soul.[40]

To take the world as it is means to take it as a vast field open to man's activity. Man's true greatness lies precisely in his aptitude to act on the world, to ameliorate the conditions of human existence. To the contemplative mode, Voltaire opposes the active mode.

As Pomeau has very aptly said, Pascalian anguish was "attuned to the state of mankind at the time of and just after the Thirty Years War. It was the world of Brecht's *Mother Courage*." Voltaire, on the contrary, expresses the "new idea of happiness on earth," a confidence in man attuned to the well-being and prosperity reigning in France and especially in England under the ministries of Fleury and Walpole.[41] And the determining social force of this prosperity was, to Voltaire's mind, the middle class merchants.

---

[40] Here again we encounter the morality of English deism. It had just found a quite satisfactory expression in French, in the *Mémoires concernant la théologie et la morale* (Amsterdam, 1732) and in the *Nouveaux essais sur la bonté de Dieu, la liberté de l'homme, et l'origine du mal* (Amsterdam, 1732).

In particular, in both these books (cited but not studied by G. Bonno in his study on English influence in France) the same texts from Chubb in different translations, are to be found. Thus one could read in the "Lettre anglaise de M. Thomas Chubb à un de ses amis" that God "is toward us a *beneficent creator*" (*Mémoires* . . . 153); that "our duties to God and to our fellow-men come from the way we are constituted, the circumstances and connections around us, as well as from the practice of what is just and acceptable in the nature of things" (*ibid.*, 154. The statement is to be compared to Voltaire's *Remarks III, IV, VI, XI,* and *LIV*); that "any action that has been made with the view and the intention to bring about happiness and public well-being is good and virtuous . . . whence it can be seen that virtue does not consist, as some have imagined, in a constant opposition to the inclinations of nature, by which oppositions one tends to prefer evil to good; but that it consists in making generous efforts to procure well-being to one's fellow-men. . . ." (*ibid.*, 178–179. To be compared with Voltaire's *Remarks X, XXIV,* and *XXVI*).

This collection of *Mémoires* from 1732 also contained a "Letter to a Friend about the Progress of Deism in England" in which a deist was made to conclude "that he would be wary lest he became a zealous Christian, if only to be less unhappy and not to lose his humanity" (*ibid.*, 331).

[41] R. Pomeau, preface to the edition of the *Lettres philosophiques* (1964), 10. "The example of England served precisely to demonstrate that it is possible to arrange collective

The reader has been prepared to understand that the human type set up by Voltaire to confront Pascal's idea of man is the one represented by the English merchant. The tenth letter, "On Trade," which begins with warm praise of trade and ends with mockery of the idle aristocrats, is quite clear: "All this," Voltaire wants to stress, "makes an English merchant justly proud and allows him boldly to compare himself, not without some reason, to a Roman citizen." One can imagine the impression produced by such a comparison on a French reader, brought up in the Latin and classical tradition.

It is therefore both remarkable and understandable that in the twenty-fifth letter, Voltaire without any transition calls upon Falkener, an English merchant, to answer Pascal directly (*Remark VI*). Metaphysical anguish is judged here from the point of view of the complacent English bourgeois.

The argument against Pascal is indeed conducted from this general point of view. It seems beyond doubt that Voltaire was encouraged by the English themselves, and especially during his sojourn in London, to adopt such a point of view. He could read, for instance, in the *Spectator* of May 21, 1711: "There are no more useful Members in a Commonwealth than merchants. They knit Mankind together in a mutual Intercourse of Good offices, distribute the Gifts of Nature, find Work for the Poor, add Wealth to the Rich, and Magnificence to the Great." [42] It is indeed in the light of such a statement that the critique of Pascal's theory of *divertissement* takes on its full polemical meaning. (See *Remarks XXII, XXIV, XXV, XXVI,* and *XXVII.*)

This tradesman's point of view is a moral one: man's sociable instinct must be cultivated—that is to say must be made to bear both flower and fruit. Voltaire may have been supported in this direction by Shaftesbury or by Chubb, and also by Mandeville (whose *Fable of the Bees* was in its fifth edition in 1728). Mandeville's famous motto "Private vices, public benefits" would moreover not be out of place in an argumentation against Pascal. One should also bear in mind the works of Petty and the mercantilists, popularized in France, precisely in 1734, by Jean-François Melon's small book, *Essais politiques sur le commerce*. Melon, defending the utilitarian thesis of the economists, notes with almost Voltairian irony the divorce between political economy and Christian morality; speaking of the lavish expenses of those who live in luxury, he remarks: "God forbid that we should want to compare [these expenses] with the great motive of charity which gives to the shameful poor and to hospitals. Everything else is outshone by this virtue, the

existence so that each individual may enjoy the share of happiness that human nature is capable of enjoying" (*ibid.*, p. 11).

[42] *The Spectator*, Nr. 69. (Ninth edition, 1929), I, 271. This text would be translated by Voltaire's contemporaries as follows: ". . . il n'y a pas de Membres plus utiles dans la Société que les Marchands. Ils unissent les hommes par un trafic mutuel de bons offices; ils distribuent les dons de la nature, ils occupent les pauvres, augmentent les biens des riches, et suppléent à la magnificence des grands." (*Le Spectateur* . . . 9 vols. [Paris, 1754], I, 433–434.) See also Lanson's commentary on the letter "On Trade" (I, 123–129).

greatest of virtues, always attended by justice and benevolence. But . . . men are rarely led by religion; religion must strive to destroy luxury and the State must turn it to its advantage." [43]

With Melon, as with Voltaire, the reader is on the side of the optimistic bourgeois who cannot understand that human activity so profitable in its diversity can be an object of suspicion and be attributed to vain diversions. In Voltaire's work, the argumentation against Pascal will thus find its logical continuation and its confirmation in a poem written a few years later: *Le Mondain,* published in a burst of scandal in 1736. It is curious—but in the order of things—that, faced later with the task of writing a *Défense du Mondain* against his adversaries, Voltaire again adopts the same tone as in his argumentation against Pascal to plead his case.[44]

It is certain that this critical attitude in tune with bourgeois optimism gave the *Philosophical Letters* their insolent originality and their dynamism. But we may think that this bourgeois ideology—whatever its particular virtue might have been in France under *l'ancien régime*—is not without limitations, and that these limitations are discernible in the attack against Pascal.

The most notable, the most apparent limitation appears in the brief *Remark XXI,* on which the reader does not usually dwell, but which is very revealing.[45]

Pascal had written: "There is nothing more important to life than the choice of a calling: chance decides it. Custom makes masons, soldiers, roofers."

Voltaire answers: "What, after all, can lead to soldiers, masons, and all the kinds of manual laborers, except what we call chance and custom? Only in the arts of genius is the decision made by oneself. But in the kinds of works that everyone can do, it is most natural and most reasonable that custom should decide."

The meaning of this opposition is remarkable. Pascal is defending the rights of the individual (and this would draw him nearer to a Jean-Jacques Rousseau) against Voltaire who is defending the interests of the bourgeoisie. Voltaire's statement follows the logic of a class which pretends not to be aware that "for the works that everyone can do," "the most important thing in life is the choice of a calling." We know that, in keeping with this logic, manufacturers in France as in England, as early as the eighteenth

---

[43] Ed. 1734, p. 151.

[44]   "A table, hier, par un triste hasard,
        J'étais assis près d'un maître cafard . . .
        Vous insultiez, pieux atrabilaire
        Au monde entier, épuisé pour vous plaire."
                (*Oeuvres,* ed. Moland, X, 90–91).

[45] No commentary in either Lanson's or Naves's editions.

century and even more so in the nineteenth century, set very young children to work in their shops.

By underlining the links that bind the twenty-fifth letter to the other *Philosophical Letters,* I have tried to show in this study what Voltaire's argumentation against Pascal owes to his English experience. In sum, this "anti-Pascal" seems to me to be an "English letter," analogous to the others. It no doubt has a special place, through its subject as much as through the circumstances of its publication. It is nonetheless obvious that Voltaire himself, by adding the letter against Pascal to the others—afterwards indeed, but, as he said to Thiériot, "without its being in any way inapropos"—made this letter the conclusion to his reflections on England.

This encounter with Pascal was not to be Voltaire's last; we know, especially thanks to Pomeau's fine study, that in Voltaire's works the dialogue with Pascal was resumed time and again, and with variations that are beyond the scope of this study. That this dialogue answers, for Voltaire, the demands of his deeper sensibility, we cannot deny. That there were in this "English" encounter with Pascal personal reasons which impelled him to develop and publish a systematic argumentation we shall not gainsay. Pomeau thinks that Voltaire decided to publish his remarks in June 1733, shortly after meeting Mme. du Châtelet. "Voltaire is loved, and someone comes and tells him that the universe is a dungeon. Voltaire cannot stand it any longer; the time has come to put in his place the 'sublime misanthrope.' " [46] Without dismissing the idea that Voltaire may have indeed found in his experience of requited love an added encouragement to venture to take "the side of humanity" publicly, we must recognize that he had been working on his refutation of Pascal several months before meeting Mme. du Châtelet. When the meeting took place, the refutation was done. The epistle published by the *Mercure de France* in September 1732 leaves no doubt about this plan—outlined several years before but fully ripened at that time—to combat the author of the *Pensées.* The deep and decisive incentive sprang from the same impulse that led him to reflect on the example of England, probably during his stay in that country. This impulse was that of a lively and inquisitive spirit, aware of its boldness and impatience. But it was also the impulse of a social and intellectual milieu; and the spirit of the period could be felt no better than in England. Daudé wrote to Demaizeaux from Paris on December 22, 1733: "Free thinking is very rife in this town, and a northerly wind hath blown down a great spirit of freedom." [47] At that time the decision had already been taken to add the remarks on Pascal to the *English Letters.* Voltaire, we can see, was "up-to-date."

[46] R. Pomeau, *La Religion de Voltaire,* 236.
[47] British Museum, Add. Mss 4288, f. 79, quoted by G. Bonno, p. 112.

WHY WAS THE ENLIGHTENMENT?*

BY PETER GAY

1

ALL MEN HAVE IDEAS. WHATEVER CYNICS MAY SAY, THIS FACT REQUIRES NO EXPLANATION: IT IS A CONDITION OF BIOLOGICAL SURVIVAL. WHAT RE- QUIRES EXPLANATION IS WHY MEN HAVE THE IDEAS THEY HAVE WHEN, AND WHERE, THEY HAVE THEM. WHAT REQUIRES EXPLANATION ALSO, AND IS STILL MORE IMPORTANT, IS WHY CERTAIN IDEAS FIND AN ECHO AT ONE moment in history and not at another. We all know the cliché, "There is nothing so irresistible as an idea whose time has come." Why is its time when it is? I want to take for granted what the Enlightenment was; I know that we know when it was. But *why* was it? Why did it take the several shapes it did, and why did it largely succeed—and partially fail—when it did?

So far the answers to my questions have been meager. There are few areas in the history of ideas in which the Marxist roots of the sociology of knowledge have been so visible, and so damaging, as in the study of the En- lightenment. For neither vulgar Marxism nor refined Marxism at all explains what needs explaining. The vulgar Marxist argues that the philosophes, in- tentionally or not, spoke for the dominant, or the rising, class of the eigh- teenth century—that is, of course, the bourgeoisie. The refined Marxist, who can call at once upon the early Marx and the late Engels, allows the interplay of ideas and society rather greater complexity: history operates behind people's back; the superstructure of ideas reacts on the social base. The identity between the philosophes' philosophy and the structure of society is thus bound to be concealed, and the ideological components of the Enlighten- ment must be hard to establish. But they must be there: history may have its cunning, but it is not cunning enough for the sociologist of knowledge.

However refined this argument, it cannot stand the test of history. The philosophes did not spring from a single class, and they did not address a single class.[1] What is in fact striking in any collective portrait of the philo- sophes is the enormous diversity of their social origins. They included Holbach,

---

* This essay was first delivered, in somewhat different form, to the American Socio- logical Association at Denver, on August 30, 1971.

[1] Marx and Engels themselves, of course, spoke for a class other than their own. Hence class origins alone do not make the point I wish to make.

a rich German baron, and Rousseau, a near-proletarian drifter; Voltaire, the son of a sophisticated metropolitan *roturier* with aristocratic connections, and Diderot, the son of a small-town craftsman-entrepreneur; Gibbon, the affluent son of an affluent man of affairs, and Lessing, the impecunious son of an impecunious minister of the gospel; Lichtenberg and Kant who (among other things) were professors, and Jefferson and Franklin who (among other things) were statesmen. Their collective name, "philosophe," testifies that their contemporaries, like their historians later, perceived them as a group. But whatever brought them together, it was not common status. Nor was it a common aspiration to status: Voltaire manufactured for himself an aristocratic-sounding name and dearly loved a lord; Hume moved across the social landscape with ease and always remained plain Mr. Hume; Rousseau bit the noble hands that caressed and fed him, while Grimm poured tears of gratitude on the same hands. Some philosophes sought freedom to say what they wanted by selling their services, and almost their souls, to the great; others sought the same freedom by very different means: through keeping their expenses modest and their letters free from servility. The affinity of the philosophes for one another was intellectual and professional; they formed what Samuel Johnson called, in a different connection, a "community of mind." [2] The philosophes were, together, men of ideas and men of words, and they were together because they were both.

Their public was as diverse as their origins. It is impossible to discover a single social rubric under which the principal consumers of the Enlightenment belonged. They were united mainly in this, that they were consumers of the Enlightenment. They had among them continental monarchs like Catherine of Russia and English aristocrats like Lord Chesterfield, French provincial nobles of the robe, Tuscan priests, Genevan plutocrats, Viennese professors. And there were others in this approving public as well, though who they were is something we cannot yet say with any confidence. We lack monographs in European social history of the eighteenth century; we know too little of the circulation of Nicolai's periodicals or the influence of Lessing's plays. Until we have such studies for the whole of Europe, country by country or, preferably, town by town, we are reduced to impressionistic generalizations. But the evidence from France, where such studies are just beginning, fortifies my sense that the public for the philosophes' writings was spread across the social map. French provincial academies, which were receptive to new ideas and could afford to subscribe to Diderot's *Encyclopédie*, repeated in their pyramid of membership the social elite in their region. They were dominated, these academies, by nobles: by landowners, ennobled magistrates, members of the service nobility. Financiers and merchants were rare

2 *Boswell's Life of Johnson* . . . , ed. George Birkbeck Hill, rev. by L. F. Powell, 6 vols. (Oxford, 1934–50), IV, 102, under May 8, 1781.

and subordinate. Similarly, the contributors to the *Encyclopédie*, that presumed great engine of bourgeois consciousness, had few bourgeois among their ranks. Obviously, Diderot sought out men expert enough to write the specialized, often technical articles he needed. But (at least among those we can identify) he did not seek out tradesmen, even to write about trades. Many of his contributors were, naturally enough, physicians; many were scientists or civil servants; and his cast was rounded out with a generous sprinkling of noblemen, presumably knowledgeable amateurs.[3] Our information is too fragmentary and our statistics are too inconclusive to permit any generalization except one: the consumers of the Enlightenment were distributed across educated society, unevenly but very widely.

Indeed, there was no single class, either in being or in being born, to which the philosophes could have addressed themselves even if they had wanted to do so. The century produced a few spectacular spokesmen for the merchant and his mentality: Defoe gave eloquent witness to the virtues of traders. But historians, looking back at the eighteenth century with their own preoccupations, have vastly overestimated the influence, and even the representative quality, of such polemicists. What little "bourgeois ideology" there was in the eighteenth century was scarcely ideological, and it was not the monopoly of the bourgeoisie. As Robert Forster's little book on the nobility in eighteenth-century Toulouse has shown, there were French aristocrats with thrifty habits and calculating minds, sober and businesslike; these Roman Catholic nobles embodied the bourgeois Protestant ethic to perfection.[4] But to say this, to deny that eighteenth-century Europe was a class society, is obviously not to assert that all were equal or that social ascent was easy. It was a society pervaded by privilege and, in consequence, a deferential society in which the ladder was narrow and steep, social discrimination exceedingly fine, mobility rare and restricted. The further eastward the traveler moved in those days, the fewer cities he would find; in Prussia, in the Hapsburg domains, in Russia, merchants, manufacturers, professional men were scarce and obedient. Even in the liberal Free German cities, or the proud little Republic of Geneva, the social hierarchy had the uncompromising form of a ziggurat; each layer was sharply segregated from, and markedly smaller than, the layer on which it rested; demands to smooth the ziggurat into a pyramid that might make movement at least a little easier, were resisted with great rhetorical passion and often with a show of force. England, too, the

3 See Jacques Proust, *Diderot et l'Encyclopédie* (Paris, 1962); *Livre et Société dans la France du XVIIIe siècle*, by G. Bollène et al., 2 vols. (Paris, 1965, 1970), *passim*, especially the articles by Daniel Roche and François Furet; see also the articles by Robert Darnton listed in note 8 below.

4 *The Nobility of Toulouse in the Eighteenth Century: A Social and Economic Study* (Baltimore, 1960).

country of Defoe, was by and large in the hands of aristocrats and squires; occasionally outsiders succeeded in forcing themselves into that restricted club, the political public, but as soon as they had done so, they did their utmost to vanish into the ranks of the squirearchy or, if at all possible, the peerage. If there was a class to which the philosophes might have addressed themselves, it was the European nobility.[5] Naive though it may sound, then, I would urge that we take the philosophes' professions seriously, recognize the diversity of their publics, and grant them their claim that they were speaking, not for a segment of society, but for all of it.

2

In seeking to answer my question, Why was the Enlightenment? I have taken a circuitous route by affirming what it was not. But my excursion has not been without use. It has demonstrated, no matter how fragmentarily, the complexity of the philosophes' world.

How are we to capture that world? A writer's world is a construct, composed of at least four subworlds that normally reinforce, though often they conflict with, one another. The first of these mental universes is the cultural atmosphere of the age, the environment that assigns positive or negative values to ideas, passions, and actions, pronouncing some exemplary, others unthinkable. This is the comprehensive world that sets the rules governing the game of living. Even rebels acknowledge its power and the most untrammeled of geniuses takes his cues from it: one leaps out of the magic circle of one's culture only so far.

But the individual does not encounter his culture without the mediation of a narrower, *his* narrower, world: the social environment into which he is born, in which he grows up and, for the most part, remains. His caste or class, his ethnic and religious loyalties, his region and family, delimit the meaning of the words he uses and the ideals he follows, define what aspirations are legitimate and what limits are inescapable. Doubtless, the most interesting ideas often emerge from a position on the margin of defined groups. But wherever ideas stand, they stand somewhere.

Ideas emerge not simply from the interplay of cultural and social environments; they carry on their backs the burden of the past, which exerts marked pressures. The writer has his literary or, more narrowly, his craft traditions, which dictate caution or encourage boldness, set permissible terms of rhetoric, establish an accepted hierarchy of genres, and in general place him into a sequence that he can hardly, and never wholly, shake off. G. E. Moore has said in his autobiography that he took his philosophical problems

---

[5] I need hardly emphasize that "nobility" meant many different things in different countries. For a dependable brief conspectus, see A. Goodwin, ed., *The European Nobility in the Eighteenth Century* (London, 1953).

not from the outside world but from other philosophers; [6] writers always write with other writers looking over their shoulders. However a writer responds, the last feeling possible for him toward tradition is indifference.

Here are three collective pressures—culture, society, tradition. They press on what is the ultimate shaper, the only carrier, of ideas: the individual. This makes the fourth of the subworlds, the self, so critically important. By "self" I mean the uneasy collaboration between genetic endowment and acquired habits, affections and neuroses, conscious purposes and unconscious wishes, skills and stratagems. Whenever a writer is seriously engaged with his work, as the philosophes normally were; whenever he is not writing purely for money, advancement, or self-protection, his work offers substantial evidence of his encounter between his private world and those three other worlds, which he reflects in his distorting mirror, relates to his needs and urges, and reproduces in his own way. Out of these strands the writer weaves the historical artifact, the work, which it is the task of the historian to interpret, which is to say, to understand.

Now what do the philosophes' works tell us? Their range was wide, wider even than their authors' social origins: they wrote history, economics, fiction, criticism, philosophy, jurisprudence, pedagogy, theology—and sociology. But they were, amidst this wealth, informed by a few central principles, addressed to a few palpable aims. In brief, the philosophes from Edinburgh to Vienna, Philadelphia to Milan, were hostile to what they were pleased to call "superstition," advocated a comprehensive humanitarianism, and deprecated the accepted legitimations of power. Even more briefly, the philosophes wanted to "rationalize" the world; they were working, in Max Weber's terminology, for its "disenchantment." The philosophes conveniently, and bellicosely, divided the world between survivals of barbarism and emergent reason. This bifurcation enabled them to enlist the scientific revolution in their cause; from our perspective, and in their own estimation, the philosophes were agents of modernity.

We must move circumspectly at this point. The most dramatic instruments of modernization have been the technological fruits of science. But these were scarcely visible in the Age of the Enlightenment. The steam engine (which multiplied men's powers), mass production (which multiplied his hands), chemical techniques (which improved the fertility of the soil), new departures in communications and transportation (which enlarged men's commercial and intellectual universe) were all barely invented in the eighteenth century and made their real impact only in the nineteenth. Yet even if these spectacular consequences of science were still in the future, even if the Enlightenment was still pre-industrial, it was not prescientific either in

6 See "An Autobiography," in *The Philosophy of G. E. Moore,* ed. Paul Arthur Schilpp (Evanston and Chicago, 1942), 14.

its methods or its goals. The philosophes' tendentious reading of science was reinforced by an intellectual and emotional temper that gives them an air of being modernizers almost by instinct.

There are, I think, five striking signs of this modern temper in their writings. (1) The philosophes had a positive attitude toward innovation, which had hitherto been a *Schimpfwort*. In marked contrast with the fearful caution of past ages, the philosophes refused to admire what was old because it was old, or to deplore what was new because it was new. And this pervasive attitude was a sign of a deep confidence in the possibilities of scientific knowledge. (2) In consequence, the philosophes believed—though with notable reservations—in the possibility of a long-range and permanent improvement in man's lot. Few of them had a theory of progress; most of them recognized the power of unreason, the precariousness of any gain, the continuing hardship of life.[7] But they thought the struggle worthwhile, and hope realistic. (3) As men of hope, the philosophes oriented themselves to the future, exploiting the past as a storehouse of excellent advice and unsurpassable art and literature, but also, and mainly, as a towering warning of what to avoid. (4) This commitment to the future—a mental reorientation as subtle, and as decisive, as the welcoming of innovation—did not commit them to Utopian dreams. However later judges might estimate their hopes, the philosophes themselves thought their only hope lay in realism. (5) Finally, the philosophes, to realize their aims, subjected their society, even its most sensitive areas (sexual morality, political authority, religious belief), to that most corrosive of solvents—criticism. With this modernity, the men of the Enlightenment treated, and thus converted, their age into an age of intellectual takeoff, an age that laid the foundations for the most far-reaching changes in years to come.

3

In concentrating on the philosophes themselves, I have offered a description, not an explanation. I want now to move toward an explanation by placing the philosophes into their world—or worlds. Before I do so, I want to insist on two obvious but easily neglected facts: the Age of the Enlightenment predates not merely the Industrial Revolution, it predates also that watershed of Western history, the French Revolution and, as well, the formation of the mass public. This double negative has two significant consequences. Since the philosophes developed their ideas before the French Revolution, they aimed to change society largely from within, to improve it perhaps out of all recognition, but to work in a framework that would

[7] Here, and elsewhere in this essay, I have drawn on my long study, *The Enlightenment: An Interpretation*, 2 vols. (New York, 1966, 1969), each of which has an extensive bibliographical essay.

guarantee the survival, with suitable improvement, of what was valuable in current life. Rousseau apart (and even he is only a partial exception), they wanted to retain their place, or improve their place, in existing society, and to enact their reforms gradually. True, the "low" Enlightenment—the Grub Street of Paris and other publishing centers—pushed the revolutionary possibilities of the Old Regimes much further. But the efforts of these true radicals did not make themselves visible until events overtook them in the 1790s. There were few Revolutionaries before the fact; the philosophes were reformers within the system.[8]

In the second place, since the philosophes spread their ideas before the emergence of "mass culture," their relations with their public, actual and potential, were essentially cordial. Indeed, when that public was embodied in figures of power, these relations were largely servile. In other words, the philosophes were not an avant-garde.

This point is worth pursuing for a moment. By definition, an avant-garde is antagonistic to the general public. Its purpose is to affront the philistine, to be deliberately offensive to, even destructive of, reigning pieties, to be studiedly difficult. Avant-gardes are coteries, clubs of disdain, held together by poverty, neglect, a shared defensive pride, a search for novel forms, in a word, by failure. They must nurse grievances as their life's blood; success, as Renato Poggioli has so elegantly demonstrated, is their death.[9] Now the philosophes' family was not that sort of coterie; its adversaries to the contrary, it was not a coterie at all. It was an intellectual fraternity, a "community of mind," highly sociable and, in moments of crisis, hysterically self-protective. But in calmer times it was open, steadily in search of allies or, more modestly, of supporters on specific issues. Unlike an avant-garde, the philosophes found their success in success. Unlike an avant-garde, the philosophes, far from shunning, cultivated popularity. And they could do this in the eighteenth century because the educated public they addressed and hoped to persuade was relatively clear-cut, fairly homogeneous, still narrowly circumscribed.

Here, then, is one side of the philosophes' social situation: as self-appointed leaders of an advanced movement, they lived in a fostering environ-

8 For the "low" Enlightenment in France, see Robert Darnton, "The Grub Street Style of Revolution: J.-P. Brissot, Police Spy," *The Journal of Modern History,* XL (September 1968), 301–27; "Reading, Writing, and Publishing in Eighteenth-Century France: A Case Study in the Sociology of Literature," *Daedalus,* December 1970; "The High Enlightenment and the Low-Life of Literature in Pre-Revolutionary France," *Past and Present,* 51 (May 1971), 81–115; and "In Search of the Enlightenment: Recent Attempts to Create a Social History of Ideas," *The Journal of Modern History* XLIII (March 1971), 113–32. This last article takes a critical look at my way of doing history.

9 *The Theory of the Avant-Garde,* tr. Gerald Fitzgerald (Cambridge, Mass., 1968), a brilliant book to which I am deeply in debt.

Peter Gay

ment. They were radical mainly in the sense that they pushed emerging
values and rising hopes and novel ideas to unexpected and unconventional
conclusions. For in truth the philosophes found wide sympathy for many
of their aims. Even their campaign against "superstition," especially in the
hands of adroit and unscrupulous campaigners like Voltaire, found echoes
among moderate Anglicans and "modern" Roman Catholics: these too
detested "fanaticism," feared "enthusiasm," hoped to end persecution. Even
more, the humanity of the philosophes struck responsive chords among men
and women no longer highly diverted by public executions; Voltaire's self-
advertised, celebrated effort to clear the posthumous name of Jean Calas
secured vocal support among pious French Catholics, some of them highly
placed. Again, the philosophes' campaign in behalf of legal reform and economic rationality was in no way offensive, let alone threatening, to rulers
and statesmen eager to pursue similar lines of policy on purely pragmatic
grounds. Persons in power wanted to modernize commercial life or ease the
ferocity of the criminal law or improve the bureaucracy because such policies
did no harm, and might do much good, to their effort at surviving in the
international competition for power. It was no surprise that in such an atmosphere, the scientific world view should advance in many imperceptible
steps right into the citadels of belief; rational Christians radically reduced
the number of articles they must believe to remain Christians; miracles grew
more and more remote as scientists (most of them good Christians) demonstrated the regularity of the universe. This was a time of weakening in mythical thinking and in cultural parochialism. Traders and (ironically enough)
missionaries brought reports of alien cultures that knew no Christ without
being barbarian; tolerance, relativism, humaneness were on the march. When
the philosophes looked back upon their followers, they saw them closing the
distance and swelling the ranks. As wars grew less devastating, medicine
(apparently) more effective, civilization more secure, the age became an
Age of Enlightenment, a fertile soil in which the philosophes could flourish.

But this was only one side of the relationship between the philosophes
and their century. In a well-known observation, Immanuel Kant asserted
in 1784 that men were living "in a Age of Enlightenment," but not "in an
enlightened age." [10] Which is to say that the philosophes, in addition to living at ease in their age, also stood off from it. There was peace, and there was
tension, and it is the coexistence of these two that gave the Enlightenment
its particular shape and explains its particular career. The most obvious,
and most dangerous, symptom of tension lay in the all-important area of
religion: scientists and statesmen who delighted in the philosophes' wit, ap-
plauded the philosophes' humanitarianism, and echoed the philosophes' call

[10] "Beantwortung der Frage: Was ist Aufklärung?" *Immanuel Kants Werke*, ed. Ernst
Cassirer et al., 11 vols. (Berlin, 1912–22), IV, 174.

68

for reasonableness, rejected and even feared the philosophes' ventures into irreligion. Less obvious, but no less dangerous, was the philosophes' political radicalism, which emerged at striking moments, often greatly to the irritation of the rulers who fancied themselves the patrons and friends of the philosophes: Diderot's peculiarly unsatisfactory friendship with Catherine of Russia exhibits this sort of tension to perfection.[11]

The philosophes' sense of ease gave them the confident conviction that realistic proposals for change had a chance of realization; the philosophes' sense of tension underscored their conviction that there was much work to be done. The late eighteenth century was an Age of Enlightenment: a time when philosophes found support. But it was also far from being an enlightened age: a time when philosophes were not simply the spokesmen, but also the goads of their time. Thus, the Enlightenment represents a conjunction rare in human affairs, a time when reformers were close enough to the core of events to think their efforts worthwhile, yet far enough from that core to think their efforts necessary.

This dialectic of ease and tension informed not merely the philosophes' reading of their age; it pervaded, palpably and intimately, their very vocation. I said before, and want to stress again, that the philosophes were professional men of words, men of letters. This meant that they experienced the decisive, if often subterranean, changes of their age in their own persons, and at a most sensitive spot: their careers. A man of letters in the eighteenth century could testify to improvement and complain of continuing trouble. In the seventeenth century, men of letters had been, by and large, the paid servants of the great, with whom they often lived, and to whom they normally dedicated their works. In the eighteenth century, men of letters gradually liberated themselves from patronage and sought precarious freedom in the arms of an anonymous public. They improved their status, enhanced their income, and enlarged their freedom. At the same time, they suffered from the caprice of censors, feared the interference of stringent libel laws, and often found themselves reduced to silence. Lessing and Kant ended their careers unable to speak about the religious questions that had agitated them all their lives, Hume refused to publish his *Dialogues Concerning Natural Religion* in his lifetime, Diderot practiced circumspection in his *Encyclopédie*, and Voltaire cheerfully developed a veritable industry of lying to the authorities. The world was very much with the philosophes.

4

This intimate and continuing engagement of the philosophes with their world put a premium on realism in their perception of the political, social,

---

11 This is now best followed in Arthur M. Wilson, *Diderot* (New York, 1972).

intellectual, and religious structures of their day. They were not always realistic in their realism: like other realists, they often failed to discriminate between wishes and realities. But their efforts, at least, were toward unillusioned clarity and flexibility. Catherine's refusal to permit Voltaire, her devoted admirer and unpaid propagandist, to visit Russia is one of the most amusing, and most instructive, testimonials to the philosophes' powers of realistic observation. Catherine understood clearly enough that, sharp-sighted and inquisitive as he was, Voltaire would abandon his idealized portrait of Russia once he had seen the seedy realities with his own eyes. Like all intellectuals, the philosophes had considerable capacity for self-deception, but at least they did not deceive themselves on principle. When they had an opportunity to observe, they practiced the "philosophical modesty" they so prized in their hero, Newton, by offering proposals adapted to a single time and a single place. Even Rousseau, speculative Platonist that he was, found it possible to differentiate among Corsica, Poland, and Geneva.

This principled realism, this modesty, and this flexibility explain yet another distinctive characteristic of the Enlightenment: the variety of its shapes across the Western world. Nothing, after all, is more evident than the divergence of the philosophes' views, especially on politics. They all agreed about decency: they were for it. And they all agreed about religion: they were against it. But their political ideas and ideals cover a wide spectrum of possibilities. Voltaire is the model here, as so often: he was a republican in the Dutch Republic, a royalist in France, an absolutist in Russia; in Geneva, which he came to know intimately, he shifted his politics twice, from the plutocracy to the middle-class republicans, from the middle-class republicans to the disfranchised aspirants to political rights.[12] Other philosophes were not far different from Voltaire: they adjusted their aspirations to their estimate of local possibilities. This is why Hume and Gibbon sound different from Diderot and Holbach, or Beccaria and the Verri brothers different from Franklin and Jefferson, or Wieland and Kant different from Martini and Sonnenfels. But this variety of enlightened politics should not compel us to abandon the category of a single Enlightenment: variety itself was one of the principles implicit in the philosophes' philosophy. Why, then, did the Enlightenment take the particular form it did in each country? Each country had the Enlightenment it deserved. And so did the century as a whole.

5

Where do these reflections leave the sociology of knowledge? Worse off, I fear, than before. Traditionally, sociologists of knowledge have recog-

12 For a detailed demonstration, I refer to my *Voltaire's Politics: The Poet as Realist* (New York, 1959).

nized the multiplicity of worlds from which ideas emerge, though they have generally insisted that one of these worlds—the social—is the cause of which the others are mere effects. My brief account of the Enlightenment offers a tentative refutation of this position; the relation of ideas to their environments is not quite so predictable as all that. I have no general theory to substitute; I would argue, in fact, that there can be no such theory. The causes and careers of ideas are too diverse, too complex, to permit us to formulate a causal generalization that is valid for them all. The social history of ideas is, like all history, the science of the concrete, exacting the most circumstantial inquiry. Only such inquiry permits us to pronounce with any confidence on the relative weight of elements in the formation and survival of ideas.

An effective social history of ideas cannot stop with merely tinkering with the sociology of knowledge. It must go further and abolish it. I agree with sociologists like Raymond Aron who have said that there is, and can be, no sociology of knowledge. For knowledge has neither class nor time. It is a logical relation; it can be precise or vague, exhaustive or partial, but it cannot be bourgeois or proletarian, Protestant or Catholic, French or German. A knower has a social status, his ideas have existential roots, but the truth or falsity of his ideas is wholly independent of this status and these roots. It is dependent, rather, on the correspondence of their formulation with the reality they purport to describe. But while there is no sociology of knowledge, there *is* a sociology of ideas—first cousin to the social history of ideas. And this sociology must undertake its work with a principled disclaimer: it must abandon the confident automatic claim to the primacy of the social. It may be the social dimension that has primacy, it may be the status of technology, or the internal history of the intellectual tradition. It all depends.

This is a conclusion which the philosophes—the first to analyze the ideological foundations of ideas—would have understood and, I think, shared. They detested dogmatism and ceaselessly polemicized against the kind of system-making that takes for granted what empirical research must first establish. They believed that a science of man is possible, and that such a science will lead through, and beyond, relativism to truths on which reasonable men can agree. It is perhaps in the force of this idea that the final answer to my question, Why was the Enlightenment?, may be found, in the very vigor of the philosophes' conviction that man, freed from the trammels of superstition, could devise a social science that would lead from interminable squabbles over phantoms to firm consensus on realities. It seems hard to believe in our own malaise-ridden day, but intellectuals, when conditions are right, have a momentum of their own.

HUME'S REPUBLIC AND THE UNIVERSE OF NEWTON

BY RICHARD KUHNS

> While Newton seemed to draw off
> the veil from some of the mysteries
> of nature, he showed at the same
> time the imperfections of the
> mechanical philosophy; and thereby
> restored her ultimate secrets to
> that obscurity, in which they ever
> did and ever will remain.
>
> HUME, *The History of England*

1

RECENT CRITICAL EVALUATIONS OF HUME'S PHILOSOPHY HAVE ALTER-
NATED BETWEEN SUSPICION THAT PART OF HIS ARGUMENT IS "RUBBISH"
AND THE VIEW THAT HUME CARRIES FORWARD THE EMPIRICIST TRADITION
TOWARD MODERN CLARITY. WHILE C. D. BROAD AND H. A. PRICHARD SHARE
THE BELIEF THAT HUME, RATHER THAN A GREAT PHILOSOPHER, WAS SIM-
ply a very clever man,[1] the positivistic and linguistic schools of recent years
have appreciated Hume for his subtlety and *his* suspicion that much that
went under the guise of natural and moral philosophy was sophistry. Those
who derogate Hume point to his discussion of physical concepts, for the
analysis of Newtonian ideas in the *Treatise* often seems fatuous. We must
be careful not to dismiss Hume's thought in this fashion, for though we
may be historically more knowing than Hume was about Newtonian problems, he had purposes of his own as a *moral* philosopher which must be recognized if we are to understand his treatment of concepts such as causality,
space, and time. Hume's interest in these categories of natural philosophy
goes beyond showing that Newton misconstrued them, for these fundamental concepts are as necessary to moral philosophy as to natural, and they
must receive careful analysis on the part of a philosopher whose task is to
demonstrate the logical and ontological priority of moral philosophy to natural philosophy.

In Hume's view, the Newtonian universe of mechanical necessity was
not only an incomplete representation of nature, it made clear at last that
natural philosophy had reached the limit of its power to reveal the order of
the universe. Yet the philosophical needs of human beings were not satisfied,
and Hume believed he could give an account of our universe in terms of an
older, yet parallel, tradition that he terms a "Republic of Letters."

[1] C. D. Broad, "Hume's Doctrine of Space and Time," *Dawes Hicks Lectures on
Philosophy*, British Academy, 1961; H. A. Prichard, *Knowledge and Perception* (Oxford,
1950). A. E. Taylor shares these doubts about Hume's philosophical power ("David Hume
and the miraculous," *Leslie Stephen Lecture* [Cambridge, 1927], *passim*).

Richard Kuhns

In this discussion I shall be concerned with Hume's criticism of Newtonian concepts of space and time, and with his efforts to reconstruct those
concepts in accordance with the needs of moral philosophy, and in the tradition to which moral philosophy has always looked, that of letters. One lesson that tradition impressed upon Hume was that here on earth our experimental interests can best be satisfied in moral subjects; that is the proper
exercise for a man of letters who offers his thought to a tribunal of reason.
That Hume regarded himself as a dweller in the republic of letters is made
clear by his remarks about his career. His brief autobiography states that he
was "seized very early with a passion for literature, which has been the ruling
passion of my life and the great source of my enjoyments." [2] He refers to
his *Treatise,* the first book he published, as a "literary attempt," [3] and finally,
after mentioning his essays, the second of his publications, refers to the *Inquiry Concerning the Principles of Morals* as "of all my writings, historical,
philosophical, or literary, incomparably the best." [4] Although he here distinguishes the three genres of his writing career, the most common means of
reference to the tradition into which his work fits is "letters." When he
refers to Berkeley's arguments against abstract ideas, he writes: "As I look
upon this to be one of the greatest and most valuables discoveries that has
been made of late years in the republic of letters, I shall here endeavor to
confirm it by some arguments which I hope will put it beyond doubt and
controversy." [5] Of course, Berkeley's "discovery" provides the foundation
for Hume's criticism of Newtonian concepts of space and time.

To establish oneself as a member of the republic of letters requires a
lifelong devotion to a variety of literary tasks, among which Hume counted
ethical theory, political and critical essays, and of course history, in addition
to the philosophical books he considered his most thoughtful works. These
are the genres by means of which we articulate our moral being; their concern is *human* nature, and together they define the moral philosopher as distinct from the natural philosopher whose interest is in the order of nature.
Yet the natural philosopher necessarily inquires into much that concerns
the moral philosopher, and one of Hume's most challenging tasks in working
out his moral philosophy is to demonstrate that moral philosophy is obliged
to analyze afresh concepts central to natural philosophy. Causality, space,
time, probability are crucial to both natural and moral philosophy, but the

[2] *My Own Life,* in *An Inquiry Concerning Human Understanding,* ed. Charles W.
Hendel (New York, 1955), 3.

[3] *Ibid.,* 4.

[4] *Ibid.,* 7.

[5] *A Treatise of Human Nature: Being an Attempt to Introduce the Experimental
Method of Reasoning into Moral Subjects,* 17. All references to the *Treatise* are to the
edition edited by L. A. Selby-Bigge (Oxford, various dates).

natural philosopher misconstrues the meaning and importance of these concepts. It remains for the moral philosopher to redefine, and to provide a reconstruction of these concepts, in which undertaking both natural and moral philosophy benefit.

Prior to the critiques of Leibniz and Berkeley, the philosophical discussions of space and time had been centered on the Newtonian model. But these celebrated oppositions still failed to ask if space and time as dealt with by natural philosophy satisfied the needs of a "universe" within which human agents performed. It was Hume who recognized that space and time are central to a moral theory, for Newton's universe lies beyond experience, a diversion from our philosophically interpretable realm. Recognition of the need to bring Newtonian precision into moral problems is stated by Hume's intention to "introduce the experimental method of reasoning into moral subjects." However, we must note that Hume's criticism of natural philosophy is far different from the criticism of science we have come to know in our own time. Hume admires the competence of Newtonian cosmology and wants to transfer its model and method to the study of human nature. Our criticism of science today may reject science entirely and in some cases embraces the irrationalities of the occult. Hume would have been horrified at this turn, for it is an excess he attacked in his own day with the utmost severity and contempt.

Newton not only failed to account for human experience but found it necessary to add to his model of the cosmos a traditional theism, to Hume a reiteration of the irrationalities of superstition. Hume sets out to demonstrate that we can account for all the Newtonian structure by a psychology of human nature and need not retain elements of philosophical absurdity; the coupling of Newtonian cosmology with what amounts to a superstitious belief posed a problem Hume sought to resolve. There must be a deep confusion if a science of the heavens and of light can accept a metaphysical extravagance such as Newton's belief in the design of the universe by a deity.

Hume believed he could expose this contradiction by a fresh analysis of fundamental cosmological concepts according to the principles of his moral psychology. When this is done, a universe of human experience is revealed, and within that universe are all the basic data (impressions and ideas) every philosopher, including Newton, has to work with. All we can know as human beings is what we find in our awareness; from that we fashion a world. But there is something more we can borrow from Newton: the mechanics of Newtonian physics coupled with the color theory of Newtonian optics provides the moral philosopher with a model he can use to give a full account of human experience.

In the place of the unacceptable metaphysical notions of absolute space and time, the moral philosopher puts the relative conceptions of space and time derived from the psychological principles of association.[6] In the place of religious superstition, the moral philosopher establishes human reason and the controlled dogmatism of the passions. Here is a republic reconstructed along thoroughly human lines, in the best humanistic tradition. It is the ancients, and French thinkers like Montaigne and Bayle, who inspire Hume to attempt philosophy without theology.

This philosophical dedication to the primacy of morality puts Newton's conclusions in a peripheral position so far as the focus of human learning is concerned. We ought not to stand and stare at the heavens; rather we ought to look within ourselves and to the interaction of human bodies. We travel in our own small orbits, propelled by feelings, drawn together and repelled by sentiments. In place of the gross, overwhelmingly brute forces of the universe with its gigantic material objects wheeling about one another, we can enjoy the finer, more delicate, and infinitely more interesting circulation of persons in society. Hume, in his effort to get us back into the sociable republic, might echo Pascal's cry that the emptiness of universal space frightens him, were he given to such melancholic fits. But temperamentally Hume was not an anxious person; he was unable to generate the anxiety that leads so often to philosophic excess. Rather, he found the deepest values in human relationships, in society, in the sensitive response to actions as delicate gradations of moral colors. The optics of sentiment can be explained in terms of the mechanics of association.

Both Newtonian models—the optics of color and the mechanics of events—provide structures for Hume's analysis of human nature. The first is applied to the life of feeling, the second to the structure of consciousness. Every literary genre provides a subject to which these organizing structures can be applied. Moral philosophy examines the organization of consciousness which underlies judgment and choice; natural religion shows the way to the destruction of religious enthusiasm and mysticism; history exhibits the evolution of society towards artificial virtues of justice and concern for human kind as a whole. Together these works constitute Hume's republic, a world he has made, constructed from actions, moral qualities, beliefs, approbations and disapprobations. Describing such a realm, it is necessary for the moral philosopher to provide a reconstruction of space and time, taking these categories away from the metaphysical extravagances of the natural philosopher, and from the comminuting exercises of the mathematician. He restores them to their experiential wholeness. In humanizing space and time, the moral

---

6 ". . . if anything can entitle the author [of *A Treatise of Human Nature*] to so glorious a name as that of 'inventor,' it is the use he makes of the principles of association of ideas, which enters most of his philosophy." Hume's comment on his own originality is thus formulated in the review he wrote of his own book. See "An Abstract of a Treatise of Human Nature," in Hendel, 198.

philosopher shows us how they are known in action, how we understand them in the exercise of will.

2

Hume turns to the tasks of analyzing the concepts of space and time in book one, part two of the *Treatise*. The importance to him of the undertaking can be seen from the early introduction of these arguments and the thematic development accorded to space and time throughout the book. Book one, part one, only seventeen pages long, makes the fundamental distinction between impressions and ideas and argues that there are no abstract ideas in the rationalist sense. All mental content can be traced back to immediate givens, that is, impressions. Part two of book one, a lengthy discussion of forty pages, is entitled "Of the Ideas of Space and Time." These concepts are the first to be subjected to Hume's epistemological method because they constitute the medium of human action, therefore are fundamental to a moral inquiry.

Hume believed that Newton dealt with space and time by means of two conceptual absurdities: first, that space and time are absolute, independent realities; second, that space and time are infinitely divisible. The first contributes to the Newtonian cosmology, the second to the theory of fluxions. Hume's first move is to argue the absurdity of the belief in infinitesimals. Invoking his method of verification (all meaningful ideas must be traceable to corresponding impressions), he argues that since all meaningful ideas rest upon a sensory given, the idea of the infinitely small must be so based as well. But experience shows us that there is a point in perceptual awareness when we reach the least discriminable impression; beyond that there is, experientially, "nothing." Hence the belief that we can subdivide impressions indefinitely makes no sense. Divisibility *ad infinitum* is absurd.

Hume supposes this attack to dispense with a mathematical notion that contradicts his analysis of experience. But out of fairness to Hume's arguments, and with regard to the historical conditions of Hume's thought, we ought to recognize how varied were eighteenth century attempts to give a satisfactory philosophical account of infinitesimals. Although Hume's arguments are based on psychological observations and not made with the logical intention of putting order into the philosophy of mathematics, his interpretation of infinitesimals as meaning least minima of perception is in accord with the logical arguments expressed by the sophisticated mathematician Jean Le Rond d'Alembert. In his *Mélanges de littérature, d'histoire, et de philosophie*, he writes:

> Some mathematicians have defined the infinitely small quantity as that which vanishes, considered not before it vanishes, not after it has vanished, but at the exact moment when it vanishes. I would

like to know what clear and precise idea one can hope to entertain
in the mind by such a definition? A quantity is something or nothing; if it is something it has not vanished; if it is nothing, it has
literally vanished. The supposition that there is an intermediate state
between the two is a chimera.[7]

"A quantity is something or nothing." These words state the logical
problem Hume is trying to deal with by means of his psychological experiment. Both arguments are directed to the confusion we cannot avoid when
we speak of infinitesimals. But it is not enough to simply point out the
confusion; the rejection of the concept of the infinitely small impression
does not provide Hume with a satisfactory way of dealing with space and
time. He has rejected one theory to search for another, and here, as so often
in the *Treatise*, Hume's critical rejection leaves us without a philosophical
alternative. Left with the troublesome realities of space and time, Hume
consoles himself in this way: "Many of our ideas are so obscure, that 'tis almost impossible even for the mind, which forms them, to tell exactly their
nature and composition." (*Treatise*, 33) Yet he boldly asserts that time is
"always discovered by some *perceivable* succession of changeable objects,"
(*Treatise*, 38), and space by the perceived coexistence of objects. Neither
space nor time is perceivable as a separate entity; they therefore constitute
(though Hume never explicitly recognizes this) important exceptions to
the principle of verification by reference to impressions, and like the missing
shade of blue mentioned earlier in the *Treatise*, they are "known" without
the mediation of impressions of themselves. They are therefore relations
among impressions, apprehended in the succession and coexistence of impressions. In offering this "solution," Hume has denied both the mathematicians
and his own epistemology.

Yet his objective is clear: he wants to hold on to the reality of space
and time without falling into Newtonian paradoxes. In some sense of "real,"
space and time are real for us, and that sense is distinct from the unsatisfactory interpretations given us by natural philosophy. While it seems convenient for Hume to fall back on Berkeley's critique of infinite divisibility,
this interpretation of space and time as relational does not prepare the way
for the moral requirements soon to be encountered. Another inadequacy of
the analysis Hume offers is its indifference to the status of space and the
status of time in the theory he himself elaborates. Hume requires the category of temporal succession and its corellative notions of priority, posterior-
ity, and contiguity. The last, of course, suggests as well a spatial relationship.
Since from the start Hume has conceived experience as composed of temporally related impressions and ideas, his rejection of space and time in the
same terms leaves his theory without careful modulation of the differences

[7] (Amsterdam, 1767), V, 249–250.

in space and time for human experience. He never makes up for this assumed indifference.

So far, then, Hume has an account of space and time as the succession and coexistence of impressions which provides a crude explanation based on gross physical objects as they are experienced, but for anything more than that, where sentiment, passion, and moral and aesthetic events are concerned, and after all, this is what interests the moral philosopher, his is no satisfactory account. Hume, of course, sees this failing, and as he further considers location in space, he supplements the first account with a second having to do with the location of impressions which are not, in an obvious sense, "out there." This is his first attempt to bend the conception of space to a theory that will do justice to human awareness.

The second step in Hume's argument is surprising since it is formulated in one of his bizarre assertions: "That an object may exist and yet be nowhere." (*Treatise*, 235) Since the Newtonian doctrine of space and time leaves no place for the interior space and time of human experience, the moral philosopher has to establish the genuine presence of such aspects of awareness. What to the natural philosopher are "secondary qualities" are to us the primary stuff of our affective and sensible lives. Consequently Hume formulates his paradoxical assertion "that an object may exist and yet be nowhere." What Hume means is this: moral qualities, and some sensory qualities like taste, smell, sound, cannot be described as possessing spatial location. If one tries to describe them in terms of spatial location, *where* are they? Assuming that the "where" means three-dimensional space, in that sense of "where" they are "nowhere," and yet they are "there." In the case of moral qualities this nonspatial presence is particularly important: "A moral reflection cannot be placed on the right or on the left of a passion, nor can the smell or sound be either of a circular or a square figure. These objects and perceptions, so far from requiring any particular place, are absolutely incompatible with it, and even the imagination cannot attribute it to them." (*Treatise*, 236)

To support this observation, Hume junkets about in one of his most argumentative moods, traversing a strange route that might be described this way: If we try to explain how we arrive at the belief that the taste of an olive or fig is located within the object, we find that the human mind performs according to the root principles of association which the early part of the *Treatise* has defined. We learn that the taste or smell of a piece of fruit is always conjoined with its other (spatial) properties. Hence by association we group them together, and where we find one, expect the others. By contiguity and causation, we strengthen the bonds between these qualities, some of which are spatial and some not. Then we add to the first two relationships a third, that of *conjunction in place* (p. 237) so we may make the transition from one property to another more easily. Odd as this sounds, it is justified by Hume in the following way: "For 'tis a quality, which I shall often have occasion to remark in human nature, and shall explain more fully in its proper place, that when objects are united by any relation, we have a strong propensity to add some new relation to them, in order to compleat the union." (*Treatise*, 237) We do this because "we feel a satisfaction in joining the relation of contiguity to that of resemblance, or the resemblance of situation to that of qualities. The effects of this propensity have already been observed in that resemblance, which we so readily suppose betwixt particular impressions and their external causes. But we shall not find a more evident effect of it, than in the present instance, where from the relation of causation and contiguity in time betwixt two objects, we feign likewise that of a conjunction in place, in order to strengthen the connexion." (*Treatise*, 237–238)

Two critical comments are relevant here. (1) By this argument Hume has added to the principles of association a set of higher order principles which we might call dispositions. Human beings are endowed with dispositions to strengthen all connections made through association. This constitutes a new hypothesis to the effect that the moral world is structured by principles whose origin is not the impressions of immediate experience, nor the principles of association. Human beings find pleasure in reinforcing, strengthening, and enlarging associations quite beyond anything experience, as first conceived by Hume, can allow. Such higher order "connexions" are required to account for moral values. (2) Hume is naive about the structure of impressions, for he conceives the nonspatial properties as related to the spatial by a "conjunction in place," clearly a spatial metaphor. I suspect Hume is recreating a philosophical problem paralleling the Cartesian puzzle over how spatial and nonspatial substances can be thought to interact. As I shall show, Hume believes he can dispose of the puzzles of Cartesian dualism, but he falls into a like dualism in which moral sentiments stand in causal relationship to human action.

To complete Hume's argument before taking up the next aspect I shall consider, namely the need to defend the nonlocatable qualities of experience, I note that he concludes his argument concerning the presence of the nonspatial in the spatial with an amusing choice: one of the following must be true. (1) "Some beings exist without any place"; (2) some beings like taste and smell are "figured and extended"; (3) some qualities "are incorporated with extended objects, the whole is in the whole, and the whole in every part." Since the last two, Hume believes, are manifestly absurd, we are left with the first, and as a consequence can dispose of a typical materialist thesis, for the materialists "conjoin all thought with extension," (*Treatise*, 239) and since thought is a being without any place, we can dispose of their confusion. At the same time, Hume believes he has disposed of the arguments used by those who oppose the materialists, and "conjoin all thought with a simple and indivisible substance." At one stroke Hume rids himself of atomistic materialism and subjective idealism.

There are further consequences of this resolution, according to Hume, for he believes that the discovery on the part of the experimental moral philosopher of the existence of nonspatial qualities gives us insight into a basic distinction of faculties within human nature. He refers to them as "*inclination* of our fancy," and "our *reason.*" (*Treatise,* 238) The inclination of fancy compels us to conjoin and strengthen, and to solidify and make more compact our experiential world; at the same time, reason shows us how tenuous the connections made by inclination really are. On the one side then we tend to think of properties as welded together into objects; and on the other that properties have no "reason" to be so welded together. The contrary commitments then, flowing from our different faculties, are on the one hand to an orderly necessary arrangement, and on the other hand to a fragmented accidental arrangement. In this conflict, reason may overcome fancy by showing the absurdity of our attributing spatial location to certain qualities, but the attribution is an experiential fact and therefore must be accounted for. It is all the more a crucial fact to the moral philosopher because it shows us how we may explain moral qualities. It is to this end that the "experiment" with the olive and the fig have been introduced. It has shown us something profound about human nature: we introduce metaphysics by our natural propensity to create for ourselves a coherent world. Thus the tendency on the part of materialists and idealists to construct extreme and fanciful explanations is accounted for by our need to have a dependable experience, but it is unjustified by the rules of reason. Hence when we try to introduce reasoning into metaphysical suppositions we pervert our own capacities, pretending to possess arguable positions while in fact we are reifying the natural propensities of a consoling fancy.

Hume draws ironic consequences from this, for example, that those who argue for the existence of the substance of the soul as a simple, indivisible, thinking substance are atheistical, shockingly aping Spinoza. For the Spinozistic view (as Hume takes it from unreliable secondary sources, particularly Bayle's *Dictionary*) is one which asserts the modification of a single substance to account for physical events; and the idealistic view assumes, in a parallel way, the modification of a single substance (soul) to account for mental events; but since there is no distinction to be made between objects and impressions, the latter position, beloved of theologians, collapses into the former, and if Spinoza be an atheist, why then so are the theists. (*Treatise,* 241–246)

Such derogations, nicely argued, result from the deep insight into human nature which the "experiment" with the olive and the fig have made possible, for by the simple expedient of asking *where* are nonextensible qualities, we are brought to see not only how human nature works but are able as well to show the absurdity of metaphysical positions so loudly defended. The experimental method accomplishes two things at once: shows us what we are and the absurdity of what we believe. The consequences are deflating.

But Hume has a serious purpose to which this discussion opens a way: our experience contains nonspatial properties whose "location" is not to be accounted for either by material nor by spiritual substance. Both sides of Descartes's dualism are disposed of and all the variations of idealism, and of materialism, put to rout. We are compelled, therefore, to consider the position Hume offers to us and to accept the puzzle he poses about space and time. This forces us to ask what kind of an interpretation can be given to categories whose previous philosophical incarnation has been declared a delusion. Space and time, up to this point in the argument, have been reinterpreted first through an attack on infinite divisibility, and second through a rejection of space and time as separate from events. Finally, all varieties of materialism and idealism have been shown to be confusions, so now we can argue for the existence of moral qualities (as well as some sensory qualities) without the ontological commitment demanded by traditional natural philosophy. But more of the past must be undermined before Hume is in a position to reintroduce the concepts of space and time in book three of the *Treatise.*

The next step in Hume's destruction of Newtonianism is the defense of the proposition that "any thing may produce any thing, and that we shall never discover a reason why any object may or may not be the cause of any other, however great, or however little the resemblance may be betwixt them." (*Treatise,* 247) Again, reason disposes of metaphysics by showing that the need (natural, to be sure, but perilous) to erect positions on the foundation of human propensities throws to reason the resolution of varying philosophical positions that in fact do not differ from one another in significant ways. Conjoining the two propositions that "anything may produce anything," and "a body may exist and yet be nowhere," Hume has proposed a philosophical "answer" to all metaphysical disputes, for if we accept this conjunction of propositions, we make reason, and its instrument, deductive inference, powerless, unable to tell us how the world "really" is. For reason has shown us that our natural philosophies are all absurd and yet has itself reached conclusions which from the assumptions of the power of natural philosophy to give us the truth are themselves absurd. Reason has led us to conclude that anything may produce anything, and that a body may exist and yet be nowhere.

Together these propositions convince Hume that he has disposed of those philosophical positions which rested upon Newtonian natural philosophy, Cartesian dualism, theology, and Spinozistic atheism. Having disposed of the traditional points of view to his satisfaction, by means of a shockingly sophisticated polemic, Hume is ready to reintroduce space and time with the purpose of explaining them according to our needs as moral beings. But the unrelenting use of reason to destroy philosophical beliefs has an unfortunate consequence for Hume: he must explain how it is that we function as moving, acting, willing beings and do this without the help of those philosophies which at least gave an account of human action. Hume is in the position of a contemporary scientist who must explain the material universe without the benefit of accepted physical theory. He faces the task of explaining human action upon the premise that "reason alone can never be a motive to any action of the will." (*Treatise*, 413) Further, he has already "proved" that we are possessed of moral sentiments which are nowhere. On these grounds, then, he must explain how we move, act, choose, accomplish, how we bring anything to pass in the natural world around us.

At this point in his argument Hume is in no better a position than a dualist like Descartes who must explain how spiritual, nonspatial, nonextended substance can cause material substance to move. Descartes devised a "mechanism" for this unlikely conjunction, Berkeley called upon mind to account for causal sequence in thoughts, but Hume has neither the mechanical finesse of Descartes nor the spiritual consolation which came to the believing Berkeley's aid. Hume is possessed of inert reason and nonlocatable sentiment. Given that combination, how can we be agents?

Hume's problem, like those encountered by so many other philosophers, is the crisis he created through his challenge to natural philosophy. In this respect, his problem is like that faced by contemporary philosophers who find a discrepancy between human experience and the objectifications of science. In reviewing Hume's efforts to deal with a new understanding of space and time I am reminded of the later attempt by Husserl to overcome the mathematical idealization of the physical world which he believed characterized modern science. Husserl and Hume face similar problems, and, surprisingly, they offer similar solutions, even though stated in profoundly different languages and flowing from radically different temperaments. For the proposed solution to Hume's philosophical troubles we must turn to books two and three of the *Treatise*.

3

The solution we find is in one respect a deep disappointment, for it consists in assuming the Newtonian model and metaphor; in another respect it completes Hume's philosophical project by applying that model and metaphor to consciousness and thereby effecting a rapprochement with the position he could never really evade; he merely "overcame" it by making it serve as a model for a different order of functioning. One is reminded of the efforts on the part of some contemporary philosophers to bend relativity theory and quantum theory to their own philosophical purposes.

Perhaps Hume's feeling that he at last succeeded in bending Newtonian philosophy to his own needs accounts for the fact that part three of book two is one of the best written sections of the *Treatise*, with an ease of expression, a flowing style of argument, and a touch of humor all balanced to present a radical position without shock. It abounds in paradoxical statements, such as the infamous, "Reason is, and ought only to be the slave of the passions, and can never pretend to any other office than to serve and obey them." (Treatise, 415) What uniquely characterizes the section is its thoroughgoing Newtonianism; every principle, every explanation, every description of mind and action is predicated on a Newtonian conception of necessity and causal rigor. After all the labor to rid philosophy of Newton's particular point of view, his spirit seems to have seized Hume's thought.

The argument moves through three stages, culminating in the final discussion of space and time. Stage one is the famous argument for attributing necessity to human action, based on Hume's analysis of the ordinary accounts we give of human conduct. Paradox appeals to Hume as the mode of formulation most appropriate to his revolution: "I do not ascribe to the will that unintelligible necessity, which is supposed to lie in matter. But I ascribe to matter that intelligible quality, call it necessity or not, which the most rigorous orthodoxy does or must allow to the will. I change, therefore, nothing in the receiv'd systems, with regard to the will, but only with regard to material objects." (*Treatise*, 410) Hume argues his case by appeal to what we in fact invoke when we characterize ourselves as "responsible." Both religion and morality would fail if there were indeterminism and unpredictability in human action. " 'Tis indeed certain, that as all human laws are founded on rewards and punishments, 'tis suppos'd as a fundamental principle, that these motives have an influence on the mind, and both produce the good and prevent the evil actions." (*Treatise*, 410)

Three historical comments are relevant to this stage of the argument. First, Hume builds his case for a necessity in human action by analogy with the Newtonian models: the will is a force, and moral rules are the laws of (human) motion. The analogy is constructed with the Newtonian universe and the Humean republic as its two orders of comparison. Extending this analogy to the philosophy Hume's thought stimulated, we might call this Hume's "Copernican revolution," as Kant called his philosophical turnabout a "Copernican revolution."

Second, Hume establishes with this argument for the determinism of human conduct and its function as the source for our attribution of determinism to nature, a species of argument which we see again and again in the history of modern thought. Its most recent manifestation is in the study of myth now being carried out by Claude Lévi-Strauss, whose thesis is that the study of mythic structures allows us to see into the structures of mental processes in general. While from a superficial inspection, it seems the work of the mind is free and inventive, the study of myth demonstrates, Lévi-Strauss believes, that there are "laws which operate at a deeper level," and that the mind, "rescued from the obligation of dealing with objects, finds itself reduced in some way to imitating itself as an object. Since the laws of its operations are no longer fundamentally different from those it manifests in its other functions, it avers its nature as a thing among things." [8] It may seem far-fetched to draw a comparison between Hume's philosophy of psychic life and and the theory of Lévi-Strauss, yet I believe the revolution Hume was attempting to bring about in the way we understand human thought and action is the first intelligible statement of a profound change in intellectual perspective, one which was elaborated by Kant, and thereafter by Kant's heirs, of whom Lévi-Strauss is one.

I interpret Lévi-Strauss's comment in this way: there has been a general retreat from the simple, realistic interpretations of experience and an increasing separation of the inner world of experience from the outer world of events. Hume's epistemology exhibits this separation and in the process takes the mind as a thing, that is, takes the mind as the natural world. Hence "reality" is described by the account of how the mind works. In postulating principles of association as "the cement of our universe," Hume is putting rules of mind functioning in place of the physical descriptions of the natural philosophers.

Finally, at this stage in Hume's argument, we can put into perspective the criticism of Hume's treatment of space and time formulated by C. D. Broad and mentioned in the introduction to this essay. It appears that the most serious philosophical inadequacy of Hume's analysis is not that he failed to understand the categories of Newtonian physics, not that he cannot resolve the contradictions in the theory of fluxions, but rather that he was content to accept and work with a grave contradiction, which grew out of his reductive analysis of human nature and left him with an inert reason and with sentiments whose relationship to an effect upon action are never explained. Yet with all this, Hume proceeds with great good humor and benevolent conviction in philosophical resolution to a thoroughly Newtonian determinism as an explanation of the will and human conduct.

Having concluded that the principle of necessity is only meaningful if thoroughgoing, applied to every aspect of reality, which means in effect to

8 "Overture to *Le cru et le cuit*," trans. Joseph. H. McMahon, *Yale French Studies*, 36–37, 1966, pp. 53–54.

human conduct and thought, Hume is ready to take the next step. Still arguing from a Newtonian analogy, Hume asserts that since the idea of necessity arises from the constant conjunction of events, by parity of reasoning and from the principle of philosophical parsimony, we are led to apply the principle of determinism to psychological events, and there we find the same sort of conjunction which originally was attributed by Newton to cosmic events. But now, in this stage of the argument, Hume must deal with impressions in order to explain what causes one impression to move and be replaced by another impression. His conclusion is a further extension of the Newtonian analogy: the motion of the mind, like the motion of natural bodies, can be explained in terms of impressions working upon one another with varying degrees of force. His language becomes that of the natural philosopher: "For 'tis observable that an opposition of passions commonly causes a new emotion in the spirits, and produces more disorder than the concurrence of any two affections of equal force." (*Treatise*, 421)

The system of psychic life as Hume describes it becomes more and more a Newtonian universe in which bodies acting and reacting, combining and separating, creating components of force, and diminishing forces through inertia and friction, are impressions of the mind. From this Hume moves on to the next step in his argument which begins in book two, part three, section seven, "Of contiguity and distance in space and time." Hume's opening statement contrasts markedly with the discussion of space and time in book one. "There is an easy reason," he writes, "why every thing contiguous to us, either in space or time, shou'd be conceived with a peculiar force and vivacity, and excel every other object, in its influence on the imagination. Ourself is intimately present to us, and whatever is related to self must partake of that quality. But where an object is so far remov'd as to have lost the advantage of this relation, why, as it is farther remov'd, its idea becomes still fainter and more obscure, wou'd, perhaps, require a more particular examination." (*Treatise*, 427)

Not only is Hume's easy avowal of the presence of the self and of "ourself," remarkable given his strictures on what we may mean by the idea of the self, but the way of describing space and time seems to restore all the false conceptions of those terms which he labored to remove in book one: " 'Tis obvious, that the imagination can never totally forget the points of space and time, in which we are existent; but receives such frequent advertisements of them from the passions and senses, that however it may turn its attention to foreign and remote objects, it is necessitated every moment to reflect on the present." (*Treatise*, 427–428)

Hume then goes on to describe in a strange way the process of memory: "When we reflect, therefore, on any object distant from ourselves, we are oblig'd not only to reach it at first by passing thro' all the intermediate space betwixt ourselves and the object, but also to renew our progress every moment; being every moment recall'd to the consideration of ourselves and our present situation." (*Treatise*, 428) Then Hume contrasts space and time in their distinction of parts, space being a collection of present parts available to sight and feeling, time being but one part, never any two coexistent. Hence it is more difficult to sustain the vivacity of impressions temporally separated than it is to sustain the vivacity of impressions spatially separated. The model of a Newtonian universe is obvious, but the willingness to use it in describing the way the human consciousness functions strikes us with its simplemindedness, quite at odds with the sophistication of Hume's arguments on free will.

If we recall the discussion of space and time at the beginning of the *Treatise*, we entertain a relativistic interpretation, in the manner of Leibniz, which makes space and time functions of events. Now, however, in this heavily Newtonian section of the *Treatise*, where human behavior is under discussion, the model remains Newtonian even for space and time. Something much closer to the absolute space and time of Newton's universe is called upon: "In our common way of thinking, we are plac'd in a kind of middle station, betwixt the past and future; and as our imagination finds a kind of difficulty in running along the former, and a facility in following the course of the latter, the difficulty conveys the notion of ascent, and the facility of the contrary. Hence we imagine our ancestors to be, in a manner, mounted above us, and our posterity to lie below us." (*Treatise*, 437) Crudely, Hume conceives of human life in a space-time environment through which the individual passes. History is real for us as creatures of the republic of letters because it tells of past events in the space-time envelope. Anticipations of the future in human behavior are analogous to predictions in a Newtonian cosmos.

Continuing the analogy, there ought to be a probability function appropriate to causal relationships in the moral realm. Indeed there is, and Hume describes this species of moral probability in book three where he analyzes moral action. We are, by our nature as human beings whose sense of life's urgencies drives us to create a moral universe, compelled to go beyond the evidence of immediate experience. We strengthen observed conjunctions by formulating rules regarding them. We would give order to our acting, aspiring selves just as the deity, according to some beliefs, gave order to the physical universe.

> For there is a principle of human nature, which we have frequently taken notice of, that men are mightily addicted to *general rules,* and that we often carry our maxims beyond those reasons, which first induc'd us to establish them. Where cases are similar in many circumstances, we are apt to put them on the same footing, without

considering, that they differ in the most material circumstances, and
that the resemblance is more apparent than real.[9]

The enunciation of this basic principle of human nature—as much a part of
Hume's psychological theory as the principles of association presented in
book one—opens the way for further experiment on constancies in behavior.
Hume gives them the status of "discoveries," and tests them with examples
from history and the moral behavior of individuals. Most of his "experiments"
seem commonplace to us because superficial or trivially obvious. However,
they provide evidence of the strengthening of causal relationships by a species
of moral probability which it is Hume's purpose to construct in his defense
of the republic of letters.

A corollary to the first principle concerning the human tendency to
make general rules, and to strengthen relationships by the addition of further
relationships, is the natural interest we have in the useful:

> The imagination has a set of passions belonging to it, upon which
> our sentiments of beauty much depend. These passions are mov'd
> by degrees of liveliness and strength, which are inferior to *belief*,
> and independent of the real existence of their objects. Where a
> character is, in every respect, fitted to be beneficial to society, the
> imagination passes easily from the cause to the effect, without con-
> sidering that there are still some circumstances wanting to render
> the cause a compleat one. *General rules* create a species of proba-
> bility which sometimes influences the judgment, and always the
> imagination. (*Treatise*, 585)

Belief, properly speaking, is the passion aroused by actual physical presences
and leads to our assertions of causal interaction. Less lively, but just as important, are the passions we feel when we perceive what we might call
utile and moral possibilities—those conditions which a sensitive and sharp
mind sees are fit for development in the direction of moral and aesthetic
comeliness. Here is another species of *probability*, not the probability of
causes which works in the experience of the external world, or what we
might call the probability of natural philosophy, those relationships of events
studied by the physicist, astronomer, chemist, and other scientists who are
interested in nature. This second species of probability we might call *the
probability of moral philosophy*, those relationships of a moral and aesthetic
kind—in short, value probabilities—on which we base our judgments of
value. It is this kind of probability, derived, Hume believes, from our tendency to make general rules, which underlies our value expectations.

Our feelings, whose presence cannot be doubted, but whose location
cannot be given in spatial terms, move with a force "inferior to belief," yet

[9] *Treatise*, Book III, Part II, Sec. IX, 551. See also p. 555.

they create relationships genuinely of a causal kind, and these connections can be described by means of general rules, though vaguer than the general rules which describe the ways in which our experience of externally related objects leads us to postulate cause in the world. General rules of feeling "create a species of probability which sometimes influences the judgment, and always the imagination." This constitutes Hume's defense of a species of probability appropriate to our sentimental life. It is distinguished from the probability of causes as understood by the natural philosopher by being looser and less precise about cause, assuming that events are "compleat" when they are not. Here then is a defense—weak to be sure—of how we are moved as moral beings. We are moved to act by the passions of the imagination through our propensity to create general rules for ourselves. The mind makes itself into an orderly universe. Just as the Newtonian universe "moves" according to the laws of motion, so the moral universe "moves" by means of the peculiar laws we forge for ourselves.

Morality, then, contradicts the conclusions of reason by giving us the rules, through a mysterious human propensity, according to which we can work as predictable agents. This concludes Hume's model of human behavior in space and time. However, it fails to bring out a further purpose in Hume's effort to argue the primacy of moral philosophy. This is what I take to be a therapeutic power of philosophy, rather like avowedly psychological therapies of the century following Hume. In the concluding section I shall comment on this conception of philosophy.

4

Hume's challenge to Newtonian philosophy concludes its argument by proposing a model of human action constructed in terms of Newtonian metaphors. The need to understand ourselves in terms of a nonorganic model had once again triumphed. One is reminded of a comment attributed to Wittgenstein: "If people imagine a psychology, their ideal is a mechanics of the soul." (*Lectures on Aesthetics*, IV, 1.) But Hume had the further purpose of showing that psychology necessarily precedes cosmology, and that philosophical concern has had a profound influence on later thought. It is therefore helpful to see what is peculiar to Hume in his Newtonianism, and how it relates to recent psychological thought.

I shall mention briefly three original arguments that ought to be disentangled from the Newtonian metaphors. The first is the theme pursued here, a theme stated clearly in Hume's *Abstract of The Treatise of Human Nature*: natural philosophy rests on moral philosophy. Whatever the discoveries of natural philosophy, moral philosophy has its own special interests in space and time and requires an analysis of those categories quite distinct from that offered by a physicist. Human experience is both in and out of space and time.

Feelings, passions, moral sensibilities exist yet are nowhere insofar as natural philosophy is concerned. In contrast, the reality of human actions—the only "reality" philosophers can meaningfully talk about—is structured historically. This requires a reconstruction of space and time in accordance with our moral needs and the recasting of our concept of probability. Therefore Hume distinguishes a moral probability from a natural probability.

The moral philosopher shows us how memory and anticipation, hope and regret, all the virtues and vices (to an analysis of which the last two parts of book three of the *Treatise* are devoted) become categories of experience. Through the moral philosopher the spatiotemporal world becomes the world of human action and the world in which we feel ourselves related to our ancestors and our progeny. By relating our present awareness to that of the past, the moral philosopher demonstrates continuity in history, and history shows us the great men of the past moved by understandable moral concerns. Thus Alexander the Great's contempt for his troops' faint-heartedness illustrates that pride and self-esteem are basic to conduct. (*Treatise*, 599) But most important, the moral philosopher gives our natural faculties a place in an ordered world. Memory and anticipation, hope and regret, the virtues and vices are not idle feelings but responses to the commitment we naturally have to what is both pleasant and useful to ourselves and to others.

The concluding sections of book three of the *Treatise* are concerned to show us how we modulate our behavior under the forces of pride, humility, and sympathy. These are the great forces which move us through the space and time of moral action, although the ultimate principles which move us as moral beings are as mysterious and hidden as are the "secret springs and principles of nature" lying behind the natural philosopher's account of events.

The second argument which is Hume's own is this: moral philosophy moderates our pathological relationship to events, showing us a middle way between the dangerous aberrations of enthusiasm and superstition. Hume explores this middle way in those writings which made him famous, the *Essays Moral, Political, and Literary*, published in 1742. A good example of the moderation he claims for moral philosophy is presented in the introductory essay, "Of The Delicacy of Taste and Passion."

> There is a *delicacy of taste* observable in some men, which very much resembles this *delicacy of passion,* and produces the same sensibility to beauty and deformity of every kind, as that does to prosperity and adversity, obligations and injuries. When you present a poem or a picture to a man possessed of this talent, the delicacy of his feelings makes him be sensibly touched with every part of it; nor are the masterly strokes perceived with more exquisite relish and satisfaction, than the negligences or absurdities with disgust and uneasiness. . . . In short, delicacy of taste has the same effect

as delicacy of passion: it enlarges the sphere both of our happiness and of our misery, and makes us sensible to pains as well as pleasures, which escape the rest of mankind.[10]

The affectively mature person has developed to the full his capacity to respond to moral qualities. His world is highly colored, rich in nuances, delicately modulated by his discriminations. All that is fine, as well as all that is foolish and absurd, becomes separated out in experience. Thus he actively structures the events peculiar to human beings. But human beings are liable to fall into perversions, the most obvious those of enthusiasm and superstition. (See the essay, "Of Superstition and Enthusiasm.") Enthusiasm results from the loss of the control of sentiments; superstition from the loss of control of passions. The superstitious man is beset by fears of all sorts; he imagines a world of threatening events and of causalities for which there is no foundation in regularity of occurrences. The enthusiast, on the other side, lives wholly in terms of his inward passions. Wholly subjective, like the romantic artist, he expresses only himself and makes a reality of his agitations.

The moral philosopher, on the ancient model, is a person of developed taste whose experience defines the genuine human universe. It is at this point that Hume reverts to the Newtonian metaphor, for the genuine human universe is organized like the mechanical universe of objects in motion. Yet the description of the human universe requires a literary genre of its own. In the moral-political essays, and in the *History of England,* Hume displays human nature in those positions, oppositions, conjunctions, aberrations, and cataclysms peculiar to its universe of sentiments and moral values.

Finally, Hume suggests that philosophy written with moral concern has a therapeutic effect. Philosophy cures us of our delusions. In this respect I see a parallel between Hume's moral philosophy and more recent efforts to develop techniques of self-consciousness. There is a fascinating likeness in some of Hume's therapeutic interests and those of psychoanalysis. Two points can be made in this brief comment. The first concerns the reconstructions we make in psychoanalysis and in letters; the second, the way we see ourselves in relationship to the external world. Once we make our reconstructions, through psychoanalysis or through moral philosophy, we are forcefully compelled to entertain a particular view of the way human experience and the external world are related.

The reconstruction in psychoanalysis was referred to by Freud as "construction" and "interpretation." Freud argued that the process of construction in psychoanalytic treatment was "effective because it recovers a fragment of lost experience, so the delusion [of the patient] owes its convincing

10 *Philosophical Works*, eds. T. H. Green and T. H. Grose, 4 vols. (London, 1882), III, 92.

power to the element of historical truth which it inserts in the place of the rejected reality." [11] The job of the moral philosopher, as Hume conceives it, is to disabuse us of our delusions and to replace them with historical truths and with new insights into our value filled judgments. It is, if you will, to bring the affective life back into the center of consciousness and action. In this process extreme aberrations are replaced by humane normality. There is a similar evaluation of human experience on the part of Freud: "If we consider mankind as a whole and substitute it for the single human individual, we discover that it too has developed delusions which are inaccessible to logical criticism and which contradict reality." [12] Although in his first writings (books one and two of the *Treatise*) Hume obviously believed human delusions were accessible to logical criticism, and proceeded optimistically to apply his method of analysis to them, by the time he published book three, and from then on to the end of his life, he saw that one could only be deeply skeptical about the cure philosophy advertised. Both Hume's literary essays and his history were devoted to an analysis of the human past in an effort to bring clarification into the consciousness of the present. But, like Freud, Hume came to see that there are inevitable, perhaps logical, limitations on what we as human beings can know, for the access we have to the world is limited by our psychological endowment. The description Freud gives of "reality," when critically analyzed, could serve as well for a summation of Hume's philosophical views:

> The hypothesis we have adopted of a psychical apparatus extended in space, expediently put together, developed by the exigencies of life, which gives rise to the phenomena of consciousness only at one particular point and under certain conditions—this hypothesis has put us in a position to establish psychology on foundations similar to those of any other science, such, for instance, as physics. In our science as in the others the problem is the same: behind the attributes (qualities) of the object under examination which are presented directly to our perception, we have to discover something else which is more independent of the particular receptive capacity of our sense organs and which approximates more closely to what may be supposed to be the real state of affairs. We have no hope of being able to reach the latter itself, since it is evident that everything now that we have inferred must nevertheless be translated back into the language of our perceptions, from which it is simply impossible for us to free ourselves. But herein lies the very nature and limitation of our science. It is as though we were to say in physics: "If we could see clearly enough we should find that what

---

[11] "Construction in Analysis," Standard Edition, *The Complete Psychological Works of Sigmund Freud*, (London, 1964), XXIII, 268.
[12] *Ibid.*, 269.

appears to be a solid body is made up of particles of such and such a shape and size and occupying such and such relative positions." In the meantime we try to increase the efficiency of our sense organs to the furthest possible extent by artificial aids; but it may be expected that all such efforts will fail to affect the ultimate outcome. Reality will always remain "unknowable." [13]

When philosophy succeeds, it, like psychoanalysis, exhibits therapeutic powers and actually changes human consciousness. Hume believed that philosophy can replace delusion in two respects: historically it brings up for review our false beliefs, often of considerable antiquity, and through careful analysis shows us what our true beliefs ought to be. Ontologically, it replaces the unintelligible categories of natural philosophy with the humanely relevant categories of moral philosophy. Of such categories space and time are most fundamental, for they define our universe, which is to say, their reconstruction in the republic of letters defines the nature and the limitation of our science of human nature.

[13] *Ibid.*, "An Outline of Psychoanalysis," XXIII, 196.

JOHNSON AND FOREIGN VISITORS TO LONDON: BARETTI AND OTHERS

BY JAMES L. CLIFFORD

1

SAMUEL JOHNSON HAS OFTEN BEEN LOOKED UPON AS THE EPITOME OF BRITISH CHARACTER. BLUNT, DOGGED, IRASCIBLE, FULL OF COMMON SENSE, HE IS SUPPOSED TO REPRESENT THE PROVERBIAL JOHN BULL, THE ESSENCE OF INSULAR DOGMATISM AND ESSENTIAL HONESTY. ALTHOUGH IN OUR DAY SCHOLARS HAVE BEEN POINTING OUT THE NARROWNESS OF SUCH a characterization, stressing the complexity of his personality and the wide variety of his interests, still in many parts of the world the image persists. And it has some justification. He was certainly not an urbane, universal author or a polite man-of-the-world. As a result, he has never had a wide appeal for continental readers, either as a talker or as a writer. There is no complete French or German translation of Boswell's *Life of Johnson,* and none of Johnson's complete published works. Although such works as *Rasselas* have been widely admired and read, his minor works are almost unknown on the Continent. He remains, for all intents and purposes, an English author.

Perhaps one reason was Johnson's own well-publicized antipathy for other contemporary cultures. As Giuseppe Baretti once put it, "Johnson was a real *true-born Englishman.* He hated the Scotch, the French, the Dutch, the Hanoverians, and had the greatest contempt for all other European Nations." [1] And Boswell at the beginning of his *Tour to the Hebrides* confessed that Johnson "allowed himself to look upon all nations but his own as barbarians." [2] Indeed, one could go on and on citing instances where Johnson castigated foreigners. Bennet Langton, in a long series of reminiscences given to Boswell, which the latter used to fill up his account for the year 1780, wrote that Johnson's "contempt for foreigners was indeed extreme. One evening at Old Slaughter's Coffeehouse when a number of them were talking loud about little matters he said 'Does not this confirm Old Meynell's ob-

[1] Boswell's *Life of Johnson,* ed. Hill-Powell (Oxford, 1934–50), hereafter called *Life,* IV, 15, n.3.
[2] *Life,* V, 20.

servation "For any thing I see, foreigners are fools." ' " [3] When he printed this in the *Life,* Boswell, perhaps wishing to make clear that he did not himself agree, inserted the word "unjust" before "contempt."

Although it is quite true that most of the evidence of Johnson's attitude comes through Boswell, who had a special interest in the matter, there can be little doubt of the Doctor's quite open hostility to foreigners *en masse.* It had become part of his public image. But this did not mean that he carried his prejudice over to individual members of other nations. Many of his closest friends came from nations which he publicly attacked. Boswell was a Scot. Baretti was an Italian. Goldsmith and Burke were born in Ireland. He had tremendous admiration for George Psalmanazar, the reformed impostor, who had claimed he was a Formosan. Sir Joshua Reynolds put it very well: "The prejudices he had to countries did not extend to individuals. . . . In respect to Frenchmen he rather laughed at himself, but it was insurmountable. He considered every foreigner as a fool till they had convinced him of the contrary." [4] And, indeed, time and again we find Johnson changing his mind. Once the new acquaintance showed that he was a scholar or a man of sense, Johnson forgot completely the man's origin and welcomed him as a friend. But the proof had to be undeniable.

One basic reason which is often given for Johnson's strong insular prejudices is that he did not leave England until he was over sixty-five years old. Because of poverty and the continual pressures of commitments to booksellers in order to keep alive, he never had the opportunity to travel on his own. And his temperament was scarcely suited to the only other possibility, a post as traveling tutor to some nobleman's son. Johnson may have dreamed of someday going to Rome, or wandering through France, but the opportunity never turned up. It was not until he was an elderly man that the Thrales carried him to Paris for his first view of continental culture. Even then he insisted on conversing in Latin with scholarly people he met. Although he could read French fluently, he never attempted to speak it. But it is not about these later years that I am writing now. For most of his early and middle life whatever foreigners he saw were those who had come to London.

Obviously it is impossible to estimate how many visiting scholars Johnson may have met in the coffeehouses and taverns, or in the drawing rooms of friends. He kept no day-to-day diary, and his letters did not generally record such inconsequential meetings. Occasionally there is some rec-

[3] *The Correspondence and Other Papers of James Boswell Relating to the Making of the "Life of Jonson,"* ed. Marshall Waingrow (New York, 1969), p. 366; *Life,* IV, 15.

[4] C. R. Leslie and T. Taylor, *The Life and Times of Sir Joshua Reynolds* (London, 1865), II, 460.

ord, and sometimes the visitor himself noted the meeting. It is on these random records that we must depend for our account.

Johnson's relations with visiting foreigners were chiefly of two kinds —with those who settled in London for a long stay, like Baretti, Paoli, and others, who became close friends—and those who came to London merely for a few months and happened to be introduced to Johnson by mutual friends. To be sure, after the appearance of the *Dictionary* in 1755 Johnson's reputation as a scholar and lexicographer quickly spread to the Continent, and visitors might well have asked to meet him.

2

Because so much has been written about Johnson's long friendship with Giuseppe (in England called Joseph) Marc'Antonio Baretti there is no need to present all the evidence here. But because it shows so well how Johnson did became involved in the life of a visiting Italian something might be said of the early years of their relationship. Baretti first came to England in 1751 and met Johnson not long afterwards. Apparently it was through Charlotte Lennox that the two first came together. There seems no reason to doubt the circumstantial account, obviously coming from Baretti, and first printed in the *European Magazine* in May 1789, just after his death. According to this version:

> Mrs. Lennox, the authoress of "The Female Quixote," having an intention to publish a translation of the novels from whence Shakespeare had taken some of his plays, wished to acquire a sufficient knowledge of the Italian language to enable her to execute the work with some degree of credit. To accomplish this point Mr. Lennox, her husband, went to the Orange coffee house to learn whether any foreigner was desirous of improving himself in the English language, and by that means receive the same advantage as he should communicate. Mr. Baretti happened to be present when the enquiry was made, and eagerly accepted the offer. After some time he was introduced to Dr. Johnson. An intimacy commenced between them, which appears to have continued until nearly the end of Dr. Johnson's life.[5]

Since the first volume of the lady's *Shakespear Illustrated*, including six translations from the Italian, appeared in May 1753, it may be safe to say that Johnson met Baretti sometime late in 1752 or early 1753.[6] Years later,

[5] *European Mag.*, XV (May 1789), 349.

[6] Allen T. Hazen, *Samuel Johnson's Prefaces and Dedications* (New Haven and London, 1937), p. 104. See also Lacy Collison-Morley, *Giuseppe Baretti* (London, 1909), p. 82. Although not up-to-date in spots and lacking much evidence, this is still the best introduction to the life of Baretti.

when giving testimony at Baretti's trial for murder, Johnson estimated "1753 Or 1754," but the earlier date appears more likely.

Evidently the two men took to each other at once, for by 1754 they were on excellent terms. Baretti consulted Johnson on various matters. He did not always accept the older man's advice, but the relationship was one of mutual respect. To be sure, the ties were sometimes strained to the limit. One fantastic episode will show the kind of problems Johnson had in defending this high-strung and emotional southern European friend.

Sometime in the spring of 1754 Baretti was approached by William Huggins, who had been working for some twenty years on a translation of Ariosto's *Orlando Furioso* into English *ottava rima*, and asked to look over the version. Huggins had read Baretti's *Dissertation upon the Italian Poetry* published the year before and was eager to secure his expert help. So he sent a young clergyman, the Rev. Temple Henry Croker, who was possibly acting as his chaplain, to see Baretti, with instructions to fetch the Italian visitor by any means he could. Evidently some agreement was reached, for Baretti wrote to Croker, who was staying at Huggins's estate, Headley Park, near Farnham, Surrey, on May 24 indicating that he was quite ready to come down and look over the manuscript according to their agreement.[7] Since in the letter Baretti asked further questions about plans for publication, it is obvious that the translation must have been virtually completed. Unfortunately Baretti had been suffering from a stubborn fever and a week later wrote apologizing for his failure to show up. He hoped to see him shortly.

Early in June, then, Baretti traveled out to Headley Park for about a two months' delightful stay in the English country side. The temperate climate and the cider and beer cooled his fiery blood, and he evidently enjoyed his visit very much, while he and his host struggled valiantly with the English verse rendering of Ariosto's lines. We know all this because on August 8, just after returning to London, Baretti wrote a long enthusiastic letter to a friend in Milan.[8] As part of his reward, so Baretti described the whole matter, Huggins paid all his expenses, generously gave him a handsome gold watch worth at least forty guineas, as well as a note for a similar amount. In addition, Huggins had offered him the use of a little neighboring house and garden with the right to as many deer from the park as he needed for his table. He even tried to saddle him with a relation as a wife. When the

[7] In the Hyde Collection at Four Oaks Farm, near Somerville, New Jersey, there are four manuscript letters by Baretti, three to Croker and the fourth apparently to Huggins, all at least partly connected with this episode. I am indebted to Mrs. Donald F. Hyde for permission to see and quote a few passages, though I do not have space to include all the details.

[8] See Collison-Morley, pp. 90–93. The letter in the original Italian may be found in Giuseppe Baretti, *Epistolario*, ed. Luigi Piccioni (Bari, 1936), I, 100–7.

translation was published it was to have an English preface by Baretti, and he was to receive the chief share of the royalties. At least that was Baretti's understanding of the arrangement, as described in detail in his letter. When he left the Huggins ménage, so Baretti insisted, the whole family had been in tears and made him promise to return for Christmas.

Unfortunately, Baretti must have misunderstood some of Huggins's remarks. Indeed, most of his assumptions appear to have been unfounded, since Baretti and Huggins were soon at each other's throats. Apparently it all started over the matter of the watch. Huggins thought he had merely lent it to Baretti to take with him when he went for a walk before dinner. Baretti thought it had been given him as a present. He certainly failed to give it back, and he took it with him when he finally left Headley Park. Despite all of Huggins's later efforts Baretti steadfastly refused to return the watch and later pawned it. Then the web becomes even more tangled. To be sure, Baretti later told a friend that it had all been caused by a jealous huntsman and that he had "instantly" given back the watch when Huggins demanded it,[9] but the affair was not as simple as that.

Again it appears to have been Temple Henry Croker who acted as one of Huggins's emissaries in the matter of the watch. Inevitably Croker was viewed by Baretti as one of his mortal enemies. Once threats were used, Baretti secured protection from the Sardinian ambassador and thought he was safe.[10] There may even have been attempts to force Baretti's landlord to allow a search of his premises. In any event, both sides were soon furious.

At this point Samuel Johnson was brought in as a neutral adjudicator. Most of the participants apparently consulted him, and he tried for awhile to remain in the center. He wrote to Huggins and advised Croker and at the same time read Baretti's communications. But nothing seemed to resolve the argument. Johnson gradually became even more deeply involved. Thus he wrote again to Huggins on 9 November 1754, trying as best he could to make clear his position:

> Sir
> I find that I am likely to suffer the common fate of intermedlers, and receive no thanks on either side. I can however solace myself with my good intentions without any disturbance from the event of a transaction in which nothing but my benevolence gave me any interest. I supposed You desirous to recover a favourite watch, and proposed a way which is certainly the most speedy, and I believe the cheapest; if you are more affected by the provocation than the loss, and more intent on resentment than the disputed property, I have no means of pacification to offer. But your letter

9 Collison-Morley, p. 94.
10 For various accounts of this episode see Collison-Morley, pp. 91–95; *Life*, IV, 473–75; B.M. Add. MS. 42, 560, I, ff. 37–38.

makes it necessary for me to tell you, that neither the loss nor the provocation is my fault. The Loss I endeavoured to repair, and should have procured restitution, or willingness in restitution, had not this new expedient been found out, by which the only conviction, which I pretend to have raised, conviction of inability to defend himself, was for a time suspended, without the least knowledge or cooperation of mine. The Provocation I endeavoured to prevent, by making up the quarrel in which I was wholly on the side of Mr. Croker. In this attempt I failed and the feud proceeded. Mr. Baretti showed me his letter before he sent it, but he did not show it for advice, and I observed neutrality so scrupulously as not even to mend his English lest he should have it to say that I concurred with him. The second letter he did not bring until he had sent it, and when he gave it to me told me 'You will not like it'. He told the truth.

Your warm assertion of yourself to me is therefore unnecessary for I never pretended to think you in the wrong. The particular question about which I remember myself quoted, you have justly distinguished in your letter to Mr. Croker, and I have nothing to object further. Your vindication of Mr. Croker is yet less proper, for I have always maintained him to be in the right, and endeavoured to convince him how easily he might prosecute the work without the help which he regretted to have lost. Mr. Croker was indeed the man for whom I was chiefly solicitous, as he was the only man that could be much hurt. I have opposed Mr. Baretti in the whole process of this difference and in the proposal meant him no favour, nor as any favour did he acknowledge it, what I said of his condition he would resent more, than he would thank me for my interposition.

One angry paragraph seems to be the consequence of an oversight in You or Me. You have read, or I have written *Hospitality* for *Hostility*, if you look on my letter you will find that *hospitality* could not or should not be the word. The laws of *Hospitality* no man ever within my knowledge charged you with breaking, the *rules of generous hostility* Mr. Croker has certainly broken if not by his application to the Sardinian Envoy, which I mentioned with with no great vehemence because at worst I thought it only circumstantially blameable, yet surely by his attempt on the landlord, of which I might speak more harshly, and speak truth. He is however a good man who in such a quarrel does but one thing wrong.

I will repeat it again that I have endeavoured honestly and, what is more, kindly, to moderate the violence of this dispute, if I had succeeded I should at least have spared you the impropriety of such a letter as you have been pleased to send to . . .[11]

[11] See *Letters of Samuel Johnson*, ed. R. W. Chapman (Oxford, 1952), I, 442–44

When his correspondent replied with further allegations, Johnson bowed out of the controversy. On 14 November he wrote again to Huggins:

> Sir
>
> I should very much blame my own negligence, if I should delay a single post to declare that I am more than satisfied, and that I shall always set the highest value on a mind so ready to receive conviction, and so candid to acknowledge it.
>
> I was led by your letter to suspect that you had received some misinformation, but I could not conceive what might be charged upon me. I see that fiction has no limits, to show you on what allegations some will venture, I assure you that I never in my life saw either the Venetian Resident, or the Landlord, nor ever sent a message to either, nor have any reason to be certain that either knows my name, or knows of my existence. I think, Sir, I may fairly claim that whatever shall be said to my disadvantage in this affair, may be judged by this Specimen. I hinted before that Mr. Croker has, I sincerely think without his fault, whisperers or clamourers about him, who want only to do mischief, or make themselves sport. If I had not happened to have written, what must I not have been thought?
>
> I hope, Sir, to have now made an end to this subject, which shall no longer disturb me, and I sincerely wish that it may cease likewise to disturb you. I should be glad that every good Mind were left to the enjoyment of itself.
>
> If you shall please to continue this correspondence upon more pleasing topicks, it will be considered as a favour by . . .[12]

Yet although Johnson refused to do any more negotiating, this was not the end of the violent controversy. When it became evident to Huggins and his associates that Baretti thought himself safe under the protection of the Sardinian ambassador, they applied to Sir Thomas Robinson, one of the Secretaries of State, to force the ambassador to withdraw his protection, which he did. Thus finally the watch was secured from the pawnbroker and returned to Huggins.

Joseph Warton, when summarizing the sequence of events for his brother Thomas at Oxford, commented: "What a Strange story! & how difficult to be beleived!" And he added some further gossip which he thought rendered the whole story more incredible.

(No. 53.1). Because this and the following letter do not appear in the normal chronological sequence of the volumes they tend to be overlooked.

12 *Ibid.,* pp. 444–45 (No. 53.2).

> Huggins wanted to get an approbation of his translation from John-
> son but Johnson would not tho Huggins says it was only to get
> money from Him. To crown all he says—that Barretti—wanted to
> poison Croker. . . . By some means or other Johnson must know
> this story of Huggins. How infamous is it if it should be false! [13]

Huggins apparently was unsure of how his translation would be received in the scholarly world and took a strange method of allowing it to appear. When a privately printed version appeared in April 1755, no translator's name was given, but there was a dedication to George II signed by Croker. Since the work was advertised in the *Gentleman's Magazine* as being "Sold at Mrs. Croker's in Rupert Street," [14] many readers assumed that he was respon-sible for the whole work. But whether this private printing was unauthorized or a trial balloon which Huggins himself had planned, and whether Huggins, once the work was favorably received, regretted his maneuver and turned on Croker is difficult to establish. All that we know with certainty is that sometime in 1756 or 1757 the translation of *Orlando Furioso* was reissued with Huggins's name as translator and with Croker's dedication omitted. Later Huggins even brought out a separate pamphlet in which he provided translations of his own to take the place of some portions of the original version done by someone else. As a reviewer in the *Critical Review* put it, "piqued, as it appears, at some particulars in the private conduct of the gentleman whose assistance he had accepted," Huggins "has been at the trouble to re-translate those few cantos done by his auxiliary." [15] The whole affair is too complicated to go into here, but it seems clear that Huggins and Croker must have quarreled somewhere along the way. In 1759, when Baretti wrote to Huggins, grudgingly trying to reestablish relations, he could refer to the "cunning of a fellow who did his utmost to set us against one another." [16]

One thing is evident: the whole involved affair brought nothing further to Baretti and was only an annoying episode for Johnson. Whose fault was it? Huggins's? Or Baretti's? Was Croker really the villain? How can we tell? The evidence is too fragmentary. Johnson, while trying to be neutral, and even for a time taking Croker's part, did not think Baretti dishonest. Johnson knew that his Italian friend was difficult to deal with and may merely have misunderstood his host. If Johnson did refuse to look at Hug-

---

[13] B.M. Add. MS. 42,560, I, ff. 37–38 (28 April 1755).

[14] *Gent. Mag.*, XXV (April 1755), 190.

[15] *Critical Review*, VI (December 1758), 506. There had been a complimentary review of the translation, perhaps by Smollett, in the *Critical Review* for May 1757, which may have encouraged Huggins to make his complete break with Croker.

[16] 10 January 1759. See note 7.

gins's translation it was not, as Huggins suspected, because he wanted to be paid handsomely to do the job, but because he did not wish to be any more involved. No doubt he later remembered the whole affair with great distaste. Late in 1762, when writing to Baretti in Italy and mentioning the deaths of Huggins and Richardson, he commented: "When we see our enemies and friends gliding away before us, let us not forget that we are subject to the general law of mortality, and shall soon be where our doom will be fixed for ever." [17] Here Johnson is quite obviously placing himself on Baretti's side. Moreover, the later reaction of the Warton brothers shows that they thought Huggins had been foolish throughout.

Certainly, the Italian, with his hot temper, his fierce pride, his quick changes of mood, must at times have been difficult for Johnson to accept. Baretti was an independent spirit, and one had to take him as he was. Once when he and Johnson had been invited to Miss Cotterell's, who was in the city in the middle of the summer, Johnson wrote to her that Baretti would not wait for him:

> Mr Baretti being a single Being in this part of the world, and entirely clear from all engagements, takes the advantage of his independence and will come before me, for which if I could blame him, I should punish him, but my own heart tells me that he only does to me, what, if I could, I should do to him.[18]

Yet when a foreigner had a fine mind and was such an admirable scholar, Johnson was quite willing to forgive him his minor eccentricities. Thus he and Baretti remained close friends and associates for almost twenty years, although it must be admitted that Johnson never proposed Baretti as a member of The Club. That would have required more social graces and dependability than Baretti possessed. But he did help Baretti in many ways. He wrote letters to Oxford introducing him to his learned friends and helped him borrow books there. He advised him and aided him in every way he could with a number of works. Allen T. Hazen sums it all up admirably in his *Johnson's Prefaces and Dedications* [19] and there is no need for me to repeat all the evidence here. For Baretti Johnson wrote dedications to important personages, prefaces, some opening sentences to set the style and pace of a work, one proposal, and we may suspect other instances which cannot be documented.

Johnson, in return, obviously learned much from Baretti about the Italian language and culture, though it was the visitor who benefitted most from the friendship. One interchange between the two men we would love

17 *Letters of Samuel Johnson,* I, 147.
18 *Ibid.,* I, 74 (letter of 19 July 1755).
19 Pp. 4–18.

to have overheard. When Baretti decided to translate Johnson's *Rasselas* into French, he was baffled as to how to reproduce the long and formal opening sentence. He tried various ways but never could get it the way he wanted. Later he told the story to Edmond Malone, who passed it on this way:

> Mentioning this to Johnson, the latter said after thinking two or three minutes, "Well, take up the pen, and if you can understand my pronunciation, I will see what I can do." He then dictated the sentence to the translator, which proved admirable, and was immediately adopted.[20]

By chance the unpublished manuscript of this French translation still survives, and it was seen by Baretti's biographer Collison-Morley. Here is how it begins:

> Mortels! vous qui prêtez l'oreille à la douce voix d'une imagination séduisante et qui poursuivez vivement les fantômes de l'espoir: vous qui attendez de l'automne de la vie l'accomplissement des promesses, que son printems vous a faites, et qui croyez, que le lendemain vous donnera ce qui vous manque aujourd'hui, écoutez l'histoire de Rasselas, prince d'Abissinie.[21]

Even in a foreign language the stately quality still persists, at least when dictated by the author.

The two friends must have seen a good deal of each other during this period, even though Baretti later insisted that he dined with Johnson at his house as seldom as he could because he "hated to see the victuals pawed by poor Miss Williams, that would often carve, though stone-blind." [22]

According to Baretti, during these years he and Johnson used sometimes to walk through the streets at night, and occasionally would talk to stray prostitutes, "for the sake of hearing their stories." But Baretti's claim that one of these tales, heard under a tree in the King's Bench Walk in the Temple, became the story of Misella in *Ramblers* 170 and 171 can hardly be true. Here Baretti must be mixed in his chronology, for he probably did not know Johnson until some time after the ending of the *Rambler*.[23]

When Baretti went back to Italy for some four years Johnson wrote him some of his best letters, addressing him affectionately as "my Baretti."

[20] James Prior, *Life of Edmond Malone* (London, 1860), pp. 160–61; Collison-Morley, pp. 361–62.

[21] Collison-Morley prints this sentence from the surviving manuscript in the possession of Avvocato Ferdinando Caire. Why Baretti chose French and not Italian is not clear. Perhaps it would have been more easily marketed, but it does not appear ever to have been printed.

[22] Collison-Morley, pp. 95–96.

[23] Prior, p. 161. *Rambler* No. 170, which begins the story of Misella, is dated 2 November 1751, and Baretti probably did not meet Johnson that early.

And later, after Baretti's return to London, when he was involved in a trial for murder, the result of a street brawl when he killed one of his attackers with a fruit knife, Johnson willingly appeared in court as a defense witness. His friend, Baretti, so he testified, was "a man of literature, a very studious man, a man of great diligence. He gets his living by study. I have no reason to think he was ever disordered with liquor in his life. A man that I never knew to be otherwise than peaceable, and a man that I take to be rather timorous." [24] When asked about his eyesight, Johnson replied, "He does not see me now, nor I do not see him. I do not believe he could be capable of assaulting any body in the street, without great provocation."

There is no need here to follow the friendship through the 1770s and 1780s, or to argue about their final quarrel, a year before Johnson's death, apparently the result of a blatant lie which Johnson had caught Baretti making.[25] With all the ups and downs, through the middle period of Johnson's life, the quarrelsome, tactless, unpredictable Italian from Piedmont was one of his closest and admired friends.

In the later years only General Paoli of the resident continentals permanently residing in London ever matched Baretti in Johnson's affection. And with Paoli there was never the same easy give-and-take.

3

With visiting foreigners staying only a few months in London during the mid-eighteenth century, it is difficult to estimate Johnson's relations. Evidently he met quite a few, and there are casual mentions of some of them in his letters, usually only when he was introducing them to one of his scholarly friends. Thus in June 1757 he wrote to Thomas Warton of Trinity College that "Dr Marsili of Padua, a learned Gentleman, and good Latin Poet, has a mind to see Oxford." [26] Johnson gladly gave him an introduction to Dr. Huddesford, recently Vice Chancellor, and also introduced him to Warton. Another time in June 1760 he wrote to Robert Chambers at Lincoln College, "The Gentleman who brings this is [a] very learned and celebrated Mathematician of Italy" [27]

Unfortunately very few anecdotes survive of Johnson's real opinion of these distinguished visitors met casually at some friend's house or possibly at a tavern. If they impressed him favorably he was quite willing to help them meet other learned men in England.

[24] See *A Constellation of Genius; Being a Full Account of the Trial of Joseph Baretti for the Murder of Evan Morgan Held at Justice-Hall in the Old-Bailey, on 20 October 1769*, ed. Herman W. Liebert (privately printed, New Haven, 1958).

[25] Collison-Morley, pp. 330–33.

[26] *Letters of Samuel Johnson*, I, 102–3.

[27] *Ibid.*, p. 127.

There is one story, perhaps not quite accurate in all details, which Boswell had from Langton. Referring to an eminent foreigner who had been shown the British Museum and was very troublesome with many absurd inquiries, Johnson commented: "Now, there Sir, is the difference between an Englishman and a frenchman. A Frenchman must be allways talking whether he knows any thing of the matter or not. An Englishman is content to say nothing when he has nothing to say." [28]

It would be amusing if we could somehow connect this anecdote with the single time that we are sure Johnson met a foreigner at the British Museum. This is the meeting of Johnson and Casanova, two men whom one hardly thinks of as moving in the same circles. The record of this meeting comes neither from Johnson nor from Casanova's full *Memoirs,* which describe in detail Casanova's stay in London from 13 June 1763 to the middle of March 1764. The entries in the *Memoirs* for this nine-month period are mostly devoted to describing his difficulties in finding suitable mistresses, the noble people he met, or notorious figures like Lord Pembroke, a gay British rake, Kitty Fisher, or the Chevalier d'Éon. Yet, strangely enough, we do know that Casanova and Johnson, who had such widely divergent views on life, did have a long talk probably in the autumn of 1763, and that it occurred in the British Museum. Somehow one does not normally think of Casanova going to museums, or Johnson either, for that matter. Anyway, it happened this way. At the Prince of Orange Coffeehouse, opposite the King's theatre at the bottom of the Haymarket, Casanova ran into Vincenzio Martinelli, well-known translator and scholar, who was at the time collecting subscriptions for an edition of *The Decameron.* Through him Casanova was introduced to Matthew Maty, and it was in the latter's rooms at the British Museum that he met Johnson. How do we know all this? Happily in a rare philological work called *A Leonard Snetlage* (published in Dresden in 1797), Casanova tells of the meeting and described one long discussion they had over the etymology of a word.[29] Whether the meeting was accidental or the result of Casanova's curiosity to meet the author of the best English dictionary, is not clear. Perhaps he had somewhere expressed his wish to see what Johnson was like, and Martinelli, or even Maty, was the go-between. To be sure, Johnson had no friendly regard for Maty. "Damn Maty—little dirty-faced dog. I'll throw him into the Thames," he had once exploded when Dr. Adams had proposed some cooperation between them.[30]

---

[28] Waingrow, p. 366; *Life of Johnson,* IV, 14. The name of the foreigner has been crossed out in the manuscript, and has not yet been deciphered.

[29] See C. W. Stollery, "Casanova's Meeting with Samuel Johnson," *Casanova Gleanings,* VII (1964), 1–4. Both the original French version and a translation into English are provided by Stollery.

[30] Waingrow, p. 24. For a slightly censored version see *Life,* I, 284.

But he might have been willing to come to the museum to meet a visiting foreigner.

Since Casanova was not fluent in English, the conversation probably was carried on in Latin. In his later account Casanova begins by describing Johnson as the "author of the dictionary, of which one criticizes the excessive erudition. *Ne quid nimis.* No less." [31] Then he proceeds to report a long discussion as to the origin of the word *comité* (committee). At first Johnson insisted that the word was derived from the verb *commettre* (commit), even in the sense where it is applied to venial sins or misdeeds. Nor did he believe that it came from the Latin word *comitas* or from *comis*, from which comes *comitas* meaning affability, politeness, urbanity. Johnson found the latter definition improbable: "for our committees are hardly gentle nor extremely polite." Then Johnson, so Casanova reported, suggested that the word came from the illness which we call epilepsy and the Romans called *morbus comitialis.* "Those same Romans used the name *homines comitiales* for all the great disputants and pettifoggers who wrangled to the point that their jaws locked, causing them to fall down, outstretched as if dead, stiff upon the ground." Thus the English passed on the name to groups of members of Parliament who came to no agreement.

It is impossible for us to guess what Johnson had in mind in this strange argument. Was he really serious? Or was he trying to be funny and thought he was pulling the fashionable foreigner's leg? Or did Casanova somehow miss the point? Or was he consciously twisting the story and being ironic about this so-called eminent lexicographer? The whole affair is puzzling to the extreme. In any event, Casanova ends his account: "It was thus that Johnson who was called the *walking library,* spoke to me, and it is altogether singular that this example of his intellect is not to be found among the too great riches of his dictionary."

In some instances we know more about the confrontations from other Englishmen who were present than from either of the central figures. As an example, there is the famous Roger Joseph Bošković, the Jesuit scholar, mathematician, and astronomer from the shores of the Adriatic, who was in England from 24 May to 20 December 1760. Although the events occurred before he knew Johnson, James Boswell records in various places three meetings of Johnson and Bošković.[32] The two men dined together at the house of Mrs. Cholmondeley, at Sir Joshua Reynolds's and Dr. Douglas's. They talked, as was Johnson's custom, in Latin, "with a dignity and elo-

[31] See note 29. I know nothing further of this meeting except what is presented by Stollery.
[32] *Life,* II, 125, 406.

quence" that surprised the visiting dignitary. Evidently the two men took to each other at once. Bošković, so Cornelia Knight put it, was universally admired. "There was something so natural and good natured in his manner it was impossible not to like him." [33] He had also a remarkable talent for making extempore Latin verses.

Arthur Murphy gives a fuller account than does Boswell of the dinner at Dr. Douglas's.[34] At first the conversation was mostly in French, and Johnson, uncertain as to his pronunciation, kept quiet. But later the topics changed as did the language. "For the rest of the evening the talk was in Latin. Bošković had a ready current flow of that flimsy phraseology with which a priest may travel through Italy, Spain, and Germany. Johnson scorned what he called colloquial barbarisms. It was his pride to speak his best. He went on, after a little practice, with as much facility as if it was his native tongue. One sentence this writer well remembers. Observing that Fontenelle at first opposed the Newtonian philosophy, and embraced it afterwards, his words were: *Fontenellus, ni fallor, in extremâ senectute fuit transfuga ad castra Newtoniana.*"

During this visit to England Bošković wrote full letters back to his brother and friends, and these, happily, have survived.[35] They allow us to date some of these meetings fairly well. Apparently he first met Johnson at the home of Sir Joshua Reynolds on 29 June 1760. Just when the two men were at Mrs. Cholmondeley's cannot be documented, but the visiting Serbo-Croat had been taken to her house in early June by Edmund Burke shortly after his arrival in England. The last meeting at the home of Dr. Douglas, which occurred just before Bošković left England, probably occurred on 12 December.

If the traveler's letters do help with chronology, they add little to our knowledge of what Bošković really thought of Johnson, for he simply mouths the customary generalizations—"one of the leading men of letters in England, author of a celebrated dictionary," or "one of the great men of letters of the country," "who has made one of the most celebrated dictionaries of the English language." [36] But there is nothing about his appearance or his obvious idiosyncrasies.

At Sir Joshua Reynolds's Johnson gave Bošković a letter to young

[33] *Autobiography of Miss Cornelia Knight, Lady Companion to the Princess Charlotte of Wales* (London, 1861), I, 26.

[34] *An Essay on the Life and Genius of Samuel Johnson* (1792); reprinted in *Johnsonian Miscellanies,* ed. G. B. Hill (Oxford, 1897), I, 416–17.

[35] J. Torbarina, "The Meeting of Bošković with Dr. Johnson," *Studia Romanica et Anglica Zagrabiensia,* No. 13–14 (July–December 1962), 3–12.

[36] *Ibid.,* pp. 5, 7. The original comments were in Italian.

Robert Chambers, who was to become the successor to Blackstone as Vinerian Professor of Law at Oxford, and whom Johnson would later help to write his law lectures. In 1760 Chambers was a youthful fellow of Lincoln College, who liked to show visiting dignitaries around. Bošković found him delightful —"a young man of the highest parts, and a nature so sweet, modest at the same time, charming and gracious, that he is enchanting." Thus if he failed disappointingly to provide any frank comments on Johnson, Bošković was not sparing in praise of others with more obvious graces.

Although Casanova, in his supposedly scholarly etymological treatise, and Bošković in his letters make no mention of Johnson's unattractive exterior, the usual reaction of foreign visitors was one of astonishment and revulsion, combined with obvious acceptance of his fame as the author of the greatest English dictionary. Perhaps Elie de Beaumont, one of the lesser *philosophes,* might be taken as an example.[37] In the autumn of 1764 he visited England and in October was in Oxford (he received a D.C.L. on the fifteenth). On the thirteenth Elie de Beaumont noted that he had "dined with the celebrated Johnson, author of the best English Dictionary, and who was enabled to cease writing pamphlets by a court pension of 300 pieces. I have never seen a face less revealing of wit and profound knowledge."

Another instance of this combination of praise and revulsion might be the German visitor Helfrich Peter Sturz, who wrote from London on 18 August 1768:

> I am just returned from a visit to Samuel Johnson, the colossus of English Literature, who combines profound knowledge with wit, and humour with serious wisdom, and whose exterior announces nothing of these qualities; for in the proportions of his form are exactly those of the sturdy drayman. . . . His manners are boorish; and his eye cold as his raillery; never is it animated with a glance that betrays archness or acuteness; he constantly seems to be, and not seldom he really is, absent and distracted. . . . He received us in a friendly manner, though a certain air of solemness and pomposity never left him, which is interwoven with his manners as well as with his style. In conversation he rounds his periods, and speaks with a tone almost theatrical; but whatever he says, becomes interesting by a certain peculiar character with which it is stamped.[38]

---

[37] I owe this information to Dr. Robert Shackleton of Brasenose College, Oxford. He sent me this quotation in the original French from *Revue Britannique* VI (November 1895), 78.

[38] *Schriften von Helfrich Peter Sturz* (1779), I, 113–14; translated, *Monthly Magazine*, March 1, 1800, pp. 149–50. I use this translation. The German version has been reprinted in *Kleine Schriften* (Leipzig, 1904).

Sturz then set down various remarks of Johnson on language, on *The Re-hearsal*, Hume, his edition of Shakespeare, Boswell, and then Sturz com-mented on Johnson's various works—on the fact that *Rasselas*, "a masterly, cold, political romance," was little read in Germany, on Johnson's early poverty and present pension and his refusal to accept Ossian as genuine. The long conversation, which occurred at the Thrales' country house in Streat-ham, is full and discerning. Sturz is one of the visitors who caught admirably the spirit and manners of the Great Cham.

To be sure, for a man of fashion from the Continent it required some concentration to pierce through the unattractive surface of Johnson's ap-pearance and way of talking. Those who made a serious effort finally saw the richness underneath. Those who refused, or were casual about the whole business, might well come away from a meeting with Johnson with the opin-ion reputedly held by the Comte de Holcke, Grand-master of the Wardrobe for the king of Denmark, who visited England in 1768. Although a man of some polite learning and classical erudition, the comte failed to discern the basis of Johnson's reputation.

According to an anecdote published long afterwards in the *Monthly Magazine*, Holcke had heard much about Johnson's fame and wished to meet him.

> Through the interest of Dr. Brocklesby, he was enabled to pay Johnson a morning-visit. They had a long conversation. Next day Comte de Holcke dined with Lord Temple in Pall-Mall, where he met with Mr. W. G. Hamilton (commonly called Single-speech Hamilton), who, knowing of his visit to Johnson, asked him what he thought of Johnson? Holcke replied, that of all the literary im-posters and pedants he had ever met with, he thought Johnson the greatest—so shallow a fellow, he said, he had never seen! [39]

What, we may wonder, had they been talking about, which would have made the polite and learned Dane call Johnson "shallow?" All we can do is guess. Perhaps irked by his visitor's manners and his obvious condescension, Johnson had insisted on discussing Tom Thumb. Or ———. In any event, if the story is to be believed, and something like this may well have hap-pened, here is one instance where the blunt Englishman completely failed to impress the visiting foreigner. Undoubtedly neither saw the other again. And there must have been many others who had the same reaction.

Perhaps enough evidence has been brought forward to prove my point. Although Johnson was not basically antagonistic to all foreigners, they had to take him on his own terms, and not be openly patronizing. They must

[39] *Monthly Magazine*, XV (March 1, 1803), 151.

prove their scholarship and accept his comments seriously, even when brought forward to prove a difficult point. Life for Johnson was always an argument. He was quite willing to accept a Frenchman or an Italian as one of his antagonists, provided the game was played according to his rules of serious conversation.

DIDEROT AND LEGAL THEORIES OF ANTIQUITY

BY JACQUES PROUST

"Did not in the long run,
the political theory of the Encyclopedists prevail,
or at least survive, after all?"

ARTHUR M. WILSON [1]

SINCE NO ONE HAS YET HAD THE HEART TO UNDERTAKE THE GREAT STUDY ON DIDEROT AND ANTIQUITY, IT IS NOT A BAD THING TO PURSUE, MEANWHILE, THE PATIENT SPADE WORK UNDERTAKEN IN THIS FIELD BY JEAN SEZNEC (*Essais sur Diderot et L'Antiquité*, OXFORD, 1957), E. SCHRÖDER ("DIDEROT UND DIE LITERARÄSTHETISCHE TRADITION," MARBURG dissertation, 1963) or René Trousson (*Diderot helléniste*, Vol. XII in the *Diderot Studies*, Geneva, 1969) to quote only three major contributions of the last fifteen years.

Indeed—as René Trousson has clearly demonstrated—Diderot did not read in the original all the ancient authors he mentions, far from it. But it is too often forgotten that the eighteenth century was a great period of translations and adaptations. There would even be interesting research—new for the most part—to be done into the role they played in the battle of ideas in their time. Translating and publishing Epicurus or Seneca, Juvenal or Tacitus, was not in itself an innocent action at the time of the sycophant Abraham Chaumeix and Attorney General Joly de Fleury. From the manner in which they were presented, from the commentaries that were added to them, there naturally followed a particular approach, a *reading* which in its turn was far from innocent. From Diderot's works alone one could draw many examples of this art of "revivifying" antiquity without unnecessary historiographical scruples, but, on the other hand, with an acute sense of the militant value of the texts. One is reminded of Terence translated into English by Colman [2] or into French by the abbé Le Monnier; [3] of Horace whom Diderot himself translated many times; [4] of Tacitus, of Seneca. . . . [5]

1 "Why did the political theory of the Encyclopedists not prevail? A suggestion," *French Historical Studies*, I, 3 (Spring 1960), 294.

2 See Diderot, *Oeuvres complètes*, edited by Assézat and Tourneux (hereafter cited as AT), V, 228 sq. ("Réflexions sur Térence").

3 AT, I, 47, note; cf. XIX, 359 sq. ("Lettres à l'abbé Le Monnier").

4 See AT, VI, 289 sq. ("Lettre à M. l'abbé Galiani sur la sixième ode du troisième livre d'Horace"); cf. *ibid.*, 303 sq., the "Satire dedicated to Naigeon *sur un passage de la première satire du second livre d'Horace*." etc.

5 *Essai sur les règnes de Claude et de Néron* (1782) and *Essai sur la vie et les écrits de Sénèque* (1778) critical edition by Hisayasu Nakagawa (Tokyo, 1966).

Among the *mediators* who gave him access to the best sources while saving him the trouble of reading the original work or even the translation, one must never underestimate Brucker and his *Historia critica philosophiae*. I have explained that point before and in sufficient length to be excused from discussing it here.[6] But all has not been said on Brucker, far from it, and his *Historia critica* will have to be looked at often: for instance, to evaluate his share of the responsibility for certain liberties—great in some cases—that Diderot took at the expense of historical truth. I have in mind his long articles on the history of philosophy of the Indians, the Japanese, the Chinese, the Persians—he felt more at home in the Graeco-Latin area.

In the introduction to a study on "La Contribution de Diderot à l'*Encyclopédie* et les théories du droit naturel" published sometime ago in the *Annales historiques de la Révolution française*,[7] I cited the articles *Cyrénaiques, Eléatiques, Epicurisme, Ionique* on the one hand and *Cyniques, Héraclitisme, Péripatéticienne, Platonisme, Socratisme* et *Stoïcisme* on the other, as being of considerable interest for the study of the foundations of his political philosophy. And I added: "The former bring together the principal representatives of a current of thought which can be called legal positivism for which positive laws are the measure of the just and the unjust; the latter assert, on the contrary, in various ways that the ideas of just and unjust are independent of positive laws, and that, consequently, there is a natural law." I would add today that the *fund* of reference that this reading, however cursory, allowed him to contribute, remained constantly in the background of the advances he was later to make in the ever widening and especially ever more contemporary field of his reflections on social morality and political philosophy. In a sense, it can be said that the *Encyclopédie* contains the rational nucleus of the famous pages he was later to give to Abbé Raynal for *L'Histoire des deux Indes*.[8]

1. *Héraclite*—Heraclitus's moral and political thought as Diderot found it expounded in Brucker, is governed by the notion of "universal law." This law governs the physical as well as the moral world. Whatever he does and "in whatever state he exists" man is therefore subject to it. In a world where everything is equally necessary, there is objectively neither good nor evil.

But on the other hand "man wants to be happy; pleasure is his aim." Whence then does moral evil arise? Brucker's summary does not say, but he suggests it: evil is the result of an erroneous judgment, of a confusion between false and true good. Man acts for his good "whenever by acting he can consider himself as the instrument of the gods," that is to say when he acts in the only truly necessary way, in conformity with universal law. In

[6] *Diderot et l'Encyclopédie* (Paris, 1967), 244–93 and 550–57.

[7] July–September 1963, 257–286.

[8] See Yves Benot, *Diderot. De l'athéisme à l'anticolonialisme* (Paris, 1970).

the same way, in the political order, the best government is that which rules men "as the gods govern the world, where everything is necessary and good." [9]

From such a perspective, morals and politics are thus simply the application of the knowledge of universal order to mores and government.

One understands how the rigor and simplicity of this doctrine may have appealed to the author of the *Lettre à Landois*. Diderot answered Heraclitus, so to speak, in the article *Irréligieux*, which appears in the same volume as *Héraclitisme*. For Diderot, as for Heraclitus, moral life depends on the knowledge of "universal law." [10] This law governs the physical and moral world in such a way that a kind of immanent justice makes unhappiness stem from vice and happiness from virtue. And so, for the encyclopedist as for the Greek philosopher, moral evil can only arise from man's illusions concerning the "interest and the appeal of the moment." [11]

2. *Socrate.* The doctrine summed up in the article *Socratique* develops the idea which is only suggested by Heraclitism: "There is only one good and it is knowledge, only one evil and it is ignorance." To put it differently man practices vice or virtue according to whether he is ignorant of or knows his nature and the nature of things. Moral activity is not autonomous since it is subordinated to an intellectual activity which in itself is neither moral nor immoral: if "justice and happiness are one and the same thing" and if man naturally seeks happiness, he who does evil grossly mistakes his natural end, he is ignorant or mad, but not, properly speaking, wicked. This theory of the natural law [12] is completed in the article *Socratique* by a theory of sovereignty. "Socrates' principles of political wisdom" [13] indeed distinguish fundamentally between two kinds of powers whatever form they may assume: power is tyrannical whenever it expresses the sole will of the ruler (here the Prince); it is legitimate when the ruler is the executor of the law; a free people is a people that, in obeying its ruler, submits not to a man or a group of men, but to the laws alone.

The Socratic notion of the good considered as knowledge and of evil considered as ignorance is found again for instance in the *Introduction aux grands principes*, written by Diderot at a date that seems close to that of the article *Socratique*. The *Introduction* links this notion closely to the principle

9 All the texts quoted in this paragraph are in AT, XV, 83.

10 AT, XV, 253. When Diderot says of this law that God's finger "engraved [it] in every heart" it is of course only a figure of speech.

11 AT, XV, 254.

12 AT, XVII, 159–160. Socrates, like Heraclitus, allows as well a kind of immanent justice which is only one particular case of the universality of Law: "Punishment is by necessity tied to the violation [of laws]; this necessary link between law and the punishment for the violation cannot come from man."

13 AT, XVII, 162.

of universal determinism: man, moved by his passions, is not morally responsible for the good or evil he may do. In every case, he obeys the deep-seated tendency of his being, which is to seek the greatest happiness, that is to say the greatest satisfaction of his desires. He therefore necessarily acts to that effect. Consequently, the problem of good and evil is no longer a *moral* problem but a problem of *knowledge*. "It is our mind that misleads us, . . . we are criminal only because our judgment is wrong; and it is reason, not nature that leads us astray." [14]

The Socratic distinction between tyrannical and legitimate power is for its part connected with the distinction noted in the article *Autorité politique*, written about ten years before *Socratique*: a people subjected to a tyrant is only "a herd of animals brought together by habit, driven by the law of the rod, and led by the whim of an absolute master," whereas a nation that obeys a legitimate power is "a society of men moved by reason, led to action by virtue, and governed according to the laws of justice by a ruler who is wise as well as glorious." [15] Ideal political power accepts for itself the sovereignty of the law.

3. *Les Cyniques*. From his extract of *Platonisme* Diderot does not seem to have drawn ideas that are very different from those he encountered elsewhere in the Socratic system. On the other hand, the article *Cyniques* contains details on the state of nature that were not without influence on his own conceptions. The Cynics, disciples of Socrates, think indeed, like their master, that men can reach true happiness only through "practices in conformity with their nature." Morality consists of obeying the law of nature. Here arises a fundamental distinction between natural law and positive laws, which often do not conform to it, or even deny it. Now, "if the laws are bad, man is unhappier and more wicked in society than in nature." [16] Just as enlightened reason alone can prevent the passions from going astray, so only knowledge and respect for natural law can make it possible to resist positive laws and correct them. Such is indeed the meaning of the formulas attributed to Diogenes: "One owes more to nature than to the law" [17] and "one must resist . . . law by nature, passions by reason." That does not mean that the endeavor of reason will be paradoxically to bring man back to the "imbecility" which characterizes him "in his natural state." Reason, which frees him from this imbecility and which gives him laws, is good, but this good can turn into its contrary if reason is not right and mistakes the nature of the happiness to which man necessarily aspires.

The article *Droit naturel*, which dates from shortly after *Cyniques*,

[14] AT, II, 88, note 1.
[15] AT, XIII, 397.
[16] AT, XIV, 261.
[17] *Ibid.*

echoes this very important idea that man is a reasonable being and that the moral problem is for him a question of knowledge. "Man is not only an animal," Diderot asserts, "but an animal which reasons." [18] And he repeats at the end of his article that "he who will not use his reason, renounces his human quality, and must be treated as an unnatural being." [19] The act by which man abides by the general will, if necessary against his own, is essentially "a pure act of the understanding which reasons." [20] Now this "general will" is one and the same thing as natural law. But since, to be truly general, this will must be that of the entire species, it is obvious that positive laws, which express the will of limited societies, do not necessarily coincide with it.

Several texts written after the article *Droit naturel* belong even more explicitly to the tradition of the Cynics, as for instance the letter to Sophie Volland of November 6, 1760, in which the Iroquois are given as examples of what "bad education" and "bad legislation" can do to men who by nature aspired only to their happiness.[21] In this particular case of the Iroquois, the perversion of the natural use of reason by religion explains acts of revenge, treason, and cruelty.

4. *Aristote*—From Aristotelianism, Diderot seems to have retained mainly the notion of *natural sociability*.[22] Among "Aristotle's principles of ethics or practical philosophy" which he gleaned from Brucker for his article *Péripatéticienne*, we may read at any rate this definition of sociability, or friendship: "Friendship is the companion of virtue; it is a perfect benevolence among men who reciprocate. It arises either for pleasure or for utility; it is based either on the pleasures of life or on the practice of good, and it is divided into the perfect and the imperfect." [23] There are, in addition, two distinct elements in this inclination of man for his fellow man: benevolence, which is merely an instinctive tendency, the "beginning" of friendship, and friendship proper, which is "perfect benevolence" and which implies an exchange, a commerce between individuals. In the text cited, this commerce can be disinterested ("for pleasure") as well as interested ("for utility"). But these are themes that Diderot had found outlined as early as 1745 in

---

18 *Ibid.*, 298.

19 *Ibid.*, 301.

20 *Ibid.*, 300.

21 Diderot, *Correspondance*, ed. G. Roth (CORR) III, 227.

22 It is indeed essential for Aristotle and the theoreticians of natural right to have found it in his writings. Barbeyrac, quoted by R. Derathé (*Rousseau et la science politique de son temps* [Paris, 1950], 143) writes for instance: "Man's natural inclination to live in society with his fellow-men is a principle that has always been recognised by wise and enlightened persons. Aristotle affirms it everywhere, in his works on morality and politics. *Man*, he says, *is a social animal, towards those with whom he has a natural kinship: there exists therefore a society and something just, outside any civil society*".

23 AT, XVI, 244–245.

Shaftesbury and that he had chosen to develop in the *Essai sur le mérite et la vertu*.

The *Essai* indeed discerns in man's very structure, as in that of any animal, the mechanisms which impel him toward other individuals. Sexual appetite is one of these mechanisms, material love is another.[24] On another level, the identity of structure between two individuals of the same species implies, if not benevolence, at least the absence of malevolence; he who might be tempted to harm his fellow man, must, since he is constructed in like manner, fear suffering in return a harm identical to the one he has inflicted.[25] Sociability is merely the flowering of these natural inclinations within the framework of constituted society. Here another monism, which already tends toward materialism, allows Diderot to revive an old idea: the individual is to the species what the organ is to the entire body, what the part is to the whole. "Social inclinations" in their purest form such as "gratitude" and "compassion" are an extension of the elemental social inclinations of the human animal, but these very inclinations enter into the general framework of the laws that govern the universal movement of matter.[26]

5. *Les Stoïciens.* The article *Stoïcisme* is a sort of synthesis of ancient theories founded on the idea of natural law. But if one did not know that it is a translation from Brucker one might believe that this article is, in an indirect form, a summary of Diderot's own ideas on that subject at the time when he was writing it. The article *Stoïcisme* indeed shows, better than any other text, how his moral and political philosophies mesh with his philosophy as a whole. For Stoïcism does not set the study of man's end apart from that of the place he occupies in the universe. Because man is only "a part of the great whole" his end "must be to conform his behavior to the laws of nature." [27] "To live according to nature," "to follow the general order," are two expressions of the same reality. From such a perspective, it is obvious that there is no room for moral freedom. The only freedom left to man is a purely negative freedom, that of deceiving himself about his end. Such is the meaning of these seemingly contradictory formulas: on the one hand "[the soul] is free," "it does what it wills," and on the other hand "if one considers it in relation to the world, [the soul] is subject to fate; it cannot act otherwise than it does; it follows the universal and sacred bond that links the universe and its parts." [28] There is properly speaking neither good nor evil and all is necessary; yet the reasoning individual has the awesome power of forgetting the place he necessarily occupies in the whole by mistak-

---

[24] AT, I, 25.
[25] See AT, I, 42.
[26] See AT, I, 64–65.
[27] AT, XVII, 219.
[28] *Ibid.*, 222.

ing his end. For the Stoïcs as for Socrates there is no evil other than ignorance: "Desires follow knowledge or opinion of things. The knowledge of the
true good depends on the knowledge of the universal order." [29] In a sense
one can even say that *freedom is the consequence of evil*, since it implies a
breach between the individual who goes astray and the whole of which he
was a part. Indeed "evil is a departure of the general reason from the
whole." [30] Man therefore cannot fulfill himself through the quest for a
moral freedom which is a veritable mutilation of the individual. On the
contrary, he attains his end only by submitting his will, enlightened by reason, to the law of nature that governs the ineluctable progress of the whole
in which he has his appointed place.

Along with the theories based on natural law, ancient philosophy offered
Diderot several variants of a positivism and a relativism of ethics and law,
which on close examination, did not necessarily preclude the idea of a natural
law. This positivism can be seen developing simultaneously or successively:
in Ionic philosophy with Archelaus, in Eleatic philosophy with Democritus
and Protagoras, in Cyrenaic philosophy with Aristippus, and finally in Epicureanism.

6. *Archélaüs, Démocrite, les Cyrénaïques.* Diderot read for instance in
his Brucker, that according to Archelaus "there is nothing just or unjust,
decent or indecent in itself: it is the law that makes these distinctions." [31]
He also read that for Democritus "it is the law which makes good and evil,
the just and the unjust, the decent and the improper." [32] Even more boldly,
the Cyrenaïcs asserted that "an act was just or unjust, honest or dishonest
only in so far as it was permitted or forbidden by custom or law." [33] All
these theories apparently deny what the school of natural law affirms: namely
that there exists a universal criterion for the just and the unjust. But one
can easily see how they can be integrated into a system based on the affirmation of natural law, *at least in the mind of a Diderot*. This integration is possible only through the involuntary or voluntary confusion he makes between
two different meanings of the word *law*.

For Archelaus, Democritus, and the Cyrenaics the law which decides
what is just and unjust is civil law. The Cyrenaics even seem to make a distinction between a common law and a written law. This shows that they
are not thinking in the least of natural law. But the word *law*, in its absolute
sense, is ambiguous and can as easily designate natural law as civil law.
Brucker's reader might think that the formulas we quoted above took up

[29] *Ibid.*
[30] AT, XVII, 221.
[31] AT, XV, 251.
[32] AT, XIV, 406.
[33] *Ibid.*, 271.

again in another guise those of the ancient theoreticians of natural law. Yet it is hard to believe that Diderot could have made such a serious misinterpretation. Must we assume that he correctly understood the thought of the adversaries of natural law, and that he simply reproduced their formulas, concerned only with being, like Brucker, an objective historian? The very text of these articles *Ionique, Eléatique, Cyrénaïque* might justify this hypothesis; for indeed no commentary accompanies the formulas in question. But from comparison with other earlier or contemporary texts one can conclude that he understood very well what he was reading and especially that he accepted for his own account, in a certain way, the ancient theories of positive law. In the *Essai sur le mérite et la vertu,* one can already read formulas like the following: "We will not of course be suspected of understanding by the phrase 'depriving man of the natural feeling of injustice and equity,' obliterating in him any notion of good and evil relative to society." [34] One could also read in the *Essai,* still more plainly: "Nothing is more valuable in a State than a virtuous administration and an equitable distribution of rewards and punishments. It is an iron wall against which the schemes of the wicked are almost always dashed, it is a dam which channels their efforts toward the good of society." [35] If the word *society* remains ambiguous in the first case and, in the context, refers rather to human society in general, the word *State,* in the second, is perfectly clear and indeed designates a particular society. It is true that the *Essai* immediately distinguishes between two kinds of states, those whose administration is equitable, "virtuous," and those which are subjected to an "arbitrary government," those in which tyranny brings about "an unfair distribution of rewards and punishments." [36] So the very law that decides between the just and the unjust can itself be just and unjust? It seems difficult to escape this vicious circle.

7. *A Synthesis of Epicureanism and Stoicism.* To understand how the synthesis is possible, we must go back to the *Essai sur le mérite et la vertu.* In the two texts we quoted above, we encountered the word *society,* meaning the general society of humankind, and the word *state,* designating a particular society. But in Diderot's mind these two concepts are not opposed. Nor is it correct to say that they are complementary: they mesh into each other, the first which is more extensive, so to speak, comprehending the second. Indeed the *Essai* presents—as has often been observed—the very Leibnitzian vision of a world in which individuals are integrated into particular systems that are themselves incorporated into larger systems, and so forth up to the single system in which all finally is absorbed: "A multitude of different systems are united and, so to speak, dissolve into one another to form a single order of things.

[34] AT, I, 42.
[35] *Ibid.,* 55.
[36] *Ibid.*

"[. . .] Now, if the animal system is joined to the vegetable system and the latter to the system of the other beings which cover the surface of our globe to constitute together the terrestrial system; if the earth itself has known connections with the sun and the planets, we will have to say that all these systems are but parts of a larger system. Finally if all of nature is but a single vast system composed of all other beings, none of these beings can be bad or good in relation to this great whole of which it is a part; for if this being is superfluous or out of place, that is an imperfection, and consequently an absolute evil in the general system." [37] These few lines give us the key to all of Diderot's political thought, because they contain the essence of his philosophy. It is indeed the same for moral beings as for physical beings: each individual is part of a system which is itself integrated into a larger system. Each man is part of a limited society, of a body that, joined to other bodies, in its turn makes up a vaster society, a nation. All the nations together form the general society of mankind, humanity, which in the moral order can be considered as the "whole" in which individuals and particular societies are united. In the article *Droit naturel* Diderot showed moreover that this whole is itself relative, since one can conceive, if need be, of a larger body, a concept even more general than that of humanity, the concept of animalkind.[38]

It is this partly organismic conception of society that Diderot had in mind when he read the ancient or modern theoreticians of natural law.[39] But he did not forget it when he read their adversaries, and that is what allows him to reconcile calmly—and I dare say, naively—Stoics and Epicureans. The passage of the *Essai* that we quoted above shows indeed that at every level of the structure evil and good are, for the individual or for the particular system considered, relative to the more general system in which it is inte-

[37] AT, I, 26–27. A note from Diderot refers to Cicero, cited as one of the ancient forerunners of the monistic conception of the universe. But there is an obvious relation between this universe in which systems interlock with each other to infinity, and that of Leibnitz, especially if one identifies, as did Diderot, the monad and the molecule (AT, XV, 457).

[38] AT, XIV, 299.

[39] On the organicistic theory of society in the eighteenth century and in modern theoreticians of *natural law*, see R. Derathé's clarification (*Rousseau*, 410–413). He shows that in Rousseau, as in Grotius and Hobbes, the frequent comparison of society, an artificial body, with a living organism must not be taken literally: "For Rousseau, as for Hobbes and Pufendorf [and we may add: for Diderot], the State is fundamentally an 'artificial body,' that is to say a 'mental being,' an 'intellectual entity' or a 'legal entity,' whose life consists solely in the 'union of its members' and which owes its existence to the social contract. But as the notion of 'legal entity' is difficult to grasp because of its abstractness, one can formulate an approximate idea of it by comparing the body politic to a living organism. However convenient this comparison might be it is none the less 'quite inaccurate' and organicistic metaphors are at best a poor substitute, an imagery which one must refrain from taking literally."

grated. In the economy of the universe, there is properly speaking neither good nor evil, but all is necessary. At least there is no "absolute evil," since that would imply the existence of a superfluous or misplaced being; and no such being could exist in the eyes of one who might embrace the totality of what is. If we consider life in society, it can contain absolute good or evil only in relation to the broadest system of which man is part *as* man—and not as a living being, for instance—that is to say in relation to the general society of mankind. But on a lower level there is a good and an evil relative to each particular society, the general law of that society being the "rule of the just and the unjust" for those who are part of it. *Thus the same action may be just in relation to the laws of the state, and unjust in relation to laws of the species.*

There exists therefore a hierarchy of values and laws, natural law having precedence over positive laws, and positive laws over all the others, especially over those of particular bodies, among which are religious laws. For it is quite obvious that in repeating with Archelaus, "there is nothing just or unjust, decent or indecent in itself," or with Democritus, "law makes good or evil," Diderot has above all a *polemical* intention. He has in mind the theory of innate morality. As can be seen in the article *Droit naturel* much more plainly than in the *Essai* where the concept of "a-priori notion" was still fairly ambiguous, he does not accept being "referred to the tribunal of conscience" when he asks the question, "What is right?" [40] Now, for the defenders of Christian morality, there was an immutable natural law, which God had prescribed for his creatures and engraved in the heart of each man. Chaumeix and the authors of *La Religion vengée* were to repeat it regarding the article *Droit naturel.*[41] They would also say that by rejecting innate moral ideas, Diderot denies natural law. For, in their opinion, any law that does not come from God and is not innate in the heart of his creatures is pure convention. But, for Diderot the opposite is true: the supposedly in-

[40] AT, XIV, 296.

[41] See the *Préjugés légitimes contre l' "Encyclopédia."* 1758–1759, II, 73: "Neither to the individual, nor to the species do I give legislative power in this matter. I recognize a superior being above humankind, and to his tribunal do I take my case." Chaumeix says also (*ibid.*): "[natural law] is eternal and immutable; [. . .] it preceded not only all society and all convention, but also the existence of the first man." But he says especially (*ibid.*, 82): "The first man who proposed the laws of *natural law* did it because he found them just. They have been approved by all only because everyone found them just. Therefore, both the first who proposed them and each one of those who approved them knew what is just before this approbation." One can also read in *La Religion vengée* (Paris, 1757 and following years), X, 144, about the same article *Droit naturel:* "In spite of ignorance and self-interested passions, all men have recognized and still recognize a law prior to all positive laws: indeed this law is indelibly engraved in their hearts and this law is nothing else than *natural law.*"

nate laws of religious morality are arbitrary and without natural foundations,[42] the laws of civil society and those which express the general will of
the species are the only natural rules of just and unjust at their respective
levels.

Indeed, for him, positive laws are in a sense natural laws, or rather particular applications of natural law. At least that is the way it *ought to be*:
there should not be any contradiction between the principles that govern the
legislation of each society and those that derive from the general will of the
species. Then positive law and natural law would be one and the same thing,
and it could be said either with the Cyrenaic that "an act is just or unjust,
honest or dishonest only in so far as it is permitted or forbidden by custom
or by law," or with the Stoic that "man's aim must be to make his behavior
conform to the laws of nature." [43] In other words, the ethics of sovereigns
and that of their subjects must coincide: the sovereign takes as a guiding
principle of just and unjust the general will of mankind, which is natural
law, and the positive law that he decrees is in its turn the principle of just
and unjust in his state. The subject's duty is to obey in all circumstances the
law of the collectivity to which he belongs, just as the sovereign's duty is to
obey the general will of the species. This indeed is the meaning of the article
Corruption publique that we have already examined. This also is the deeper
meaning of the apologia of the laws that Diderot inserted in the article *Grecs*,
and which was suggested to him by four lines of the Epicurean Horace,
quoted by Jacob Brucker: natural law is not self-evident to men, and a man
can get knowledge of it neither from the gods nor from listening to the
voice of his conscience. Positive laws, no matter how imperfect they may be
in view of the general will of the species, are the only expression of natural
law and they are also the only means natural law has to assert itself: "The
law! The law! It is the only barrier that can be raised against the passions of
men; the general will must be pitted against the will of individuals, and un-
less there is a sword to sweep evenly over a people, and to cut off or bow
the bold heads that dare to rise up, the weak will be subject to the offenses
of the strong." [44]

This reconciliation of Epicureanism and Stoicism may seem satisfactory

[42] See the *Essai sur le mérite et la vertu*, AT, I, 39: in it the "eternal laws of justice"
are opposed to the "vain applause of custom" and to the "whimsical laws" of religion.

[43] AT, XVII, 219.

[44] AT, XV, 57; the lines from Horace quoted by Brucker are taken from his *Ars
Poetica*. They celebrate the wisdom of the first legislators:

". . . *Fuit haec sapientia quondam,*
"*Publica privatis secernere, sacra profanis,*
"*Concubitu prohibere vago, dare jura maritis,*
"*Oppida moliri, leges incidere ligno*"
                                (*Historia critica*, I, 434)

in abstracto. But it is dangerous, to say the least: reality does not yield to ideas so easily. In reality, the tradition of the advocates of natural law and the tradition of the Ionics, Eleatics, Cyrenaics, and Epicureans were as difficult to reconcile as were, at the time of the *Encyclopédie* itself, the system of Hobbes and that of Pufendorf.[45] That explains why the *practical conclusion* of so free a work as the *Supplément au voyage de Bougainville,* for instance, will always seem so disappointing: "What shall we do?" A asks B. "Shall will return to nature? Shall we submit to the laws?" and B answers: "We shall speak out against senseless laws until they are reformed, and, in the meantime we shall submit to them. He who, on his own authority, violates a bad law allows anyone else to violate good ones. There are fewer drawbacks in being a fool among fools than in being wise all by oneself."

The limit reached by Diderot in the *Encyclopédie,* in the *Supplément,* and elsewhere is in fact that of any humanistic ideology. He is none the less very representative of those members of the French bourgeoisie who, long before the Convention or the Empire, displayed their wealth of togas, swords, civic crowns, and triumphal arches, turned to the ancients to ask them to validate their political ideas. It was beyond question, a step forward in comparison with the politics that some still drew from the Scriptures. But, in this case, the philosopher's procedure remained as tainted with idealism as that of the Sorbonne doctor. For, as Marx said: "*Ideas* cannot lead beyond an earlier state of the world; they can lead only beyond the ideas of the earlier state of the world. Ideas can in no way *realize anything.* To realize ideas, it takes men who use a practical force." [46]

If the encyclopedists' political ideals still haunt the consciousness of the French—and indeed of a part of the western world—as once did the ghosts of unburied Greeks, it is indeed because they have not, as yet, found a *body.* But how could they then or can they now—since they are the result of *a priori* reasoning and the projection into the present of a mythical representation inherited from the distant—or recent—past, rather than a critique of all ideology, through the elaboration of a theory *and* a practice, fundamental each to the other?

---

[45] See the article cited, in the *Annales historiques de la Révolution française,* 277 sq.

[46] Taken from *La Sainte Famille,* quoted in the introduction to the second volume of Marx, *Oeuvres* (Paris, 1968), XXXV.

THE CRUDELI AFFAIR: INQUISITION AND REASON OF STATE

BY PAOLO CASINI

La Maréchale: C'est donc vous
qui ne croyez rien?

Crudeli: Moi-même.

ON MONDAY MORNING, MAY 11, 1739, A FRIGHTENING RUMOR SPREAD QUICKLY THROUGH FLORENCE. ANTONIO COCCHI'S POLYGLOT JOURNAL RELATES IN ITS SHAKY ENGLISH: "AS I WAS DICTATING THE INVENTORY IN THE [MEDICEA] GALLERY, ONE OF THE WRITERS TOLD ME . . . THAT DR. C[RUDELI] HAD BEEN ARRESTED BY THE INQUISITION. I DID NOT BELIEVE IT thoroughly, not having had the least hint of the matter before, not imagining that the government would have given hand to it." [1] The public was astonished, for the newly established Lorrainer regime enjoyed a good reputation for tolerance, and even anticlericalism.

Dr. Cocchi, a learned and prominent physician, had many friends at

[1] Antonio Cocchi, *Effemeridi*, entry of May 11, 1739, n.p. The MS of this unpublished journal is in Biblioteca dell'Ospedale, Careggi, Florence. (Here and below I have quoted Cocchi's English without any change.) Cocchi was an *érudit* and a polygraph. In his long European trip (1720s) he met Newton and was elected a F.R.S.; we find him professor for Theoretical Medicine at Pisa (1726) and lecturer for Anatomy and Natural Philosophy in the Studio Fiorentino (1731 ff.); in 1738 he was elected Antiquario della Galleria Medicea. There are frequent references to him in the Walpole correspondence: see *'Mann' and Manners at the Court of Florence, 1740–1786, Founded on the Letters of Horace Mann to Horace Walpole*, ed. Dr. Doran (London, 1876), 2 vols., *passim*; Horace Walpole, *Correspondence*, ed. W. S. Lewis, W. H. Smith, and G. M. Lam (New Haven, Conn., 1961), XVII, *passim* (with an excellent commentary). On Cocchi and his many medical and literary works see Andrea Corsini, *A. Cocchi, un erudito del Settecento* (Milan, 1928).

The documents of the Crudeli affair are stored in Archivio di Stato, Firenze, Reggenza (hereafter quoted as ASFR), esp. 339, 340, and 1, 14, 328; see below, note 42. The first account based upon these papers was written when the Grand Duke Pietro Leopoldo finally abolished the Florentine Inquisition: [Modesto Rastrelli], *Fatti attenenti all'Inquisizeone e sua istoria generale e particolare* (Florence, 1783), 162 ff.; a shorter but interesting account is in F. Moisé, S. *Croce di Firenze, illustrazione storico-artistica* (Florence, 1845), 398 f., and in Antonio Zobi, *Storia civile della Toscana dal 1737 al 1848* (Florence, 1850), I, 198–205. The fullest and still valuable narration is Ferdinando Sbigoli, *Tommaso Crudeli e i primi frammassoni in Firenze* (Milan, 1884; facs. reprint, Bologna, Forni, 1969), a work characterized by a strong pro-Masonic bias; the historical background was better explored by Niccolò Rodolico, *Stato e Chiesa in Toscana durante la Reggenza lorenese, 1737–1765* (Florence, 1910; facs. reprint, *ibid.*, Le Monnier, 1971). Both Sbigoli and Rodolico reproduced some of the most interesting papers deposited in ASFR. A good short account is given by Franco Venturi, *Settecento riformatore* (Turin, 1969), 56–58.

court. Pushing on in his anxious inquiry about the fate of his friend, he was able to collect all available gossip. Competent confirmation of the news was given by Giulio Rucellai himself, the secretary of state for Ecclesiastic Affairs. The inquisitor, P. A. Ambrogi, had again and again requested the grand duke to concede the secular arm in order to seize the thirty-six-year-old poet Tommaso Crudeli and two other citizens. After some resistance, the duke gave his assent: "At last the night of May 9th, Saturday, about four, as he was returning home in Borough of S. Croce," wrote Cocchi, "he was taken by two squadras of sbirri and conducted to the public prisons, and a little after from thence to those of the Inquisition next to the Church of S. Croce." [2] The weekend proved an excellent choice for secrecy, for "his friends knew it the day after and I but the other day." [3]

The reasons for such a measure were wrapped in deep mystery not only where public opinion was concerned, but also in the eyes of the sovereign and ministers, whose consent was forced at a difficult stage of the struggle between church and state. The new grand duke, Francis of Lorraine, had just left on April 28 after a short state visit. He had spent only three months in Florence, accompanied by his young Hapsburg wife, Maria Theresa: it was the shortest trip needed to take possession of the Medici throne assigned to him by the 1735 Vienna treaty as a compensation for the Lorraine duchy handed over to Stanislaus Leszczynski. The degenerate and heirless Gian Gastone had left his ancestors' principate—amounting in 1737 to about one million subjects—in a state of intolerable anarchy, "un chaos presque impossible à débrouiller." [4] His attempts at ecclesiastical and fiscal reforms were abortive in the face of exploitation by officials and financiers, a decrepit set of laws, and an endemic economic crisis. His predecessor, the bigot Cosimo III, had left an enormous burden of privileges accumulated by the rich clergy through the legal devices of mortmain and fideicommissa. Francis started his reforms by abolishing the bureaucratic machinery of the state and creating a Consiglio Supremo di Reggenza headed by the prince of Craon. But the eminent figure—in fact the "dictator" he was to be labelled later on—was the Lorrainer Emmanuel de Richecourt, the secretary of the Conseil of Finances. He played a leading role in the Crudeli affair, as we shall see.

[2] Cocchi, *Effemeridi, ibid.* On Paolo Ambrogio Ambrogi see *Dizionario Biografico degli Italiani* (Rome, 1958), II, 689 ff.,article by E. Gencarelli.

[3] Cocchi, *Effemeridi, ibid.*

[4] Count Richecourt's statement, quoted by Niccolò Rodolico, "Emanuele di Richecourt iniziatore delle riforme lorenesi in Toscana," in *Saggi di storia medievale e moderna* (Florence, 1963), 367. For a general survey see esp. Zobi, I, 167 ff.; Alfred von Reumont, *Geschichte Toskanas* (Gotha, 1876–77), II; id., "Il principe e la principessa di Craon e i primi tempi della reggenza lorenese in Toscana," in *Archivio Storico Italiano*, serie III, vol. XXV (1877), 228–57; and also Harold Acton's brilliant *causerie, The Last Medici* (London, 1925), rev. It. ed. (Turin, 1962).

Tuscany's traditional submission to papal policy was severely challenged by the simple fact of Francis's succession, decided by the great powers against the pope's will. The duchy gravitated now within the orbit of the Hapsburg empire, and the Holy See had been frustrated in its support of Carlos of Bourbon's pretences, as stated in a former Vienna treaty. As Clemens XII, the reigning pope, was a Corsini—the richest and most influential family of Florentine aristocracy—diplomatic relationships between Rome and Florence reflected all the great powers' political tensions. In Florence people were split into two factions—the supporters of the new monarch, called *Lupi*, and those nostalgic of the Medici or partisans of the Bourbon pretender, the *Orsi*. These inner tensions were obviously exploited by the Corsinis and their friends, particularly by the very active and ambitious Neri Corsini, a shrewd diplomatist recently made cardinal by his uncle the Pope.[5]

A further element embittered the intestine struggle: Freemasonry proliferated rapidly. The first lodge had been founded in Florence in 1732 by some Englishmen. Among them, Dr. Cocchi—who was admitted as an apprentice—mentions a Mr. Shirley, a Capt. Spencer, a Mr. Clarke, the Earl of Middlesex, and Robert Montagu.[6] In mid-1737 ecclesiastical authorities were excited by the sudden growth in the number of brethren which amounted, they said, to thirty thousand in the whole duchy. The ambassadors of Lucca and Venice reported horrific tales of their mischief and debauchery.[7] The inquisitor requested of Gian Gastone, who was then close to death, a resolute purge, but he could obtain no more than an ironic refusal.[8]

In the following months the court of Rome tried to take advantage of the dynastic change and endeavored to reaffirm its traditional privileges. It found in Francis's ministers a firm opposition ranging from the enunciation of solemn principles to everyday controversy. One of the most controversial topics was the Inquisition's autonomy within the state. The inveterate abuse the former enjoyed *de facto,* the hiring of bravoes and delators called *familiari,* was checked by the edict of January 1738.[9] The concession of the secular arm for the seizing of the accused was again and again demanded by the inquisitor without success. His prestige was low. It touched bottom

5 Venturi, esp. 7, note 2, 299 ff. and *passim.*

6 Cocchi, *Effemeridi,* January 1732, n.p. Also the German Baron Philip von Stosch is mentioned here as Freemason: on him see below and note 41. Also Nicholas Hans, "The Masonic Lodge in Florence in the 18th Century," in *Transactions of the Quatuor Coronati Lodge* LXXI (1958).

7 See Lorenzo Diodati's letters to Giuseppe Niccolini, Chancellor of the Republic of Lucca, of June 12, 16, 29, July 2 and 16, published by Sbigoli, Appendix, pp. I–XI; the Venetian consul's dispatches are quoted by Rodolico, pp. 192 ff.

8 This is testified by the *Diario Settimanni,* MS in ASFR; cf. Zobi, I, 77; Sbigoli, 55.

9 ASFR, 218, entry of August 3, 1737; and Cantini, *Legislazione toscana* (Florence, 1806), XXIV, 79; Rodolico, 150 ff.

when his colleague in Siena was banished by the civil magistrate for tortur-
ing an innocent apothecary whose wife he had seduced.[10] As a result, the
Inquisition attempted to "start a clamorous case for the rescuing of the
tribunal's reputation." [11] But in December 1738 the confiscation of a set of
suspect books, including a Pufendorf and a Vitriarius, in a pro-Masonic
librarian's shop proved a shameful failure, for the inquisitor had to return
the books and his *familiari* were either banished or imprisoned.[12]

It was in this growing mood of chicanery that the zealous Father
Ambrogi obtained leave to proceed against Crudeli and two other men on the
eve of the grand duke's departure. The diplomatic reasons for the latter's
compliance are a matter of conjecture, as we will see. There is no doubt, however, that reasons of state induced him to sacrifice the victim even without
knowing the nature of his guilt. It was a deliberate withdrawal; but the
grand duke's attitude soon changed, for a few days later he refused to give up
the other two men, a certain Giuseppe Cerretesi and the abbé Buondelmonti.[13]

The inquisitor boasted of having caught the right man to reestablish the
tribunal's prestige. Crudeli was a notorious freethinker and plainspeaker. "A
tall, lean man, with small piercing eyes and a prominent nose. . . . On the
whole his profile reminded [one of] that of Dante . . ." [14]; he was at ease
in the well-to-do society as a result of "the poetic talent he possessed in an
excellent degree" [15] and his fashionable Anglomania, which opened to him
the doors of aristocratic salons. He was of good birth and breeding but pen-

---

[10] The papers concerning this trial are mounted in ASFR, 382.3; cf. Zobi, I, 195 ff.;
Sbigoli, 138 f.

[11] Giulio Rucellai, in his "Relazione al Conte di Richecourt sopra i diversi motivi, che
ha di credere illegittima ed abusiva la carcerazione del Crudeli," of July 21, 1739, ASFR,
339.1.3; Sbigoli, Appendix, XXXIII.

[12] Richecourt's letter to the grand duke of December 20, 1738, in ASFR, 13; Rodolico,
165 ff., 327 ff.

[13] This was the result of Richecourt's and Rucellai's pressure, as it emerges from their
dispatches of April 22 and May 6, 1739; ASFR, 339, 1. Cf. Francis's dispatch dated
Vienna, July 11, 1739, refusing the secular arm for Cerretesi "parce qu'il s'est trouvé
extrèmement malade"; Buondelmonti might have been given up, but if "l'arrest de Crudeli
n'avait fait un éclat qui a paru demander d'aller avec un peu plus de précaution . . . M.
l'Inquisiteur en a meme reconnu la nécessité, et il avouera sans doute que le premier
exemple a fait déjà tout le bien que l'on pouvoit experer." ASFR, 1, f° 226. Cf. also
ibid., f° 228.

[14] "Era alto di statura, scarnito, bianco, d'occhi neri piccoletti e vivacissimi, naso
grande e auzzo. . . . Il tutto insieme del suo viso non era molto dissimile dall'aria di
Dante," G. Gualberto de Soria, *Raccolta di opere inedite* (Leghorn, 1773), I, 126. Good
portraits to Crudeli are prefixed to the 1746 and 1895 eds. of his works (see below, note
63), containing an anonymous summary of his life.

[15] Rucellai, "Relazione . . . ," in Sbigoli, Appendix, p. XXXIV; cf. Richecourt's
"Mémoire" of July 21, 1739, ASFR, 14. In Horace Mann's words, "Crudeli has for some
years past served most of the English people of quality as a language master." Dispatch to
the duke of Newcastle of May 18, 1739, in the Public Record Office, London, State Papers,
98/42, f° 122.

niless and earned his living by giving Italian lessons to the English. One of the pretexts adduced by the inquisitor for his arrest was his being on good terms with Protestants. Another was his education at the University of Pisa, a nest of libertines and unbelievers, where men of letters trained in Galilean physics read Gassendi in the 1727 Tuscan edition and Lucretius in the elegant translation of Alessandro Marchetti. Crudeli, born in Poppi (Casentino) in 1703 of a family of provincial gentry, took his degree *in utroque jure* at Pisa in 1722. There Bernardo Tanucci, the future minister of Carlos of Bourbon in Naples, was his teacher and friend. Some years later Tanucci invited Crudeli to the Neapolitan court with a good pension, but the latter refused.[16] After a short stay in Padua and Venice, where he was appointed preceptor by the Contarinis, he settled in Florence. His reputation as a poet was founded almost exclusively on extemporaneous verse, such as ironic epigrams, epithalamia, and occasional pieces that he recited but did not bother to write down. Like most of his fellow citizens, he had a very sharp tongue. His railleries had made him some enemies who were ready to take revenge on him during his trial.

The only poem Crudeli had published by 1734 was a funeral ode devoted to Rucellai's predecessor on the board of Ecclesiastic Affairs, the learned antiquarian Filippo Buonarroti.[17] This is a dignified and somewhat pompous piece: Roman grandeur and contemporary Italy's narrowness are compared in the panegyric of a man who had duly drawn a living political lesson from his archaeological hobbies. The verses had been recited in the Cappella de' Pazzi, in the presence of the inquisitor and other ecclesiastical dignitaries, whose ears—the poet's friends argued—might well have been shocked by an anticlerical blunder contained in them. On July 4, almost three months after the poet's capture, the mystery had not yet been unveiled: "My private suspicion is"—again wrote Dr. Cocchi—"that his chief crime is the song for Filippo Buonarroti in which he speaks with some unrespect of the clergy. This I am afraid offended the court of Rome. And perhaps the Pope himself heard the song." [18]

In the first three months the recluse was treated very harshly. He was

---

16 For these details see the biographical sketch prefixed to the 1805 ed. of Crudeli's works (below, note 63); cf. Enrica Viviani della Robbia, *Bernardo Tanucci* (Florence, 1932), I, 85; for the University of Pisa see esp. Mario Saccenti, *Lucrezio in Toscana, Studio su Alessandro Marchetti* (Florence, 1966); and Eric W. Cochrane, *Tradition and Enlightenment in the Tuscan Academies* (Rome, 1961).

17 On him: Luigi Moretti, "Note sull'archeologo Filippo Buonarroti," in *Studi in onore di Antonio Corsano* (Manduria, Lacaita, 1970), 443 ff. The ode is also contained in all the editions of Crudeli's poems.

18 Cocchi, *Effemeridi*, entry of July 4, 1739. The incriminating lines say that Buonarroti in his office had succeeded in calming the furor of the stormy clergy: ". . . Ei calma il furore/ Del procelloso tempestar del clero." The last word was expunged from the 1746 ed.

isolated in a narrow, airless cell situated just under the roof in the west wing of the Brunelleschi chiostro.[19] He was considered as "a heresiarch of extreme danger to the Church," and was visited daily by the inquisitor's vicar, who endeavored to extract from him some sign of repentance and a full confession.[20] Crudeli's friends, including Francis's ministers, followed with growing discomfort the news leaked from the gaol. "The Inquisitor has lately examined several people"—annotated Cocchi—"about trifling circumstances relating to the life of this man even some years ago—which makes us suspect that they have not already arguments strong enough against him." [*sic*] [21] The trial ran its course, but Cocchi was wrong in this last conjecture. Many dubious witnesses had given evidence against Crudeli, but the resulting charges were of a ludicrous nature: in former years the poet had been heard uttering some unorthodox remarks about the Blessed Virgin, he did not fulfill his religious duties, he made jokes about scholastic theology and the guardian angel.[22]

However, the inquisitor kept in reserve a much more dangerous dossier. In mid-July he put his cards on the table by formally examining the recluse about Freemasonry. He was asked to confess "everything Freemasons were doing and saying, for it was suspected they talked about religion. . . . The Holy Office had promoted careful investigations into this matter since 1736, aiming at Crudeli as an adept of the said Society." [23] Impunity was promised to him in exchange for full delation, but as he denied any connection with the Freemasons, he was finally charged with "enormous mischief."

When the news spread through the town, the ministers' alarm turned into a feverish activity. First of all, the inquisitor—they said—had deceived the grand duke by passing over the real accusation in silence. Secondly, the inquisitor's behavior appeared now to be an inadmissible interference of ecclesiastic power with the sovereignty of the state. The ministers' duty was to inform the grand duke at Vienna of the gravity of the affair. The documents of the trial show a sudden change in emphasis from this moment onward, that is, when it appeared clearly that the poet was a mere scapegoat in the struggle between church and state—and perhaps in a broader international concern.

[19] Moisé, S. *Croce* . . . , 393 f.; Sbigoli, 184.

[20] [Modesto Rastrelli], *Fatti attenenti* . . . , 179 f.

[21] Entry of July 4th, 1739. On June 15 Cocchi reported as "falso o almeno caricato" a rumor about Crudeli's affiliation to Freemasonry as the main cause of his arrest, published by the *Gazette de Berne*, n° 43 of the same month.

[22] ASFR, 340, A; another copy of these interrogatories is mounted in 340 Y, ff[s] 125–32; cf. the interrogatories concerning Crudeli of September 10, 11, 17, ASFR, 339.1.2, ff[s] 1–13 and ff. The sentence issued on August 20, 1740, repeated all these charges: see below, note 61.

[23] *Fatti attenenti* . . . , 181.

2

The procedure, though incorrect even by the standards of eighteenth-century criminal law, was perfectly in tune with the long-tested Inquisition methods. Moreover, it was the literal application of the papal bull *In eminenti* of April 28, 1738. Clemens XII had here condemned in his solemn prose "nonnullas societates, coetus, conventus, collectiones, aggregationes, seu conventicula, vulgo de liberi muratori seu Franc Massons," describing them as an impending danger to the whole of Christianity. With all their secrecy and mutual solidarity, Freemasons were like "thieves" and "foxes" insinuating themselves into the Lord's vineyard, and even among the ranks of the Catholic clergy, "corrupting the hearts of simple people." The Pope therefore ordered that Freemasons of every rank be seized and prosecuted as heretics.[24]

In reality, only those of the lower levels were indicted. Highly placed adepts—the grand duke himself and his dignitaries—were obviously out of the Church's reach, and others paid for them. It is hard to believe that the Florentine lodge was a sort of democratic meetingplace for people of different social ranks.[25] It worked rather as a filter through which English travellers or residents and the Lorrainer ruling class would select their friends and clients. This may explain the sudden multiplying of the brethren in mid-1737, just when the new foreign ruler was about to gather the relics of the Medici regime and work out his anti-Roman policy. On the other hand, this opportunistic drive met a revival of the old Ghibelline spirit, an irresistible outburst of antipapalism that led so many Florentine men of letters, government officials, and liberal ecclesiastics to Masonic lodges.

In the last months of 1737 the Inquisition reacted to this phenomenon with its customary prudence. At first only some "innocent priests and monks" were prosecuted in secrecy; [26] the pretext for forcing the game was provided by the Jesuits, involved in a somewhat scurrilous literary controversy with Dr. Giovanni Lami, then a young erudite and lawyer suspected of Masonic connivance.[27] The boldness of temper of the wits grouped around

---

24 *Bullarium Romanum*, 24 vols. (Augustae Taurinorum, 1857–1872), XXIII, 366 ff. See Ludwig von Pastor, *Storia dei papi*, Ital. ed. (Roma, 1933), XV, 722 f.

25 Venturi, 54.

26 " . . . E solo è stato carcerato dal S. Offizio qualche pretino o fraticello, di poco conto, che forse né pur saranno della Lega. . . ." Lorenzo Diodati to Giuseppe Niccolini, letter dated Florence, June 29, 1737; in Sbigoli, Appendix, VIII.

27 Rodolico, 60 ff. On Lami (1697–1770) and his work see Giulio Natali, *Il settecento*, 6th ed. (Milan, 1964), I, 377 f. and 431 (bibliography); and esp. two recent articles: Mario Rosa, "Atteggiamenti culturali e religiosi di G. Lami nelle Novelle Letterarie," *Annali della Scuola Normale Superiore di Pisa*, serie II, vol. XXV (1956), fasc. 3–4: Eric W. Cochrane, "G. Lami e la storia ecclesiastica ai tempi di Benedetto XIV," *Archivio Storico Italiano*, vol. LXXXIII (1965), n. 455.

him, however, must not be overstated. The bull against Freemasonry was a political act, and the sect was formally condemned only when it presented a political danger.

This was realized by the court of Rome when Florentine policy against the Inquisition and ecclesiastical property appeared the result of a Masonic plot. In spite of the well-meant efforts of some modern historians to free the grand duke and his ministers from all suspicions of radical impiety, it can hardly be denied that they were enlightened men.[28] Francis's education at the Vienna court was directed by the maxims of absolutism and probably included freethinkers' readings. At the age of twenty-two he was received as an apprentice in the lodge of the Hague under Lord Chesterfield's auspices.[29] Giulio Rucellai was the veteran of many fierce controversies with the court of Rome, which had demanded in vain to dismiss him from his office.[30] As for Richecourt, his first approach to Italian affairs is documented by an important *Mémoire* concerning the Church, where his energetic program for the laicization of the state was fully anticipated. He stated here the inveterate abuses the Church of Rome had practiced with the connivance of the Medici government over the last two centuries through the increasing of her benefices, the bishops' jurisdictions, and above all the Inquisition:

> L'Inquisition peut faire arrester en Toscanne qui bon lui semble, sans *visa* ou *pareabis* du Grand Duc. Elle peut mesme les faire transporter hors des Etats de Toscanne sans aucune permission, sans mesme estre obligée d'en donner avis; si quelques fois l'Inquisiteur en fait part, devant ou aprez, c'est uniquement par politesse, sans aucune obligation. L'Inquisition fait le procez a ceux qu'elle arreste en secret, et comme bon lui semble sans l'intervention d'aucum officier du prince, et de suitte prononce la condamnation qu'elle fait executer; tel est l'etat des choses.[31]

[28] Rather curiously, Rodolico remarks that Francis was "sinceramente cattolico" (114); and that Richecourt in one of his writings "è pieno di devozione alla Chiesa" (129), probably taking seriously what was only lip-homage to Christianity.

[29] C. te De Villermont, *Marie Thérèse, 1717–1780* (Paris, 1895), I, 35 ff.; cf. D'Haussonville, *Histoire de la réunion de la Lorraine à la France* (Paris, 1859), IV, 277 ff.

[30] Luigi Passerini, *Genealogia e storia della famiglia Rucellai* (Florence, 1861), 162. On Giulio Rucellai (1702–1778), educated at the University of Pisa and professor of Law there, then successor to Filippo Buonarroti in the Segreteria del Regio Diritto (1734), see also Angelo Fabroni, *Historia Academiae Pisanae* (Pisa, 1795), III, 336 ff.; Venturi, 306 ff. The documents concerning his jurisdiction are mounted in ASFR, Regio Diritto, Affari Giurisdizionali, nn. 279–288. Rodolico's analysis of them (134–43) is unsatisfactory because of his preoccupation with clearing Rucellai and Richecourt from the blame of unorthodoxy (116).

[31] ASFR, 194, ff° 5–53, "Rappresentanza," dated July 13, 1737, published by Rodolico (316–26; for an unsatisfactory analysis, *ibid.*, 119–34).

This paper denounces further the wealth of cloisters and monks and the ensuing economic damage to the civil society. It culminates in a clear-cut advice to the grand duke concerning the attitude needed to face Roman intrigue: "Il est evident qu'il n'y a pour la ramener au raisonnable que la voye de fait avec de la fermeté. D'abord la Cour de Rome tonne, eclatte; si l'on reste ferme, ella prend la voye de la negotiation. . . ." [32] This was precisely the cunning strategy adopted by Richecourt against Ambrogi's interference in the public affairs. On the other hand, the anti-Masonic bull was the first answer to this challenge, a kind of deterrent to hinder the new ecclesiastic policy. And it is important to note that it was the product of the fertile political imagination of the Florentine prelates of the anti-Lorrainer faction, monsignor Ferroni and cardinal Neri Corsini himself.[33] A further round of the match was the firm refusal by the grand-ducal government to publish the bull.

Therefore clerical hostility against Freemasonry actually aimed at another goal, in Richecourt's own words: "les moines . . . en parlant des francs massons n'ont pas respecté mesme la personne auguste de S.A.R." [34] As for Crudeli, there was clearly no proportion, even by Masonic standards, between the prince (the "Lorrainer brother") and his humble subject. But if the former's Masonic solidarity found a limit in the reason of state, Richecourt behaved in a more resolute way. He saw in the affair a test of his policy. He forcefully pleaded the prisoner's cause with the Vienna court in two dramatic *Mémoires*,[35] emphasizing from a political and humanitarian viewpoint his obvious innocence, the trifling charges made against him, and the

[32] Rodolico, p. 324. Richecourt ends his account of the exploitation of the country by the high clergy remarking: "Enfin l'on peut comparer l'Eglise en Toscanne, s'il ny est remedié, a une mer qui emporte tout dans son flux, et qui n'a point de reflux, ou dont le reflux ne rapporte rien, mais vient seulement pour engloutir de nouveau." *Ibid.*, p. 321. In 1738 there were in Tuscany 27,108 monks and nuns, in a total population of 900,000, i.e. 3%. In 1751 Richecourt computed that this clerical 3% of the population received 33½% of the national income while 97% of the population shared the remaining 66½%. See the documents in ASFR, 236 and 869, n. 4; Zobi, I, Appendix, 97 ff.

[33] Sbigoli, p. 61. ". . . Le promoteur de touttes les rumeurs, que l'on a fait a Rome et ici, viennent (*sic*) de mgr Ferroni, nouvel assesseur du S. Office, le quel est l'autheur de la bulle contre les franc massons, par la quelle il a voulu signaler son entrée dans cet employ," wrote Richecourt to the grand duke on July 21, 1739, in ASFR, 14; another copy in ASFR, 339.2.7.

[34] Richecourt's letter to the grand duke of October 20, 1739, in ASFR, 14; another copy in ASFR, 339.2.8.

[35] These are quoted above, notes 33 and 34, and are reproduced in part by Rodolico, Appendix, 352–66. Richecourt's arguments reflect those of Rucellai, as stated in his "Relazione . . ." quoted above, note 11, and in his important sketch of the history of the Inquisition in Tuscany, probably written in September 1738, in ASFR, 339, 23; another copy in ASFR, 328.4.

premeditated climax of the trial. The anticlerical puns and other "bagattelles" Crudeli was reproached of were mere pretexts, Richecourt argued, "car si plaisanter sur l'ignorance et la vie des moines, parler contre la manière de proceder du S. Office est un crime, il y a peu de gens en cette ville qui ne soient dans le cas d'estre mis à l'Inquisition." [36]

Apart from the poet's case, there was a widespread freethinking spirit, and the Lorrainer minister felt himself the spokesman of the public opinion. He depicted in the blackest colors the cruelty of a trial where "le calomniateur n'est ny connu ny puny," the secrecy and perfidy of the inquest.[37] For Crudeli was convicted before the trial. Witnesses were heard only to keep up appearances. The only way to set precise boundaries on such abuses in the future, Richecourt thought, was to introduce a laic judge-assistant—a proposal already adopted in Venice, which showed that the minister knew his Sarpi well.[38] Moreover, Richecourt's remarks on the political strategy of the Catholic Church, on the furor and fanaticism of the inquisitors,[39] betray in him the straightforward disciple of freethinkers in the analysis of the impostures connected to political religion.

3

The most odious side of the Crudeli affair, Richecourt and Rucellai repeated in their dispatches, was the premature judgment passed upon him before the formal trial.[40] In fact, by taking a look behind the diplomatic scene of the struggle between Rome and Florence, it is easy for us to realize

[36] Letter of July 21; Rodolico, 353.

[37] *Ibid.*, 358.

[38] Richecourt, *ibid.*; cf. his letter to the grand duke of July 14, 1739: "Je la supplie de vouloir bien lire la relation que fit le siècle passé le doge de Venise par fra Paolo Sarpi. . . . V.A.R. y reconnoitra combien un Souverain doit estre attentif aux demarches de ce tribunal qui ne s'est occupé qu'à étendre sa jurisdiction au depens de la souveraineté soubs pretexte de relligion," ASFR, 14. The thesis of Paolo Sarpi (1552–1623) was adopted also in Florence in 1754, after tedious negotiations with the new Pope Benedict XIV: see his *Istruzioni* of March 16, 1754, ASFR, 339. 16; Rodolico, 235–56.

[39] "Rome n'a pas meme respecté les testes couronnées dans les siècles d'ignorance, où l'on croyoit l'authorité du pape superieure a toutes les puissances . . . . Elle a proscrit les meilleurs livres de lorsque ils ont traitez de diminuer la puissance temporelle qu'elle avoit usurpé dans les temps passez." (Rodolico, 354); ". . . Le judgement que l'on porte contre [Crudeli] est pareillement secret, un homme pouvant estre condamné pour des delicts imaginaires par l'ignorance et le fanatisme de ceux qui composent ce tribunal." (*ibid.*, 359); ". . . Les inquisiteurs pour la plus part et particulièrement celui de Florence sont trop ignorants. . ." (*ibid.*, 363) etc. On Richecourt's education and character see Henri Woelmont de Brumagne, *Notices généalogiques*, Ve série (Paris, 1927), 698; G. de Soria, *Elogio* (Pisa, 1783); Zobi, esp. 360 ff. and *passim*; and his letters to Toussaint, of Dec. 11, 1749, and Jan. 31, 1751, in ASFR, 23 and 25. Cf. also Walpole's *Correspondence*, XVII, *passim*.

[40] Esp. Rucellai's "Relazione . . . ," ASFR, 339.23; and Richecourt's letter of July 21, 1739, already quoted.

that the main designated victim of the Inquisition campaign behind the poet was Britain's secret agent in Florence, the abominable Baron Philip von Stosch, a famous German-born art connoisseur and a notorious spy and thief.[41] A remarkable portion of the trial record concerns Crudeli's suspected relations with this curious character and other so-called Freemasons. As soon as the most serious charge against the poet emerged from the interrogatories' mists, it became more and more evident that von Stosch was the Inquisition's second true target behind Crudeli. Ambrogi endeavored to involve them both in the same accusation of impiety and Masonic conspiracy.

Forgeries and false witnesses were largely used to this end. It is not easy to reconstruct the trial in every detail, for delators and their interrogatories appear sometimes unidentifiable and not fully reliable.[42] However, among the lists of queries still extant in various copies and addressed by the inquisitor to different witnesses and to Crudeli himself (who could only reply "yes" and sign), those concerning the latter's relationships with von Stosch are recurrent and particularly pressing. One has the impression that the chief task Ambrogi had been entrusted with in Rome was to *demonstrate* at any cost the Crudeli-von Stosch connivance, as it was already assumed to exist in higher quarters.

A month before Crudeli's arrest, the inquisitor had submitted his set of questions to the notoriously silly cavaliere Andrea Minerbetti and had succeeded in extracting from him, partly by threat and partly through flattery, a full statement of the poet's guilt. Minerbetti testified to having been present at the obscene rites of Masonic initiations, just as they were imagined in all their absurd details by the fertile mind of the inquisitor. He had been some twelve times in von Stosch's museum and library, where such assemblies were held, and with his own ears had heard a lot of blasphemy pouring from Crudeli's mouth. Moreover, he named one by one all the lodge's adepts, who were in due course to be interrogated by the inquisitor.[43] At this very

41 See on him Carl Justi, *Winckelmann und seine Zeitgenossen* (Leipzig, 1923), 3d ed., II, 263 ff.; id., "Philipp von Stosch und seine Zeit," *Zeitschrift für bildende Kunst* (1872), 293 ff., 333 ff.; D. M. Quynn, "Philip von Stosch: Collector, Bibliophile, Spy, Thief," *Catholic Historical Review* XXVII (1941), 3, 332–44; and esp. Lesley Lewis, *Connoisseurs and Secret Agents in Eighteenth-Century Rome* (London, 1961), 39 ff.

42 The Inquisition Archives were transferred from S. Croce to the Arcivescovado in Florence, where perhaps they now are, still secluded from profane eyes (like those of the S. Uffizio in Rome). The documents extant in ASFR are of two different species: in 339.1.2., we have the interrogatories of Crudeli and various witnesses, some of them in an almost illegible handwriting (e.g. nn° 13 ff.). As it is unlikely that these are the originals, they probably are copies taken by Luca Corsi and other friends to prepare the poet's defense. Excellent MS copies of a good portion of these papers are mounted in the bundle 340.A–H and Y, ff⁸ 125–69, 177–290: they are in a later handwriting and well ordered. The lists of queries are mounted in 340.A, ff⁸ 8–10, and 339.2.5.

43 ASFR, 340.B. ff⁸ 12–15, and E. 25–28; Sbigoli, 156 ff.

time, around about Easter 1739 (which fell on March 29), a similar confession was obtained by an Inquisition official from the twenty-nine-year-old physician Bernardino Pupiliani. As this man spent some days in the Jesuit convent at San Miniato al Monte for his Easter spiritual exercises, it proved an easy task to get from him under confessional secrecy fantastical accounts of the Masonic activities. Rather honestly, however, Pupiliani declared he had never been present at these meetings, ceremonies, and suppers; but he confirmed by hearsay all the questions put to him. He too described in every detail von Stosch's flat and library, as though he were an habitué, and subscribed to all the inquisitor's suggestions concerning the Freemasons' atheism, obscenity, and roguery.[44]

In July 1740, just before the prisoner was released, both Minerbetti and Pupiliani were to sign full retractions of their accusations, disclosing how they had been forced to give their assent to false depositions. The doctor was particularly explicit in exonerating Crudeli and in denying any relationship between the latter and von Stosch.[45] But this was exactly the point closest to the inquisitor's heart in April 1739. It was apparently on the basis of the Minerbetti and Pupiliani forgeries, that in a diplomatic dispatch signed by cardinal Neri Corsini, Rome in a solemn way requested the grand duke "de chasser immédiatement de ses Etats le B. Stosch . . . et de permettre à l'inquisiteur d'arrester deux ou trois des principaux coupables, pour arracher les racines naissantes de cette secte et reduire les autres a penitence." [46]

In the light of this complex background, von Stosch's role appears to be paramount. He enjoyed the high protection of Whitehall, which had for a long time been paying him for his intelligence delating Jacobite plots in Italy. This could, in fact, be the clue to the arrest of Crudeli and the compliance of the grand duke.[47] Even if cardinal Corsini confined himself to the

---

[44] ASFR, 340.F. ff⁸ 34–38, and G. 74–81, 84–85. These papers were published by Sbigoli, Appendix, pp. XXXIX–XLVI; for a good analysis, *ibid.*, 148 ff.

[45] Sbigoli, Appendix, Documents VII, VIII, pp. L–LX. ". . . Siccome non è mai venuto il D. Crudeli, così non posso dire né ho detto di avere il med.° veduto in Casa del Baron di Stosce. . . ." *Ibid.*, LVI.

[46] "Extrait d'une lettre de M. le Cardinal Corsini a S.A.R. du 16 avril 1739," ASFR, 340.C. Corsini wrote also: "S.A.R. scavant donc que le B. Stock qu'il connoit de longue main et en hollande et a rome, pour un homme sans moeurs et sans religion; tient dans la maison une Ecole de pur deisme, avec quelques professeurs les plus corrompus de l'université de pise, et les ecoliers les plus pervers qui sortent de cette université joignant a ces principes la debauche la plus dissolue. Stoch se croira a couvert de tont soubs la protection de la cour qui regne en angleterre. . . ." The letter's content reflects *verbatim* the Minerbetti and Pupiliani depositions of the end of March.

[47] Missing the point, Sbigoli speaks vaguely of "l'avarizia e la continua necessità di denaro" as the motives of the delivery of Crudeli (p. 171); and Rodolico candidly objects to him "io non credo che da avarizia fosse mosso Francesco Stefano, ma dal sincero convincimento della degenerazione avvenuta nella massoneria per opera di persone corrotte, come

usual charges of atheism and Masonic proselytism, Baron von Stosch was an intimate and longstanding acquaintance of prelates and popes, and Rome was once more anxious to get rid of him.

As a young man he had paid his first visit to Rome in 1715 and was pensioned and befriended by Pope Clemens XI. He shared with his friend Alessandro Albani, the future Maecenas and leading figure in Vatican diplomacy, that enthusiasm for archaeology which made the latter turn up the whole soil of Rome in search of antiquities. Von Stosch soon enjoyed an international fame as an art expert and a man of great wit, but he also had a very bad press for his cynical behavior in the gem or antique trade and in political intrigues. His career as a diplomatist began with some obscure missions in the Low Countries in 1710, and later in Vienna he arranged collections of antiquities for Charles VI and Prince Eugene; in 1718 he was appointed Royal Antiquarian by Augustus II of Saxony. In those decades "the cloak of real or simulated scholarship was a convenient and not unusual disguise for secret agents," [48] and von Stosch resolved to devote himself entirely to espionage after his patron's death. In 1721 he entered His British Majesty's secret service and was appointed to Rome with the task of spying and reporting to Whitehall the intrigues and moves of the Old Pretender James III and of his shadow court in Palazzo Balestra. L. Lewis has examined his dispatches signed John Walton, now in the Public Record Office in London, and has carefully detected the patchwork of his ambiguous activities in the Roman underworld during the 1721–1731 decade.

Von Stosch was on good terms with a choice set of cardinals, and through their confidence he was able not only to report Jacobite plans, but he also boasted of having had some influence in the Conclave of 1724.[49] From then on, his position in Rome became more and more difficult: his spying activities were no longer a secret and he was considered as "the author of all the Pretender's misfortunes." [50] His friendship with Cardinal Albani, the leader of a pro-British and pro-Hapsburg faction within the Sacred College, proved extremely dangerous when the Corsini pope was elected by the opposite faction in 1730. Von Stosch was threatened with death and was obliged to leave Rome in a hurry. Somebody suspected him of having simulated the attack in the hope of getting rid of his uncomfortable position, but it is almost certain that the threat came from the Holy See itself. Von Stosch

lo Stock." (p. 178) Von Stosch's role was not focused by these writers. The link between von Stosch and Crudeli was underlined by the Inquisitor himself, who boasted that, if the former had escaped him, he had at least caught the latter: "[Ambrogi] disse che se non aveva potuto spuntare l'esilio di Stoch, almeno aveva concluso l'arresto di Crudeli." Rucellai's "Relazione. . . . ," in Sbigoli, Appendix, XXXIV.

48 Lewis, 51.

49 *Ibid.*, 74. In 1724 was elected Benedict XIII.

50 *Ibid.*, 73.

settled in Florence in February 1731, going on to give a weekly report on
all the rumors concerning the Pretender's doings he was able to collect from
a network of minor spies. His salary was low and he suffered from the dila-
toriness and niggardliness of his employers, so that his intelligence lost in ef-
fectiveness and had to be corrected by the British Resident in Florence, Charles
Fane, and later by Horace Mann.[51] Fane even suspected him of "treachery
and false reports," [52] and Mann's remarks about him were likewise un-
favorable. However, his reports were still appreciated by the duke of Newcastle, the British minister for Foreign Affairs, in 1737, when the Pretender's
son's visit to Florence (Charles Eduard Stuart was particularly welcomed by
the Corsinis) aroused some concern in London. L. Lewis gives no details of
von Stosch's correspondence for the year of the Crudeli trial, remarking
only that "the Pretender . . . was extremely apprehensive" of the Masonic
meetings organized by von Stosch in his home.[53] It may be doubted whether
those meetings were Masonic at all—but it is plausible that the Pretender
had some share in cardinal Corsini's step.

Indeed, from his own point of view the latter must have had very strong
reasons for demanding von Stosch's ban so peremptorily on April 16, 1739.
On the other hand, the grand duke appears to have been prevented by even
stronger reasons from bowing to the injunction. English diplomacy set
suddenly about protecting its ambiguous creature. On April 22 the grand
duke intimated that von Stosch "get out of the State within three days";
upon Horace Mann's protest he prolonged this term to eight days. Evidently
putting aside all rivalry with his shameful clandestine colleague, Mann protested again that von Stosch was under the "particular protection" of George
II. The grand duke was eventually obliged to suspend his order, though
making known to the British Resident "les motifs pressans" and "des très
fortes raisons" which were behind it,[54] obviously alluding to pressure from
Rome.

Francis's delicate diplomatic position emerges once more from his own
embarrassed prose. On the eve of the European war around his father-in-law's
throne that he was to inherit—the struggle for the Austrian Succession was
already on the horizon—he was greatly concerned with Britain's benevolence.
On the other hand, it was extremely dangerous for him to resist such a

[51] On Fane and Mann see Walpole's *Correspondence,* XVII, the Editor's introduction,
XXIX–XXXIII; the letters (1740 and ff.) and the notes frequently refer to "John
Walton"—*i.e.,* von Stosch—and his dispatches. Horace Mann "took over his duties on 4 April
1738 OS, as chargé d'affaires, becoming entitled on 24 April 1740 OS . . . to the rank
of Resident as Fane's successor." *Ibid.,* XXXI.

[52] Fane to the duke of Newcastle, 3 Sept. 1736, quoted by Lewis, 110.

[53] *Ibid.,* 111.

[54] Grand-ducal dispatch to the duke of Newcastle of April 26, 1739, in ASFR, 1, f°
218. Cf. the letter to Corsini of April 27, *ibid.*

peremptory request from Rome, coupled by the threat of a more spectacular diplomatic accident, the recall of the papal nuncio in Florence. Pressed between Rome and London, the little monarch sacrificed Crudeli but as for von Stosch managed to gain time. As apparently the duke of Newcastle had denied British protection for von Stosch only in the case that he would be guilty of public religious scandal, the grand duke gave instruction "de s'informer à fond si cet homme tient des discours, ou propositions contre Notre Religion." [55] This investigation seems never to have been accomplished. Von Stosch was able to live in Florence, collect gems, and receive distinguished guests in his museum notwithstanding recurrent threats until his death in 1757.

4

The task of testing and even formulating Crudeli's crime proved so difficult that the customary arbitrariness of the Inquisition procedure soon turned into a tragic farce. In mid-October 1739 the documents of the trial were submitted to the supreme commission of the Holy Office in Rome, which was composed of seventeen cardinals. Some of them were bent on getting rid of the poet with a light penalty, while others preferred to disguise the affair under a cloak of lawfulness by allowing him a defender. The debate was composed by a Solomonic oracle: *impinguatur*. Crudeli was allowed to choose a lawyer, the eighty-three-year-old Bartolomeo Archi, who, although a habitual solicitor in the Inquisition causes, protested energetically against the tribunal's abuses. [56] The poet's behavior in the prison was stoic, in spite of his frequent attacks of consumption. The denial of any medical assistance for all his blood spitting made Richecourt suspect that this was a premeditated way of "letting the prisoner perish in order to avoid a *dementi*." [57] In fact, as he was exposed to the first frosts in his roof cell, a more serious bleeding almost killed him. An unsuccessful attempt to escape from the gaol was organized by Luca Corsi and other friends. They held a clandestine correspondence with the prisoner and were able to arrange every detail of the escape in a somewhat romantic way. [58] The plot was easily discovered

---

[55] Grand-ducal dispatches of July 8 and November 21 (ASFR, 1, ff* 223 and 250) referring to "notre lettre au Roy d'Angleterre" and to a "Lettre venue d'Angleterre, dont vous [*i.e.*, Richecourt] avez copie." I could not find the diplomatic correspondence between Florence and London. Further study of the papers concerning "Walton" in the Public Record Office, London, should better explain von Stosch's position in this period.

[56] See his declaration of January 2, 1740, supporting Crudeli's innocence, ASFR. 340. F. Cf. *Fatti attenenti* . . . , 214 ff.

[57] Dispatch of October 20, 1739, ASFR, 14; Rodolico, 362. Cf. *Fatti attenenti* . . . , 194.

[58] See the plan in ASFR, 339.2; *Fatti attenenti* . . . , 190 ff.; Sbigoli, 220 ff. A slightly different version is given by Antonio Cocchi in his journal, entry of December 5, 1739.

and consequently the prisoner's treatment was made more severe for a while. It is interesting to observe that the escape had been secretly authorized by the grand duke.[59]

On the monarch's part, this was certainly a way of making amends for the former weakness in delivering the poet to the tribunal. But Francis's behavior was dictated by political opportunism once more. It was now a resolute intervention in favor of Crudeli that turned the scales of his prudent diplomatic balance. Horace Mann had represented to Richecourt his government's peculiar interest in the Crudeli case. The duke of Newcastle was personally eager to know the present state of the affair, he said, thinking that it was intolerable that a man should be prosecuted only because "he was a Freemason and frequented some Englishmen." This was an offense not only to the duke's sovereignty, but to Britain herself.[60]

Richecourt and Mann's energetic defense might have been ineffective without timely changes in the court of Rome. In December the nuncio Stoppani who had patronized the Inquisition's attack, was dismissed, and a broader-minded prelate, Alberigo Archinto, succeeded him. Two months later Clemens XII died. The Conclave for the election of his successor—the enlightened Prospero Lambertini, Benedict XIV—lasted until August 16, 1740. In the meanwhile a lot of water had passed under the bridges of the Arno and Tiber. The grand-ducal government managed to transfer the prisoner to a state prison, the Fortezza da Basso. The *impinguatur* formula was hypocritical, but it proved to be a useful screen for the Church, for it had cleared the way to an almost painless denouement of the trial. This took place on August twentieth—the new Pope had been proclaimed on the sixteenth—with the farcical apparatus of a formal "abjuration." In an almost clandestine meeting in the church of San Pietro Scheraggio near the Uffizi (no longer extant), Ambrogi enumerated one by one the various crimes Crudeli had been charged of, placing his jests, his blasphemy, his insolence against the Pope, the Inquisition, the saints, and God on the same level. Items three and four of the sentence insisted once more on Crudeli's complicity in the Masonic misdeeds at von Stosch's home.[61] Crudeli protested in vain against this charge which had even been retracted by his accusers, and nobody had been able to prove.[62] He was probably right, and guilty only of

[59] The grand duke to Richecourt, October 24, 1739: "Le reste du contenu de toutes vos lettres regarde l'affaire de Crudeli, qui paroit vous tenir tant à coeur; quoique nous ne l'envisagions pas tout à fait comme vous; pour la finir, et ne plus en entendre parler, si cela se peut, Nous voulons bien permettre qu'il s'évade. . . . Cette évasion doit se faire sans paraitre qu'elle est tolerée, et encore moins insinuée. . . ." ASFR, 1. f° 240.

[60] Richecourt's dispatch to the grand duke of October 20, 1739; Rodolico, p. 356. Cf. above, note 55.

[61] ASFR, 340. Y. ff⁸ 132–33.

[62] We may believe two unsuspected Masonic witnesses, Richecourt and Cocchi. Richecourt's dispatch of October 20: ". . . Tout le crime de Crudeli est d'estre franc masson

imprudent plainspeaking. Surely, he had been involved in a political game he was scarcely conscious of, and paid for others.

5

Tommaso Crudeli obviously lacked the stuff of an intellectual hero. Nor was he such a radical philosopher as the eighteenth-century reader of Diderot's *Entretien avec la Maréchale de * * * * might believe him to have been. His poetic work consists of no more than forty pieces: epithalamia, odes, love idyls, fables, canzonettas, and some satirical verse and prose composition. These are the relics and fragments of a truly ingenious improvisator, whose authentic poetic gifts were dissipated in a frivolous social context and brutally cut off by events. He did not even write down his compositions, which were recorded and published by Luca Corsi. Among these poems, critics usually praise the *Ode* to Buonarroti, the love song *A Nigella,* and two idyls, *La nuotatrice* and *La ricamatrice.* These are certainly some of the finest examples of Arcadian craftsmanship. Particularly in *La nuotatrice* the exquisite rococo elegance of the imagery is accompanied by subtle erotic overtones springing from the most sensitive cord of Crudeli's muse. The mimical virtuosity of a song describing Farinello's performance (the great *castrato* Carlo Broschi) reveals the poet's gusto for a kind of musical entertainment that had its most celebrated masters in Chiabrera, and later in Metastasio, two names to which literary historians refer in judging Crudeli's work. The poet is also rightly praised as a translator: among his finest pieces there are the prologue affixed to a lively prose translation of Destouches's comedy *Le glorieux,* essays from Shakespeare and a number of unidentified English poets, and above all his witty, masterly rendering of four fables by La Fontaine with their biting satire of absolutism and leonine justice.[63]

Insisting on the vague stereotype of Masonic observance, interpreters oddly enough have missed Crudeli's intimate moral beliefs and some political implications of his own fate alluded to in his poems. It is a curious understatement to say, as Croce did, that his frame of mind was "not very religious

et d'estre soubçonné d'avoir esté amy et dans la maison de Stoch, ce qui est un fait notoirement faux, puisqu'il estoit au contraire journellement dans la maison de M. Faine, qui ne luy auroit pas souffert, s'il avoit osé mettre les pieds dans la maison de Stoch." Rodolico, 362. Antonio Cocchi commented as follows on the charges made against Crudeli for his connivance with von Stosch: "Which two suppositions are certainly false. It is not known whether it is a calumny or a mistake. St[osch] is a really vicious man and a teller of fables invented by him[self], which might have given occasion to the 1st supposition. The 2nd [concerning Masonic rites] seems to be utterly false." *Effemeridi,* entry of September 21, 1739. Cf. Pupiliani's retraction, quoted above, note 46.

63 *Raccolta di poesie del dottor T. C. dedicata all'illustrissimo signore Orazio Mann Ministro in Toscana di S. M. Britannica appresso Sua Maestà Casarea* (Naples [but Florence], 1746); *Poesie del dottor T. C. Edizione seconda con l'aggiunta di altre composizioni dell'istesso autore tanto edite che inedite* (Naples, 1767); *Rime e prose del Dottor T. C. Toscano* (Paris [but Lucca], 1805); *Il superbo. Commedia tradotta dal dottor T.C. dedicata*

and lacked the sense of the sublime," that he was "addicted to civil progress but unable to see beyond pleasure and utility." [64] In the Buonarroti ode, in the small tract *L'arte di piacere alle donne,* and elsewhere, there are thinly disguised traces of deliberate Epicurean feelings. Buonarroti's calm in the face of death, the poet's frank appreciation of erotism, sensuality, and utilitarianism, reveal a sage educated by Lucretius, Gassendi, and the French *libertins,* authors widely read in Pisa. Crudeli's behavior and manners were likewise that of the *esprits forts*—only a bit more indiscreet, if we are to believe some of the documents of the trial.

Moreover, he was a strenuous supporter of the ideal of political freedom, which in those years shifted from the old pale shadows of the Florentine republic and of Machiavelli to Britain and Montesquieu.[65] Political allusions are very cautious and cursory in his pieces, yet they are clear, as when he compares England's freedom to Italian serfdom and praises the former "nation of heroes." [66] His Anglomania was therefore something more than a conventional mask. This is particularly evident in his ode to the countess of Orford, Margaret Walpole, Horace Walpole's sister-in-law and Richecourt's mistress, then living in Florence and certainly well acquainted with the poet. The poem has a significant title, *Il trionfo della ragione,* the lady herself being here the personification of the ruling reason:

> Ivi in dolce maestà
> Coronata di splendori
> Vincitrice di terrori
> La Ragione in trono sta.[67]

The verses are not very good, with their turgid encomiums; but the comparison of the lady with Great Britain's political influence over the continent is remarkable:

> Della sua patria gloriosa
> L'alte imagini ella imìta

all'*illustrissimo signor Conte Bernardo Pecori* (Florence, 1746). In the Biblioteca Marucelliana, Florence (C.369.1) there is a MS collection of the Crudeli poems, "Dono del Dr. Corsi," probably the basis of his 1746 edition. It contains however some unpublished pieces, for instance a fine verse translation of Hamlet's monologue.

[64] Benedetto Croce, "Le poesie di Tommaso Crudeli," in *La letteratura italiana del Settecento* (Bari, 1949), 116. For an authoritative literary appreciation see Giosué Carducci, *Poeti erotici del secolo XVIII* (Florence, 1888), XX ff.

[65] See esp. Mario Rosa; *Dispotismo e libertà nel Settecento. Interpretazioni "repubblicane" di Machiavelli* (Bari, 1964).

[66] In the poem *A Farinello.*

[67] There in sweet majesty / Splendidly crowned / Overwhelming all terror / Reason is seated in her throne.

Che possente e generosa
E' de' regi oppressi aita.[68]

The panegyric ends with the triumph of reason over superstition, a baroque allegory in which "livid and dark slavery," a kind of monster whose emblem is a skull and crossbones, is introduced as surrounded by snakes (superstition's Furies), but these are turned into stone by the lady's beneficent influence. This Masonic imagery seems to refer to the poet's own case; for, if the poem was composed just after his release, it is probably a thanksgiving for Lady Margaret's substantial contribution in inducing Richecourt and the Walpoles to act on his behalf.

The personal revenge of Ambrogi on the victim that had escaped him was a sadistic stratagem for depriving Crudeli of his friends' solidarity. He was allowed to settle anywhere in Tuscany, except in Florence, Pisa, Leghorn, or Siena. This obliged him to spend the coldest months of the 1740–41 winter at Pontedera, an uncomfortable village near Pisa, where his poor health and melancholia grew worse: "I am enduring in my mind and flesh," he wrote to Richecourt, "everything mankind can endure; harassed, though innocent, I feel that my health is vanishing day by day: I am here without doctors, without remedies, so lonely as to have not even the force to relax by reading books, deprived as I am of my friends' company. . . ." [69] His fine translation of Hamlet's monologue was probably made there. Only in April 1741 was he officially pardoned by Benedict XIV and allowed to settle in Florence. There he died on January 27, 1745.

The name Crudeli soon became a symbol: "Crudeli, si connu par ses poésies et par d'autres ouvrages, avait une manière de penser fort libre," said an anonymous preface affixed to Diderot's *Entretien,* "et ses affaires avec l'Inquisition ne prouvent que trop qu'il ne la dissimulait guère." [70] In his martyrdom and death appeared the last clamorous examples of popish wickedness and of the political dangers of the Inquisition in the countries where it was still at work. But Crudeli's name did not only provide the "mascarade italienne" to conceal the actual author of Diderot's *Entretien.*[71] In the following years the Inquisition's activity in Florence was reduced to nil, and a bill for the freedom of the press from ecclesiastic censure was passed in 1743. Tuscany set out to become the most enlightened of eighteenth-century Italian states, and d'Alembert probably makes reference to it, when he says:

68 She imitates the lofty images / Of her glorious fatherland / Of the powerful generous country / The support of oppressed kings.

69 Letter of December 19, 1740, in ASFR, 340. I. f° 74.

70 *Pensées philosophiques en français et en italien* (Londres-Amsterdam, 1777).

71 Paul Vernière, in Diderot's *Oeuvres philosophiques* (Paris, 1956), 520; cf. Manlio Busnelli, *Diderot et l'Italie* (Paris, 1925), 172.

[L'étude de la géométrie] est peut-être le seul moyen de faire sécouer peu-à-peu à certaines contrées de l'Europe le joug de l'oppression et de l'ignorance profonde sous lesquelles elles gémissent. Le petit nombre d'hommes éclairés qui habitent certains pays d'inquisition, se plaint amèrement quoiqu'en secret, du peu de progrès que les sciences on fait jusqu'ici dans tristes climats . . . Il est certain que les abus les plus intolérables d'un tribunal qui nous a toujours si justement révoltés, ne se sont produits en ne s'entretiennent que par l'ignorance et la superstition. Eclairez la nation, et les ministres de ces tribunaux renonceront d'eux-mêmes à des excès dont ils auront les premiers reconnu l'injustice et les inconvéniens. C'est ce que nous avons vu arriver dans les pays où le goût des Arts et des Sciences et des lumières de la Philosophie se sont conservés. On étudie et on raisonne en Italie; et l'inquisition y a beaucoup rabattu de la tyrannie qu'elle exerce dans ces régions, où l'on fait encore prêter serment de ne point enseigner d'autre philosophie que celle d'Aristote.[72]

In 1782 the Inquisition was finally suppressed by Pietro Leopoldo. The booklet setting out its long history, which was published on that occasion, narrated the Crudeli affair in all its details. Its outcome had been the destruction of the tribunal itself.

[72] *Encyclopédie ou dictionnaire raisonné* . . . , vol. VII (Paris, 1757), article "Géomètre," 629. Two editions of the *Encyclopédie* were issued at Lucca (1758 ff.) and Leghorn (1769 ff.), the latter under Grand Duke Pietro Leopoldo's personal patronage.

"SENSIBILITY," "NEOCLASSICISM," OR "PREROMANTICISM"?

BY ROLAND MORTIER

THE AMBIGUITIES AND THE CONTRADICTIONS OF THE NOTION OF *pre-romanticism* HAVE BEEN UNDERLINED TIME AND AGAIN. IF WE WERE TO ACCEPT THIS HISTORICAL CATEGORY, THE SO-CALLED "CENTURY, OR AGE OF ENLIGHTENMENT," WOULD EXTEND IN FRANCE AT THE MOST OVER ABOUT FORTY YEARS: STARTING IN 1715 (WITH THE DEATH OF LOUIS XIV), it would end, if we are to believe Paul Van Tieghem, in 1755.[1] Deprived of Diderot and Rousseau, of all its emotional, "sensitive," or affective content,[2] the age of Enlightenment fades in this way into a desiccated rationalism, which in its turn (in the minds of detractors) could be identified with Voltaire. In that case, Bayle and Laclos would be excluded from a period of which they were, each in his own way, illustrious examples.

One might, at least, limit these annexationist aims (of which romanticism itself, we must acknowledge, is quite innocent), and restrict the preromantic wave in France to the last third of the eighteenth century. Baculard d'Arnaud, Loaisel de Tréogate, Ramond de Carbonnières, Letourneur, Mercier, and Bernardin de Saint-Pierre are called to the witness stand and testify in its behalf. But would not this be giving short shrift to Chénier, Parny, Condorcet, Chamfort, Laclos, Volney, Beaumarchais, the abbé Delille, even to Sade, who are certainly their equals as far as literary quality and historical significance are concerned?

In such a debate, it is really too easy to pit name against name, challenger against challenger. Representativeness is too subjective a criterion to allow the establishment of sound periodization. All told, what most clearly

---

[1] *Le Romantisme dans la littérature européenne* (Paris, 1948), 40: "French preromanticism appears to us as made up at first of two successive waves, that of Diderot and Rousseau which was formed after 1755, and that of their successors . . . who came into the picture after 1769 . . ." It is significant that in his posthumous book on *Le Sentiment de la nature dans le préromantisme européen* (Paris, 1960), Paul Van Tieghem no longer speaks of a preromantic current or period in the eighteenth century, but only of preromantic writers.

[2] This kind of restrictive definition has been wittily called "definition by larceny" by Peter Gay, precisely in connection with the notion of "preromanticism." See *The Party of Humanity: Essays in the French Enlightenment* (New York, 1964), 253–254.

invalidates the notion of "preromanticism," is that in the only period during which factual arguments could be put forward in its favor, the undeniable irruption of sensibility coincides with a vigorous rebirth of classicism. The so-called preromantic era is the very one which other historians, with just as much right, call the neoclassical age. Faced with this paradox, must we renounce all attempts at synthesis, consider all period divisions as utopian visions? That would be giving up a bit too quickly, and throwing out the baby with the bath.

The last third of the eighteenth century (and we could add to it the years of the Consulate and the Empire) doubtless constitutes an entity endowed with characteristic features. The ambiguity stems from the desire on either side to reduce these features to a single one, to go from the complex to the singular, and to trim the luxuriant growth into straight lines.

In the realm of the fine arts—from architecture to the decorative arts—this is obvious. The end of the eighteenth century is stamped in its essence with a concern for rigor, purity, bareness, simple and noble truth ("edle Einfalt und stille Grösse," in Winckelmann's phrase). The easy grace, the fragile artifices of rococo, are denounced as so many expressions of decadence and perversion. It is not mere chance that the Revolution, in its harsh and pure phase, should choose to be Roman and to drape itself in Brutus's toga. David was to supplant Boucher and his adulterated charms. Houdon was to represent Voltaire and Diderot in the antique style. The latter proposed that Pigalle glorify Voltaire by sculpting him in the nude at the age of seventy-six. Bouchardon made a statue of Louis XV as a Roman emperor. The rococo style, with its languid curves, gave way to stark and grandiose creations. The desire for monumentality prevailed over the search for refinement and over the somewhat precious charm of the decoration of the *"petits appartements."* The gigantic projects of a Ledoux and a Boullée, almost cubist in their soberness, set their powerful stamp on the end of the century.

With the injustice of all reactions, criticism rejected the *"fêtes galantes,"* the boudoir scenes, Crébillon's and Voisenon's racy and adulterated sensuality, the false ingenuousness of Greuze's young maids *en bloc,* and it did so in the name of an aesthetics which called itself moral, civic, virile before openly asserting itself as republican. Antiquity was no longer offered as an example in the name of the sacrosanct doctrine of imitation or of a preeminence as evident as it was *a priori,* but because it proposed models of noble simplicity, of constant fidelity to nature and truth.

It would be wrong, however, to confine the end of the century as a whole to the severity of David's style or to the icy perfection of Canova's people. Spartan rigor is not a common denominator that can account satisfactorily for the manifold tendencies of a time that was rich and contradictory, like all creative periods in the history of man's genius.

The success of the word *preromantic,* made fashionable and founded in theory by Paul Van Tieghem,[3] has made us forget, or neglect, a fact that Louis Bertrand had stressed in his book which despite its age is still unique of its kind, *La fin du classicisme et le retour à l'antique dans la seconde moitié du XVIIIe siècle et les premières années du XIXe, en France* (Paris, 1897). Studying the literature of the Directoire and the Empire he noted with surprise: "The strangest thing is that these ultra-romantic lucubrations are contemporary with the most narrowly classical works," (p. 356) and he cited Nodier and Raynouard, Creuzé de Lesser and the abbé Delille.

We could obviously remove the contradiction by opposing these two currents as the end of one taste and the birth of another. According to this hypothesis two irreconcilable tendencies, then, coexisted for a few decades, one superimposed on the other. This would have resulted in a fuzzy, hybrid zone in which two styles and two periods crossed each other, an end point and a point of departure.

The trouble with such an interpretation, whose undeniable merit is that it is clear, simple, and didactic, is that it does not fit the facts. Chénier, Madame de Staël, Chateaubriand, just like Diderot in the preceding generation, did not feel an inner conflict between the penchant for emotion and the taste for rigor; they strove to reconcile them. The young Romantics laid claim to Chénier. In the realm of painting the group of the "bearded" or the "primitives" dressed in the Greek style, indulged in the mystique of hierophants, and called David a "Vanloo," or "rococo" (Bertrand, p. 316).

They worshipped "high taste," the "severe style," but this excludes neither emotion nor pathos. Chénier's Hellenism—had it been known around 1800—would no doubt have seemed slightly too alexandrine, and insufficiently "antique." But they also raved about "Erse" poetry, about Ossian, about the barbaric song of the Edda revealed by P.-H. Mallet, just as they rediscovered the Gothic style, or Shakespeare, and created from nothing the fascination of mountains or scientific fantasy.

Is all this as contradictory as some would have it? We would be going up a blind alley if we tried to reduce the complexity of the period to a matter of themes and motives. We will limit ourselves to two of them to be concrete and remain within the bounds of our subject; ruins on the one hand, tombs on the other.

The theme of ruins must not be identified *a priori* with a romantic or even preromantic sensibility (whatever historical extension one may wish to

---

[3] Later synthesized by André Monglond in the domain of French language. (*Le Préromantisme français,* 2 vols. [Grenoble, 1930].)

give its definition).[4] It appears after 1330, with Petrarch, in a humanistic perspective which is itself part of the vast aspiration toward the "restauratio" or "renovatio" of antique Rome. Ruins are a pretext for meditating on a past splendor whose remains, however dilapidated, fragmentary, degraded by time, are still an object of admiration and wonder. Melancholy is only a passing reaction that soon fades before the exaltation of Roman prestige and the dream of its complete restoration. This is the theme of "Roma quanta fuit, ipsa ruina docet," that was later amplified and enhanced by Du Bellay.

Not until Hubert Robert and his most eloquent expounder, the Diderot of the *Salons,* can we see a "poetry of the ruins" come into being, associated with twilight, solitude, meditation on the flight of time, and the precariousness of love.[5]

Far from pursuing that path, in 1791 Volney was to bring the theme of ruins back into the orbit of historical and philosophical reflection; he was nearer on this point to Montesquieu, Voltaire, or d'Holbach than to the exalted reveries of the *Salon* of 1767. The ghostly landscape of the forest of columns that antique Palmyra had become, led him to meditate on the causes of the fall of empires.

The literary motif of ruins, far from necessarily including nostalgia and lyricism, can adapt itself to the most diverse uses. It may, as for Diderot, be associated with intimate reveries, with an enthusiastic response to the sublime, with exaltation and the cry of the soul. In that case, in good logic, the preromantic élan should be dated about twenty-five years before the grave neoclassical meditation, and the schema too commonly adopted by literary histories should be reversed.[6]

Sepulchral inspiration also lends itself to different if not always contradictory variations.[7] On the English side, we note the recurrent appearance of the old Puritan theme of "Memento mori" and "Pulvis es, et in pulverem reverteris," so abundantly explored since the Middle Ages in didactic moralism and dances of death. Edward Young's *Night Thoughts* (1742–1745) are in the line of a constant that had generously supplied baroque art with ideas

---

[4] Which we plan to study separately, from Joachim du Bellay to the Romantics, in a work to be published later.

[5] See Hubert Burda, *Die Ruine in den Bildern Hubert Roberts* (München, 1967).

[6] The internal evolution of Diderot's esthetics takes the same direction: if the exaltation of unbridled sensibility in the *Entretiens entre Dorval et moi* (written in 1756) corresponds quite well to "preromanticism" as defined by Van Tieghem and developed by Monglond, one should consider as "classical" the preeminence given to lucidity and intelligence in *Le Paradoxe sur le comédien* (written between 1769 and 1778).

[7] In his study on *Le "Plaisir des tombeaux" au XVIIIe siècle* (R.L.C. avril–juin 1938, pp. 287–311), R. Michéa already clearly contrasted a protestant movement, coming from England, to a Latin conception in which the cult of the dead merges with that of the fatherland.

and images. As Louis Cazamian beautifully put it: "The spirit of Milton's *Penseroso,* and not that of the *Allegro,* sets the tone for landscape literature in the eighteenth century. . . ." (*Histoire de la littérature anglaise,* [Paris, 1925], p. 801). Young says nothing different from what religious orators and apologists repeat almost everywhere, but he says it with a contagious emotion which stirs tragic shudders. *Night Thoughts* nevertheless takes the form of an oratorical and discursive work, whose language is abstract and whose structure is wholly cerebral—in brief a very classical "machine" which does not substantially differ from Pope's poetry. Young is more an apologist than a poet, and only *a posteriori* did he appear as an ancestor—a very dubious one—of romantic sensibility. In France, in Italy, in Spain, in Germany, in the countries where religion was powerfully institutionalized and rationalized, this Puritan threnody on the vanity of happiness, the rewards of suffering and the quandary of unbelief, was felt as a rejuvenated and renewed form of the old Christian pessimism, somewhat neglected during the eighteenth century in favor of a desperately finalistic and reassuring theodicy.

Young's popularity corresponds to the transformation of religious sensibility which appears in parallel fashion in the *Profession de foi du Vicaire savoyard* (the only work of Rousseau's, we should note, that Voltaire always unreservedly admired). Should we, then, proclaim this as romanticism? We would be forgetting a bit too quickly that the eighteenth century, generally held to be irreligious, was also the source of modern religiosity which is subjective, lyrical, individualist, and very distant from the faith of a Bossuet, a Pascal, or a Malebranche.

It is much better, therefore, to abide by the chronological framework that we have set ourselves, which is that of the end of the century. Now, if "sepulchral" works abounded at that time,[8] they were hardly distinguished by their romantic character. Their most evident meaning tends to be either moral, or civic or national.[9] The most significant example is no doubt Ugo Foscolo's famous poem *Dei Sepolcri* (1807). That this same Foscolo is also the author of the *Ultime lettere di Jacopo Ortis* should have reminded us of the coexistence in the same mind of sentimental impulses oriented toward morose delectation, and an ardent patriotism exalted by the French Revolution. *Dei Sepolcri,* like Alessandro Verri's *Notti Romane* and Pindemonte's *Cimeteri,* is a moral amplification on national grandeur, the cult of the dead which, furthermore, merges with that of great men and with the passion for liberty.

---

[8] The sepulchral craze, around 1800, is much more than a literary theme. A veritable collective obsession could be discerned in it. We refer the reader, on this point, to Lionello Sozzi's remarkable study, *I "Sepolcri" e le discussioni francesi negli anni del Direttorio e del Consolato,* in "Giornale Storico della Letteratura Italiana," vol. CXLIV (1967), 567-588.

[9] The numerous texts quoted by Lionello Sozzi *all point in both directions.*

Far from belonging to a "lugubrious" inspiration (Van Tieghem, 37), such poetry perpetuates the austere civic and moral inspiration that imbued, in another register, David's *Marat assassiné* (1793). For Foscolo, just as for David, "fia santo e lagrimato il sangue per la patria versato."

The use of the tomb in neoclassical architecture is one of the most revealing traits of its inspiration. Boullée's imagination is obsessed with cenotaphs. They combine the ideas both of grandeur and of perpetuity: conical or pyramidal, they tend towards an almost abstract bareness that is supposed to suggest their eternity as well as their kinship with the colossal creations of Assyria and Egypt.

The visionary architects of the neoclassical age were, in the final analysis, poets.[10] In 1784 Boullée conceived an extraordinary spherical cenotaph in honor of Newton, the hero of modern science who discovered the mathematical formula for the movement of the universe.[11] "Sublime spirit! Vast and profound genius! Divine being!" he exclaimed. "Oh Newton! if, by the breadth of your enlightenment and the sublimity of your genius, you determined the shape of the earth, I have conceived the project of enclosing you in your discovery. It is in a way enclosing you with yourself." Light and shadow effects were to give this sphere a strange appearance, capable of suggesting the mystery of the cosmos. "Yes," Boullée wrote, "I believe that our buildings, especially public ones, ought, in some fashion, to be poems." [12]

The same Boullée imagined gigantic cemeteries, with a pyramidal portal, watched over by sphinxes which were to be transformed, by night, into

[10] They were literally revealed by Emil Kaufmann in his monograph *Three Revolutionary Architects* (Transactions of the American Philosophical Society, N.S., t. 42, 1952). In fact, Kaufmann had devoted articles and studies in German to them since 1929. A synthesis of these works was published in 1955 under the title *Architecture in the Age of Reason: Baroque and Post-Baroque in England, Italy, France* (Cambridge, Mass.), and was translated into French in 1963 under the title *L'Architecture au siècle des lumières*.

[11] Praise of Newton was always written in an exalted style at the end of the eighteenth century. The botanist André-Joseph Canolle, another instance of the convergence between poetry and the scientific spirit at that time, wrote in his *Délices de la solitude, puisés dans l'étude et la contemplation de la nature* ([Paris, 2d ed., 1799], p. 59), in the chapter on *Emblêmes de l'amour* "O genius of Newton! borne on your audacious wings I rise to the heavens amidst those globes whose immense ellipses you have centered in the sphere of our knowledge. Thence, through the eyes of your sublime understanding, I see these luminous bodies which command the respect of even the boldest imaginations, move according to the same laws that rule our hearts." One will not fail to be struck by the analogy between the tone of this passage and that of Chénier in *L'Invention* or in *L'Amérique*, as well as by the similarity between this theory of love-as-attraction and the conceptions developed some time later by Charles Fourier. So true it is that the literary study of that time is still to be undertaken.

[12] In E.-L. Boullée, *Essai sur l'art*, ed. J.-M. Pérouse de Montclos (Paris, 1968), 47 and 137. The commentator notes (138, n. 116) that there had been at least three other projects for a "Cenotaph to Newton" before 1800.

"shadow architecture." Diderot wrote, in the *Salon* of 1767: "A palace must be in ruins to become an object worthy of interest." Hubert Robert had applied this formula to the letter when he represented the Grande Galerie of the Louvre in a ruined state. As for Boullée, he created from nothing what he called a "buried architecture" and the example he gave was a *monument funéraire* whose low and sinking lines suggested absorption and burial.

In short, whether we consider painting, architecture, or literature, neoclassicism and sensibility, far from being exclusive or divergent, live happily together in the grand conceptions of the end of the eighteenth century. Ledoux dreams of building vast classical palaces astride a stream, on top of a cave (château of Eguière) or facing Alpine peaks (the episcopal palace at Sisteron).

Ledoux realized in the purest neoclassical style some of Rousseau's fantasies and at times foreshadowed the ground plan of the phalansteries. His project for the city of Chaux comprised a Panaretheon and a Coenobium in the heart of the forest.

The architect executes on paper the scientific and technical feats that Chénier was to exalt in *L'Amérique* and in *Hermès*. Possessed by the demon of the absolute, he draws the perfect city, the temple of Love, the palace of Concord, the house of Unity. As against this, Delille the poet exalts Ledoux's project in the fifth canto of *L'Imagination* (1806):

> "A l'honneur des Français, que n'eût point ajouté
> Le généreux projet de ta vaste cité!
> Là serait le bonheur; là de la race humaine
> Le monde eût admiré le plus beau phénomène."

But no architect's phantasmagoria more eloquently points to the unconscious of the time than the extraordinary *"Rendez-vous de Bellevue, à la pointe du rocher"* imagined by Lequeu, which unites in unbelievable confusion a small-scale Greek temple, a Renaissance tower, and a Gothic gate. The same Lequeu also imagined the romantic underground passage with hidden galleries, threatening machinery, secret corridors designed for initiation rites, that seem to foreshadow Kafka's *Penal Colony*, while in fact he quite simply referred to a few pages of the abbé Terrasson's *Séthos*, illustrating in a puerile fashion an initiation to heroism and duty.[13]

We have come a long way indeed from the graces and volutes of the rococo. The second half of the century of "Enlightenment" turned to the

---

13 All these projects, which, for the most part, are still in their author's portfolios, were the subject of a traveling exhibition (Bibliothèque Nationale de Paris, Metropolitan Museum, etc.) and they appear in the copious catalog *Visionary Architects* (University of St. Thomas, Houston, 1968.)

ancients for a lesson in grandeur, a model of rigor and majesty, and—as Peter Gay has so well demonstrated in his book *The Enlightenment: An Interpretation. The Rise of Modern Paganism* (1966)—a vision of the world which is at once grandiose, coherent, and secular in opposition to the prestige of Christian tradition.

Here is imaginary antiquity, in which memories of Plutarch mingle with those of Seneca, and which the Revolution would attempt to relive. But the enlightened age projected into this antiquity its obsessions, anxieties, and impulses. As Hugh Honour says in a recent book that excellently synthesizes the givens of the problem (*Neo-Classicism*, London: Penguin, 1968, p. 186): "The Neo-classical movement contained within itself the seeds of most of the Romantic forces that were to destroy it." Therefore he concludes his work with a brilliant analysis of Ingres's picture, *Oedipe et le Sphinx* (1808), that marks the internal split which was then forming: "A new vision of antiquity is here beginning to emerge—very different from the cool, calm land of liberty and reason described by Winckelmann and painted by David. In this grim mountain cleft there is no sign of eternal springtime. The dark irrational gods are once more closing in." (Honour, p. 190)

But we would then have to admit, at the outset, that antiquity for the neoclassicists was only this cool, calm land of liberty and reason. We have seen from the examples of Diderot, Chénier, and Boullée, that the return to antiquity could include the thrust of emotion, the throb of dreams, the call of the cosmic, the meditation on eternity and time. An attentive study of the facts reveals, we can see, that far from being incompatible, neoclassicism and sensibility were enriched by mutual contributions, that they were nurtured from the same source,[14] which became dissociated only after 1825, when this unity—precarious and confused no doubt, yet rich and varied as life itself—was to burst apart.

P.S. I had finished writing this essay when I learned of Bertrand H. Bronson's *Facets of the Enlightenment: Studies in English Literature and its Context* (Univ. of California Press, Berkeley and Los Angeles, 1968).

One may imagine how pleased I was to read, in the preface, statements like the following: "The age was, as we now recognize, extraordinarily complex, far from monolithic, and full of self-contradiction, change, and violent contrasts. Its spokesmen were notably individuated, often sharply antagonistic. . . ." (p. v), and further: "The habit of taking comparative views

---

[14] Similar conclusions are to be found in *Neo-classicism: Virtue, Reason and Nature*, by Rémy G. Saisselin (Intro. to *Neo-Classicism: Style and Motif*, Cleveland Museum of Art Exhibition, 1964, p. 3) and in *Le Néo-classicisme*, by François-Georges Pariset (*Information d'Histoire de l'Art* [Paris, 1959], n° 2, p. 47).

forces on one's attention the unevenness, relatively, in the rate of advance between the arts . . . and *how narrow and inadequate are our customary literary labels* as denotative terms in a larger context. Thus are planted the seeds of *a kind of impatience with the formalized, simplistic outlines of cultural history generated by our over-specialization* . . . a suspicion that in a retrospective view like ours the disappearance of the classical idea is ordinarily put a good deal too early" p. vi).[15]

Mr. Bronson's book opens with a study whose title is provocative: *When Was Neo-Classicism?*, which he had first thought of entitling, even more paradoxically, *From Romantic to Classic*. It is significant to see an historian of English literature forcefully protest against "the distortions arising from our obsession with interpretations *ex post facto*" and conclude that "If we did not know—or if we could awhile forget—that the Age of Romanticism followed on the heels of the Age of Enlightenment, should we not quite naturally be seeing the eighteenth century in quite another than the customary view: as in fact a period when the spirit of Classicism steadily *refined* its values, grew increasingly *assured* in its declaration of them, and never knew better their true and vital meaning and importance than when on the verge of losing them?" (p. 24).

[15] Italics mine.

THE PHILOSOPHES
AND NAPOLEON

BY ERNEST JOHN KNAPTON

THE EXTENT OF THE IMPACT MADE BY THE PHILOSOPHES UPON THE REVOLUTIONARY GENERATION WHICH SUCCEEDED THEM HAS LONG GIVEN HISTORIANS A LIVELY SUBJECT FOR DEBATE. SINCE NAPOLEON MORE THAN ANY MAN CAME TO DOMINATE THE REVOLUTION, ONE MAY WELL ASK TO WHAT EXTENT HE HAD BEEN EXPOSED IN HIS FORMATIVE YEARS TO THESE combative writers and how he had responded.

The problem has not remained unexamined. Arthur Chuquet's three substantial volumes published more than seventy years ago still constitute the most massive account of Napoleon's early years from his birth in 1769 until the siege of Toulon in 1793 where his reputation as a soldier was established.[1] The many notebooks and loose sheets in which the young officer began at the age of sixteen to annotate his reading and try his hand at authorship are now after many changes of fortune one of the treasures of the Medicean-Laurentian Library in Florence.[2] They were scrupulously transcribed, annotated, and published by Frédéric Masson and Guido Biagi (the prefect of the Laurentian Library) in 1895 and again in 1910.[3] Although a number of scholars have studied the general problem of Napoleon's literary interests and efforts, these studies have not been focused upon the particular problem of the philosophes. It is understandable also that historians have been chiefly concerned with the vast complexities of the Napoleonic epic and have tended to pass lightly over

[1] Arthur Chuquet, *La Jeunesse de Napoléon*, 3 vols. (Paris, 1897–1899), hereafter cited as Chuquet.

[2] A sealed package containing the notebooks was given by Napoleon during the Hundred Days to his uncle, Cardinal Fesch, who apparently kept it unopened until his death in 1839. The documents were then sold by his grand-vicar to Guillaume Libri, a somewhat notorious bookseller from whom the English collector, Lord Ashburnham, acquired them. On the dispersal of his library in 1884 they were purchased by the Italian government, along with other Napoleonic papers, for £23,000 and deposited in the Laurentian Library. The collection, amounting to some 700 folio manuscript pages of notebooks and loose sheets, comes to nearly 650 pages as printed by Masson and Biagi. A substantial part of the manuscripts deals with technical military matters not relevant to the present discussion.

[3] Frédéric Masson and Guido Biagi, *Napoléon inconnu: papiers inédits (1786–1793)*, 2 vols. (Paris, 1895), hereafter cited as MB; and by the same authors, *Napoléon: manuscrits inédits, 1786–1791* (1910).

the literary aspects of these early years.[4] This paper undertakes to reexamine the corpus of Napoleon's early annotations and writings in order to see very simply what works of the philosophes he had read and how much of their ideas he embodied in what he concurrently wrote. In addition and very tentatively it will suggest a few echoes of the philosophes persisting in the later period when this arch-realist and pragmatist pursued his destiny to its end.

Little need be said about the first years in Corsica. Napoleon's father, with his ancient patent of Corsican nobility and a law degree from the University of Pisa, was an easygoing dilettante. Napoleon's great-uncle Lucien, archdeacon of the cathedral in Ajaccio, made no pretence at scholarship. His mother, albeit intelligent and capable, had nothing to contribute to his literary interests.

The formal education of Napoleon began in January 1779, when at the age of nine his father took him to France from the wild and romantic setting of Corsica to begin a schooling that would prepare him for a career as a French officer of the *ancien régime*. The three preliminary months spent at the Collège of Autun in Burgundy were designed merely to give him some ease in the use of the French language, though the *cahiers* were later to show that his mastery was far from complete. Following this, at the Ecole Militaire of Brienne in Champagne (one of the twelve royal schools founded in 1776 to give training to the sons of impoverished nobles), he spent the more than five years of his adolescence. Here the conventional education was directed by the Minims, a minor and undistinguished teaching order. It gave him a little familiarity with the Latin and German languages, with French classical literature (largely in the form of extracts from the dramatists and poets), rhetoric, history, geography, and mathematics, the last being perhaps the only instruction of any substance and the subject in which he did best. Napoleon later told Roederer that he first read *La Nouvelle Héloïse* at the age of nine, and whatever doubts one may have of this, it is certain that he was to reread it until the last days at Saint Helena. Las Cases records Napoleon telling him that at Brienne he read Tasso's *Gerusalemme Liberata;* and a story has been preserved that because of his passion for the republican he-

---

[4] The most important of such works in addition to those of Chuquet, Masson, and Biagi are: F. G. Healey, *The Literary Culture of Napoleon* (Geneva, 1959), and by the same author *Rousseau et Napoléon* (Geneva, 1957); and N. Tomiche, *Napoléon écrivain* (Paris, 1952), with a valuable bibliography. Other somewhat less valuable studies are: F. Masson, *Napoléon dans sa jeunesse* (Paris, 1907, definitive ed., 1922), incorporating the earlier material; G. Mouravit, *Napoléon bibliophile* (Paris, 1905); Marquis de Sayve, *Napoléon et les livres* (Paris, 1927); A. Dansette, ed., *Napoléon: vues Politiques* (Paris, 1939), a collection of extracts; J. Holland Rose, *The Personality of Napoleon* (New York and London, 1912); and Norwood Young, *The Growth of Napoleon, A Study in Environment* (London, 1910), this leaning very heavily on Masson and Biagi.

roes of Plutarch the moody, awkward, aloof boy was nicknamed "the Spartan."[5] One can justifiably assume that the uninspired teaching of history and geography, largely concerned with names and dates, had much to do with the mechanical and factual type of note-taking which was so overwhelmingly to characterize Napoleon's *cahiers.* Chuquet writes that Napoleon was "touched by the winds of disbelief" blowing in the school at Brienne: the most popular priest, it is said, was the one who could say Mass in four minutes; the slowest and least popular took twenty.[6]

One development linking these early years with the later period when Napoleon unhesitatingly accepted the Revolution was his increasing interest in the struggle led by Paoli to win Corsica's independence from Genoa—a long conflict quickly followed by submission to France after Corsica was purchased from Genoa in 1768. In an undated letter, probably of June 1784 when Napoleon was fifteen, he asked his father to send him a French translation of Boswell's *Account of Corsica,* along with "other histories or memoirs concerning this kingdom."[7] This deep interest in the record of Corsica's struggle for freedom, along with a growing interest in Rousseau, can be taken as indicative of Napoleon's early intellectual concerns. The prophetic passage from chapter 10 of the second book of the *Social Contract* which gives some link between the two is worth citing here:

> There is still in Europe one country capable of being given laws—Corsica. The valor and persistence with which that brave people has regained and defended its liberty well deserve that some wise man should teach it how to preserve what it has won. I have a feeling that some day that little island will astonish Europe.

In October 1784, Napoleon entered the famous Ecole Militaire in Paris where he was to spend just less than a year, leaving it in the following September to enter the artillery Régiment de la Fère at the age of sixteen as a second lieutenant. Felix Markham's characterization of this school as the French Sandhurst is true only in part, for the course of study there seems to have been designed more to produce polished gentlemen than to turn out professionally skilled officers. Technical military training would be the responsibility of the regiments to which the cadets eventually were posted. Under teachers certainly much better equipped than those at Brienne, and with an elaborately organized and rigorous program of studies, Napoleon

[5] Healey, *Literary Culture of Napoleon,* p. 20; Emmanuel Las Cases, *Mémorial de Sainte-Hélène,* ed. E. Garnier, 4 vols. (Paris, 1934), I, 319; Chuquet, I, 129–130.

[6] Chuquet, I, 114.

[7] MB, I, 83. Boswell's *Account of Corsica* with its glowing tribute to the islanders first appeared in 1768 at Glasgow. According to Masson this is the second earliest known letter of Napoleon.

was exposed to conventional drill in French literature, Latin prose and poetry, some Greek excerpts in translation, outlines of history and scholastic philosophy, a little English and German, a smattering of natural history and religion, and mathematics. Such military training as was given dealt with artillery, fortifications, and plans. According to Chuquet, Napoleon did not read the famous *Traité de tactique* of the Swiss military theorist Jomini until 1806, when he complained that "in our military schools we were taught nothing like this." [8] Instruction was given also in equitation, fencing, the use of arms, and dancing. "We were fed," Napoleon later recalled, "served magnificently, and treated in every way as officers enjoying great comfort"— a striking contrast to the semimonastic discipline associated with the cell-like cubicles at Brienne.[9] Napoleon, with his eight daily hours of scheduled classes, would have had little if any time for desultory reading, and surely little opportunity to explore any of the works of the philosophes. Teaching of literature was in the hands of one Louis Domairon, whose widely used *Principes généraux des belles-lettres* (2 vols., Paris, 1785) Napoleon long admired. Essentially a manual of grammar and usage, with quotations from all the great ages of literature, including passages from Corneille, Racine, and Voltaire, Domairon's work is faintly damned by Healey as being "probably no better nor worse than that of any other 18th century schoolmaster." [10] One has to remember, moreover, that all this and other education was crowded into a space of about eleven months.

Although Napoleon had a few pleasant companions, he seems to have learned little from his fellows. Nothing during his regimental years could compare with the ferment of ideas prevalent in the salons, the publishing offices, and the literary circles of Paris. Napoleon was the first Corsican to graduate from the Ecole Militaire and probably in terms of money one of the poorest members of his class; of the eight pupils posted with him to the artillery he was the only one not eventually to emigrate; and he ranked forty-second among the fifty-eight winning commissions in 1785.[11]

Napoleon joined his regiment at Valence in October 1785. Here, and later at Auxonne, he lived the relatively easy and not untypical life of an officer of the *ancien régime*, taking frugal domestic lodgings in the town, mastering some of the important new technical works on strategy and tactics, and engaging in a variety of artillery studies and exercises. For France as a whole these were the critical years preceding the new age of the French Revolution—years that were to culminate for Napoleon in his acceptance of the Revolution, in his continued service as a commissioned officer, and in his

[8] Chuquet, I, 207.
[9] *Ibid.*, 210.
[10] Healey, *Literary Culture of Napoleon*, 23.
[11] MB, I, 115, 129; Chuquet, I, 226.

emergence from relative obscurity at the time of the siege of Toulon in the closing months of the year 1793. This was the period when the professional interests of the soldier gradually took precedence over all else. At Toulon in October 1793, he rose to command a battalion; and his nomination as general of brigade (when he was only twenty-four) came in December of the same year.[12]

A striking feature, quite typical of the general practice of the officer class of the *ancien régime,* was the amount of leave granted. In the period of more than eight years running from October 1785 to December 1793, Napoleon spent forty-one months with his regiment and fifty-eight away from it, principally in Corsica, where he made five extended visits, the shortest being about five months and the longest, seventeen. His concern with Corsican politics can be mentioned only briefly here. In essence he was turning from his early enthusiasm for Paoli to a determination that Corsica must associate itself with the new revolutionary France emerging as a result of the work of the Constituent Assembly. He spent two short leaves in Paris, one between October and December 1787, and another, at a time of critical importance in the history of the French Revolution, between May and October 1792. The actual pattern of Napoleon's life needs thus to be kept in mind, for against this background his reading and his various attempts at writing must be set.

What did Napoleon read, and under what circumstances? Not given to sociability with his fellow officers, and finding only a modest intellectual stimulus in his lodgings at Valence and Auxonne, he was thrown very much upon himself. In the Bou family with which he stayed a small literary circle of minor local officials existed. Napoleon also came to know a Madame du Colombier, a witty and intelligent woman with whose daughter Caroline, in episodes reminiscent of the youthful Goethe, he would eat cherries in an idyllic orchard setting. His memories of Caroline were to persist until the last days at Saint Helena.[13] He was more at ease in Corsica, where he was actively concerned with the financial affairs of his family and even more, as the Revolution advanced, with the political fortunes of the island. The evidence of the notebooks so painstakingly edited by Masson and Biagi makes it possible for us to follow in remarkable detail his methods of reading and his interests.

Napoleon got what books he could from the *Librairie Aurée,* a bookshop in Valence, and from the private library of a Monsieur de Josselin; he

[12] Louis Garros, *Quel Roman que ma vie! Itinéraire de Napoléon Bonaparte, 1769–1821* (Paris, 1947), 64–65. This itinerary gives the most precise and best documented account of Napoleon's moves during these early years.

[13] Chuquet, I, 287. See also François Gilbert, baron de Coston, *Biographie des premières années de Napoléon,* 2 vols. (Paris, 1840), I, 87, II, 63.

also wrote for books to Geneva.[14] At Auxonne a Bibliothèque de l'Ecole Militaire had been founded in 1781 which contained memoirs and historical works in addition to the standard treatises on military science.[15] When Napoleon went to Corsica in September 1786, he took with him, according to the *Mémoires* of his brother Joseph, a trunkful of books, among them translations of Plutarch, Plato, Cicero, Cornelius Nepos, Livy, and Tacitus, and also some of the works of Montaigne, Montesquieu, and Raynal as well as the poems of Ossian.[16] Much of his reading had little to do with the philosophes. The evidence of his note-taking shows very slight interest in the conflict of ideas and an almost complete absence of bold generalizations. Such methods of annotation obviously reflect the disciplined, factual training and rote memorization demanded at Brienne and at the Ecole Militaire in Paris. Names, dates, statistics, the facts of geography—these reappear endlessly. He took long notes, for example, on Rollin's *Ancient History*, principally concerning the governments of Persia, Athens, and Sparta, outlines of Greek geography, and observations on Egypt, Carthage, and Assyria. He made a few excerpts from Plato's *Republic*, an indication that he may have read at least the first book. He summarized, again very factually and at great length, John Barrow's *History of England*, a work going to 1688, from a French translation of 1771–73. There are brief notes from an unidentifiable history of Frederick II of Prussia, others of greater length from the memoirs of François baron du Tott dealing with the Turks and the Tartars (1784), still others from the *abbé* de Marigny's *Histoire des Arabes* (1750), and factual résumés from the widely popular *Géographie moderne* of the *abbé* de Lacroix first published in 1747. Among these last will be found at the end of the section dealing with the South Atlantic the poignant and unfinished brief entry, "Sainte-Hélène, petite île. . . ."[17] There are few such poignancies and nothing, certainly, to capture the imagination. What are we to make, for example, of a note such as the following: "Indians are yellowish. Americans are olive-colored. Africans in general are black."? A few significant points do emerge: first, an intense devotion to factual knowledge; second, a widespread interest in geography; and third, an interest in the long sweep of history almost exclusively as it was concerned with forms of government and the exercise of political authority. But there is nothing, for example in his brief annotations from Plato's *Republic*, to suggest any mature interest in the subtleties of political theory.[18]

[14] MB, I, 138, n. 1.

[15] Tomiche, *Napoléon écrivain*, p. 17.

[16] Joseph Bonaparte, *Mémoires et correspondance politique et militaire*, 10 vols. (Paris, 1853–1854), I, 32–33.

[17] MB, II, 49.

[18] A detailed account of Napoleon's method of note-taking is given in Tomiche, *Napoléon écrivain*, pp. 81–89.

Napoleon's interest in Corsica led him ambitiously to undertake a history of that island—a project never fully realized yet interesting because of the scattered evidence of some of the ideas of the philosophes, and especially of Rousseau and Raynal. This Napoleonic dedication to the history of Corsica had appeared during his schooldays at Brienne.[19] In his first year as an artillery officer at Valence he wrote to a bookseller in Geneva ordering the two volumes of the *abbé* Germanes' history of Corsica and asking for a list of other similar works.[20] The notebooks of 1786 contain a four-page fragment *Sur la Corse* notable for its strong echoes of Rousseau. It is an eloquent defence of Paoli's leadership of his people against tyranny. The duty of any government is to seek the *bonheur* of its people, and if the ruler does not so act, then "it is clear that the people returns to its primitive condition, and that the government, not providing for the aims of the *pacte social,* is automatically dissolved." [21] Napoleon concludes by saying that the Corsicans, having shaken off the Genoese yoke, can do as much against the French—a strange doctrine indeed for a newly appointed officer of the king.

A fragment of 1787 dealing with the love of country and full of Plutarchian admiration for ancient republican virtue cites Corsica and its patriotic leaders as illustrations of this love.[22] On Napoleon's second stay in Corsica in the spring of 1788 he took the occasion to visit brother officers at Bastia, one of whom found him "dry and sententious," full of comparisons between ancient and modern governments, and strongly in favor of summoning an assembly of the Corsican estates—a move which the government stubbornly opposed.[23]

On Bonaparte's return to Auxonne in June 1788, he found time amid his artillery studies to begin the reading of Raynal's *Histoire philosophique et politique des Indes.*[24] Although Raynal was a strong opponent of colonial slavery in general and a sympathizer with the cause of Corsica, the notes which Napoleon took are again dry, brief, and factual, showing little of the deeper concerns which animated Raynal. He was, however, determined to go on with his project of a Corsican history. A curious fragment, *La Nouvelle Corse,* strongly reminiscent in style of Bernardin de Saint-Pierre, emerges from this year at Auxonne.[25] It took the form of an account by an English

19 Chuquet, I, 116–117.

20 *Abbé* Germanes, *Histoire des révolutions de la Corse depuis ses premiers habitans, jusqu' à nos jours,* 3 vols. (Paris, 1771–1776). See Chuquet, II, 62.

21 MB, I, 142.

22 *Ibid.,* 185–192.

23 *Ibid.,* 199 and note.

24 Guillaume Thomas François Raynal, *L'Histoire philosophique et politique des établissements et du commerce des Européens dans les deux Indes,* first ed., 4 vols. (Amsterdam, 1770). Napoleon's notes are in MB, I, 334–339. See also note 52.

25 MB, II, 75–83.

traveller who on leaving Leghorn for Spain had been forced by storms and contrary winds to seek refuge on the desolate island of Gorgona, where he compared his situation with that of Robinson Crusoe. During the night the traveller heard voices and found his tent, which he had pitched amid the ruins of an ancient monastery, in flames. Outside were two figures, the one, an elderly Corsican, bitterly reproaching the other, his daughter, for having set fire to the tent of the stranger. The old man explained that after having fought for freedom against the Genoese he had been forced into exile in order to escape persecution at the hands of the French. Then followed a long account of the harsh sufferings endured by the Corsican at the hands of occasional French intruders on the island. The obviously incomplete composition, which had made its point, ends in midsentence.

In this same year of 1788 at Auxonne the project for a history of Corsica took more definite shape. Bonaparte had originally hoped to begin by addressing some letters to Brienne, the chief royal minister at Versailles. The fall of Brienne in August led Napoleon to plan the direction of these letters to Brienne's successor, Necker, hoping to have them available at the opening of the Estates General. In June 1789, Bonaparte wrote to Paoli, then in London, telling him of his plans "to dissipate these fogs, the product of ignorance," that hide the desperate situation in Corsica. "I wish," he wrote, "to summon to the tribunal of public opinion those who govern," and he expressed his hope that "the virtuous minister who governs the state" (Necker) could be brought to act.[26] The actual text of these first Napoleonic drafts is unknown. He sent them, however, to one of his former teachers at Brienne, a certain *Père* Dupuy, for criticisms and corrections, and the tenor of the letters can be deduced from Dupuy's replies. His two answering letters made many pedantic suggestions for minor stylistic improvements and also offered other advice concerning the substance. In general he urged Napoleon to soften his attacks. When asking favors of a king through his chief ministers, one should not, the schoolmaster urged, describe rulers as "proud tyrants of the earth."

The *Lettres sur la Corse* were put into shape on the island, whither Napoleon went in September 1789. En route he paid his respects to Raynal, then living in Marseille.[27] It is possible that he could have seen Raynal even earlier, on his passage through Marseille in 1786 or in 1788. Raynal, according to his biographer Feugère, was in the habit of holding weekly "*déjeuners philo-*

[26] *Ibid.*, 64–66.

[27] Although the fact of the visit has been questioned, it is accepted by Masson and Biagi, MB, I, 225; Chuquet, II, 52; and Garros, *Itinéraire de Napoléon,* 38. A letter of Napoleon to Raynal of June 24, 1790, introducing his brother Joseph, who brought a copy of the unpublished *Lettres sur la Corse,* speaks of himself as "a person to whom you were good enough to be courteous last year." MB, II, 106.

sophiques," at one of which Napoleon seems to have become known to him.[28] This visit can be listed as Napoleon's only personal contact with a member of the rapidly diminishing band of philosophes. The material on Corsica took the form of three long letters covering altogether seventy-three folio pages of manuscript—by far the longest of Napoleon's early writings.[29] The first letter begins with an elaborate dedication to Raynal, "a friend of free men." Corsica, having won its liberty from Genoa, has suffered twenty years of "the despotism of Versailles." Slavery must now be replaced by liberty. "Man! Man! How despised thou art in slavery, how great when inflamed by the love of liberty! Prejudices dissolve, thy soul is elevated, reason regains its empire." Corsica must follow the example of America, where "men enjoy the triumphs of Washington." A labored outline of the Corsican struggle for liberty traces this development from ancient times to the period of the medieval struggles of the Italian communes.

The second and longest of the three letters continues the history of Corsica, using an exaggerated preromantic style to record the virtues of its heroes and the vices of its enemies—a struggle carried on by "an indomitable nation."[30] The unfinished third letter deals with the increasingly dictatorial Genoese period from the middle of the sixteenth century onward, a continued period of struggle dominated by a nobility, a clergy, and a merchant class that had combined to destroy Corsican liberty. Here the echoes of Rousseau become very striking:

> Man in the state of nature knows no other law than that of his own interest. . . . But when he is united in society his sentiments are enlarged. The love of country is born, and a Curtius, a Decius, a Brutus, a Dion, a Cato, and a Leonidas come to dazzle the world. Magistrates assure him the conservation of his property and his life. The goal of his actions must be the well-being [*bonheur*] of the association. He must no longer act according to his individual interest.[31]

Despite heroic struggles the "despotism of kings" has been imposed and thus "no one can deny that the confederation would find itself dissolved and that men would consequently sink once more into the anarchy caused by the conflict of personal interests."[32] This third letter, obviously meant to be

---

28 A. Feugère, *Un Précurseur de la Révolution—l'abbé Raynal* (Angoulême, 1922), 333, accepts the story of Las Cases that Napoleon did attend one of these *déjeuners*.

29 MB, II, 127–179. The *Lettres sur la Corse* were very inadequately published in 1843 by Guillaume Libri in the French journal *Illustration*.

30 A dated revision of this second *Lettre* permits Masson to conclude that the work of writing went on in Corsica until November 1790. MB, II, 138, n. 1.

31 *Ibid.*, 174.

32 *Ibid.*, 175.

further extended, breaks off with the beginning of the great Corsican struggle against Genoa. Napoleon clearly had more to say. Yet by this time his interests and those of Paoli were beginning to separate, for Paoli, hailed as a hero when he returned from England to Corsica in 1791, was increasingly at odds with the government in Paris.

The hoped-for association with Paoli did not develop. Back at Auxonne, Napoleon wrote to him on March 16, 1791, sending a printed copy of his *Lettre à Matteo Buttafuoco*. This was a savage diatribe against the Corsican representative to the National Assembly in Paris.[33] Buttafuoco, the *Lettre* stated, has failed to represent a free people and has become simply the ally of "the soldier, the lawyer (*robin*), and the financier (*publicain*)." He should have listened to the cries of his native country, but instead he has been seduced by gold. "O Lameth! O Robespierre! O Pétion! O Volney! O Mirabeau! O Barnave! O Bailly! O Lafayette!" cries Napoleon in an interesting summary of those whom he regarded as the true leaders of France, "behold the man who dares sit beside you!" The letter was ordered printed by the revolutionary Club of Ajaccio. In addition to sending Paoli the *Lettre à Matteo Buttafuoco* Napoleon asked him for documents needed to complete his history of Corsica. Paoli replied from Bastia on April 2, urging Napoleon to waste no time on Buttafuoco; as for documents, he wrote coldly, "I cannot at present open my boxes and search my writings. Moreover, history is not written in the years of youth." [34] A further letter which Napoleon got his brother Joseph to write to Paoli resulted in a similar reply. "I have received the brochure of your brother: it would have made a greater impression if it had said less and shown less partiality. I have other things to think of now than to look for documents and have them copied." [35] Paoli was now sixty-six and his breach with Napoleon was complete.

The *Lettres sur la Corse* can give Napoleon little claim to a place among the philosophes. Marked, to be sure, by an ardent Corsican patriotism, they echo some of Rousseau's ideas on the social contract and individual liberty. In style and tone they have the strong preromantic flavor so typical of the early Napoleonic writings, though it is difficult to accept the opinion of Alphonse Aulard that they are "un des plus beaux monuments de notre langue." [36] Raynal had paid them some polite compliments and Paoli had waved them aside. They did not then achieve the dignity of print, and so, whatever their personal interest, they have no practical place in the powerful body of literature marking the last phase of the Enlightenment.

Since Napoleon's early interest in Rousseau was closely tied to his similar

[33] *Ibid.*, 180–193.
[34] *Ibid.*, 199–200.
[35] August 15, 1791. *Ibid.*, 201–202.
[36] Quoted in Tomiche, *Napoléon écrivain*, 320.

early interest in Corsica, the problem requires some further evaluation.[37] It seems evident that he had read the *Discours sur l'origine de l'inégalité, La Nouvelle Héloïse, Du Contrat social,* and the *Confessions.* While at Valence in 1786 he had written to Geneva for copies of the apocryphal memoirs of Madame de Warens (whose name he spelled "Valens") and Claude Anet, "to serve as a sequel to the *Confessions* of J. J. Rousseau." [38] A copy of *La Nouvelle Héloïse* later was included in the library he took with him to Egypt, as it was in the great imperial library at the Tuileries and in the portable Bibliothèque de Campagne. *La Nouvelle Héloïse* and the *Confessions* were in the list prepared for another contemplated Bibliothèque Portative in 1808. Among the books sold from the library at Longwood after Napoleon's death in 1821 was a twenty-volume set of Rousseau's *Oeuvres complètes.*[39]

The pervasive overtones of Rousseau are apparent in the *sensibilité* of Napoleon's early writings—in the already mentioned fragment *Sur la Corse* and in the *Sur la suicide* of 1786,[40] as well as in the curiously moving *Rencontre au Palais Royal* of 1787 in which he tells of his encounter with a young prostitute.[41] In *Sur la Corse* he speaks of a people returning to its "primitive nature" and of the original *"pacte social,"* from which a constitution is derived. In *Sur la suicide* he exclaims bitterly, "How far men are removed from nature! " His most striking championing of Rousseau is found in his refutation of the work of a Genevan pastor, Antoine Jacques Roustan, entitled *Offrande aux autels et à la patrie* (Amsterdam, 1764), which contained an essay, *Défense du Christianisme considéré du côté politique ou l'on répond en particulier au chapitre VIII du quatrième livre du Contrat Social.*[42] Rousseau had argued that a powerfully organized religion, approved and supported by the state, would destroy the social unity essential to it. Instead, Rousseau proposed his well-known simple civil profession of faith having among its dogmas or "social sentiments" the existence of a beneficent Deity, the sanctity of the social contract and the laws derived from it, and the rejection of intolerance. Napoleon vigorously attacked Roustan's argument that the constitution of a state should require it to incorporate an official religion so as to provide a strong support for its policies. Napoleon argued that a single, officially established religion would destroy *"l'unité sociale."* One can see, moreover, an interesting though not very precise suggestion of Napoleon's acquaintance with Montesquieu. Roustan, he said, appeals to Montesquieu in support of the argument that Christianity will strengthen

37 The problem is carefully studied in Healey, *Rousseau et Napoléon,* to which this section is heavily indebted.

38 MB, I, 138, n. 1.

39 Healey, *Rousseau et Napoléon,* 100–101.

40 MB, I, 145–146.

41 *Ibid.,* 181–183.

42 *Ibid.,* 147–159.

the state. In fact, replied Napoleon, Montesquieu's argument is against him, though Napoleon did not show how.[43] Although the refutation of Roustan was not clearly argued, one can agree with Masson that the work anticipated the policy of the Concordat of 1801 in that while Roman Catholicism was then given an official status other religions were tolerated and the supremacy of the state was to be unquestioned.[44]

An equally strong reflection of Rousseau's influence is seen in the interesting if minor *Projet de Constitution de la Calotte du Régiment de la Fère*, probably written at Auxonne in 1788.[45] The *Calotte* was a widely established association of regimental officers below the rank of captain intended to maintain their standards and traditions and to enable them to present their causes to higher officers. The studious Napoleon was assigned by his comrades the task of preparing a written constitution for them and did so with a vengeance. The intricately organized scheme is of interest here not so much for its detailed provisions as for the echoes of Rousseau running through it. Constitutions, Napoleon solemnly wrote, must be derived "directly from the nature of the *pacte primitif*." Any fundamental law can be annulled only by unanimous agreement. All members are equal. "The laws which derive from the nature of the pact are constitutive laws. No legislator, no authority, can derogate from them." The document seems to have caused considerable amusement among his fellow-officers, so much so that, according to a contemporary anecdote, after some sharply critical discussion one of Napoleon's friends was charitably impelled to throw it into the fire.[46]

The strong impact of Rousseau found in the preliminary sketches for a history of Corsica has already been mentioned and need not be rehearsed here. The striking new fact was to be the turning away of Napoleon, as he became more closely aware of the harsh realities of the revolutionary years, from his earlier Rousseauistic enthusiasms. Among his notes of 1791 are some which deal with Rousseau's *Discours sur l'origine et les fondements de l'inégalité*.[47] The tone is highly critical. Napoleon quotes passages in order to refute them. Summarizing Rousseau's claim that man's first and only concerns are food, the reproduction of his kind, and rest, he writes, "*Je ne crois pas cela*." To Rousseau's picture of man living aimlessly in a pure state of nature he replies, "*Je ne crois rien de tout ceci*." His own views, which were more reminiscent of those of Aristotle, were that man has always been a social animal, gradually moving from some primitive social organization to one

[43] Montesquieu does say in the *Esprit des lois*, Book XXIV, chap. 14, that religion joins with civil laws to make men into good citizens, and that when religion begins to fail in this duty the state must do more.

[44] MB, I, 158, n. 1. See also Healey, *Rousseau et Napoléon*, 24.

[45] MB, I, 227–240.

[46] *Ibid.*, 229, note.

[47] *Ibid.*, II, 285–287.

more complex. Men have always had some capacity to feel and reason. If it were true, as he held Rousseau to say, that feeling and reason did not exist before the creation of society, then these would have no natural origin and there would be no innate duty or happiness with respect to virtue. "It is not," Napoleon concluded, "the citizen of Geneva who is to tell us that."

By the time Napoleon wrote his *Discours de Lyon* in 1791, to be considered later, the echoes of Rousseau had become faint. Even so, he never in the imperial years abandoned some concept, however distorted, of equality, and it could be argued that the imperial plebiscites had a suggestion of Rousseau's *pacte primitif*.[48] "The nation," he told Roederer, "is in the throne." Healey sees in the ardent letters which Napoleon wrote to Josephine after their marriage in 1796 the continuing influence of Rousseau, though their romantic tone might equally be due to a much wider current of *sensibilité*, a legacy from the last years of the *ancien régime*.

Napoleon's criticisms of Rousseau were to grow. "Until I was sixteen," Roederer reports him saying in 1803, "I would have fought to the death for Rousseau against all the friends of Voltaire. Today it's the other way around. I am especially disgusted with Rousseau since I have seen the Orient. Savage man is a dog."[49] Lucien Bonaparte's *Mémoires* contain an indication of the mature opinion that Napoleon held of Rousseau; it fell far short of his earlier enthusiasm: "In my eyes he is a mere chatterbox—or, if you like that better, a rather eloquent ideologist. I never cared for him and, what is more, I never could quite understand him. It's true that I didn't have the courage to read all of him because he seemed, on the whole, boring."[50] Perhaps the most revealing Napoleonic commentary on Rousseau was made at the time of the Consulate when Stanislas Girardin took him to see Rousseau's grave on the estate at Ermenonville. Girardin's memoirs describe the episode as follows:

> When he reached the poplar island, Bonaparte stepped in front of Jean-Jacques' tomb and said, "It would have been better for the peace of France if this man had never lived."—"And why, Citizen Consul?"—"It was he who prepared the French Revolution."—"I should have thought, Citizen Consul, that it was not for you to complain of the Revolution."—"Well," he replied, "the future will tell us whether it would not have been better if neither I nor Rousseau had ever lived." And he resumed his walk with a thoughtful air.[51]

[48] See the discussion in Healey, *Rousseau et Napoléon*, pp. 73–78.

[49] Quoted in J. Christopher Herold, ed., *The Mind of Napoleon* (New York, 1955), p. 156.

[50] Iung, Théodore, *Lucien Bonaparte et ses mémoires, 1775-1840*, 3 vols. (Paris, 1882–1883), II, 224.

[51] Quoted in Herold, *The Mind of Napoleon*, p. 67.

The *abbé* Raynal must be put next in significance to Rousseau in his influence upon Napoleon. His *Histoire philosophique* had first appeared in 1770 and was frequently republished. Many of its attacks on slavery, on monarchical despotism, on the evils of monasticism, and on the organized Church were a *réchauffage* of views common among the philosophes, so that by reading him Napoleon would automatically be brought into contact with a wider range of ideas than those of Raynal himself. Napoleon took his notes on the *Histoire philosophique* in 1789, and if it can be assumed that the notebooks are in chronological order he followed this with reading in the previously mentioned *Mémoires* of baron de Tott dealing with the Turks and the Tartars, the *Histoire des Arabes* of the *abbé* Marigny, and the *Géographie* of Lacroix.[52] One would be hard put to demonstrate from the dry notes taken from these various works any important impact of ideas. Instead we have information such as the following from Raynal:

> Henry, King [*sic*] of Portugal, established an observatory at Sagres, a town in Algarves.

> Emanuel sent out Vasco da Gama in 1497, who reached Hindustan after thirteen months of navigation.

> Alfonso Albuquerque, viceroy and successor to Cabral, felt the necessity to seize Goa: he fortified it, making it his capital.[53]

The notes contrast the old overland routes and the new sea routes. They give a summary account of India and the East Indies, a brief account of the Portuguese arrival in China, and of Confucianism ("the agreement of Nature and Reason is its supreme Law"), and an even briefer mention of Japan and of Shintoism. Notes from the other works supplementing what he read in Raynal are equally literal and commonplace.

What Napoleon derived from Raynal in addition to factual information must remain to some extent a matter of deduction and conjecture.[54] Raynal denounced both autocratic monarchs and the despicable conquerors of the overseas world. He admired the American Revolution. He was hostile to all established religion, especially when it claimed to have power over civil gov-

[52] *Mémoires du baron de Tott sur les Trucs et les Tatars*, 4 vols. (Amsterdam, 1784); *abbé* François Augier de Marigny, *Histoire des Arabes sous le gouvernement des Califs*, 4 vols. (Paris, 1750); *abbé* Louis Antoine Nicolle de Lacroix, *Géographie moderne* (Paris, 1747 and many later eds.). According to Tomiche, *Napoléon écrivain*, 344, Napoleon's notes from Raynal appear to be taken from the first three volumes of the ten-volume Geneva edition of 1781.

[53] MB, I, 334, 337.

[54] Chuquet, II, 18–30, 219–220, claims a very large influence, both on the *Lettres sur la Corse* and on the later *Discours de Lyon*, but does not always document his arguments in a way that can be verified.

ernment. He wrote that the clergy must be subject to the state as a kind of *"gendarmerie sacrée."* [55] He attacked superstition and fanaticism and was highly critical of the wasted lives led in monasteries and nunneries. He had warm feelings for the Corsican struggle for freedom. In all these respects his views could hardly fail to strike a responsive note when Napoleon was preparing his *Lettres sur la Corse*. At a later date a copy of Raynal's *Histoire philosophique* was in the library Napoleon took with him to Egypt. One may also assume that when the First Consul undertook in 1800 to recover Louisiana from Spain he was not unaware of the importance Raynal had attached to this vast territory. [56] It seems fair to conclude that the immediate influence of Raynal in the early period of writing was substantial and that traces of it long persisted.

Napoleon's intellectual indebtedness to the other philosophes can be treated more briefly. While in school he had read extracts from Voltaire's plays and poems. The plays in particular never lost their interest for him, and in the Saint Helena years he took delight in having passages read aloud during the evening *salons*—a delight not always shared by his drowsy companions. For *Zaïre* he had what amounted to a passion. His librarian was instructed to include the *Contes* of Voltaire in the travelling library of 1808, and according to Lord Rosebery the six packing cases of books which accompanied Napoleon even to Waterloo contained all the seventy volumes of Voltaire. [57] The notes which the youthful Napoleon took from the *Essai sur les mœurs* (according to Masson, from the incomplete Paris or Geneva edition of 1756) are of little help in deriving any of the intellectual attitudes of Napoleon from those of Voltaire. [58] Yet a copy of the *Essai* went with him to Egypt, along with Voltaire's histories of Charles XII and Peter the Great. Nothing seems to indicate any familiarity with *Candide*, the *Dictionnaire philosophique*, or the *Siècle de Louis XIV*. True, the mature Napoleon, keenly aware of the foibles of men, saw much in Voltaire that may have escaped him in his youth. He made this clear to Roederer in 1803:

> What a difference between today's writing and Voltaire. The more I read of Voltaire the letter I like him. That man is always reasonable, not a charlatan, not a fanatic. . . . I even like his historical writings a great deal, although they are much criticized. His *Pucelle* is not good for young people to read, but it cheers the mature. Voltaire is for mature people. [59]

[55] Feugère, *Un Précurseur de la Révolution—l'abbé Raynal*, 248.

[56] *Ibid.*, 418–419.

[57] Lord Rosebery, Archibald Philip Primrose, *Napoleon: The Last Phase* (London, 1900), 246.

[58] MB, II, 268–274.

[59] Quoted in Herold, *The Mind of Napoleon*, 155–156.

Like Voltaire, Napoleon came to regard a powerfully organized church as a foe to civil government, and like Voltaire he saw the need for the reign of equality, if not of liberty, to replace the old era of privilege.

The links with Montesquieu are as elusive as those with Voltaire. Joseph Bonaparte lists Montesquieu as one of the authors contained in the trunkful of books taken to Corsica in 1786, and according to Chuquet Napoleon read the *Esprit des Lois* with his Corsican compatriot, Pozzo di Borgo, during one of his vacations.[60] Yet none of the published *cahiers* contains any explicit annotations of Montesquieu's works, so that his influence, such as it was, has to be determined not from the notes but from some of the early exercises in authorship. In a brief essay of 1791 entitled *République ou monarchie* Napoleon poured scorn on the monarchists and came out for a republic. "I have read all the speeches of the monarchist orators. I saw great efforts to sustain a bad cause." Napoleon seemed to echo Montesquieu's idea of a republic whose animating spirit is virtue: "Without morality [*mœurs*]," he declared, "there is no republic." [61] A later indication of his interest in Montesquieu can be found in a long letter from Italy of September 17, 1797, to Talleyrand, the new minister of foreign affairs, about the need for constitutional revision in France.[62] Talleyrand had elaborated on this need. We are, Napoleon replied to Talleyrand, very ignorant in such matters and have been misled by Montesquieu, who gives us false definitions of what legislative, executive, and judicial powers should be. Montesquieu's eyes were fixed on the government of England, with its supposed checks and balances, whereas, so Napoleon claimed, in France "where all authority emanates from the people" the central power should be prepared to act strongly. "Governmental power, in all the latitude which I give it, should be considered the true representative of the nation." Napoleon's argument need not be pursued, yet the concern with Montesquieu, if only to attempt to refute him, is worth recording.

Some of Montesquieu's emphasis on geography seems to be reflected in Napoleon's comments upon Italy recorded by Las Cases at Saint Helena. The area, position, and shape of Italy, he insisted, have undoubtedly influenced the destiny of that lovely country. If it had been wider and shorter, then "its center would have been closer to its whole periphery; there would have been a greater community of interests. . . . The cohesive tendency that has united France, England, and Spain would have acted upon Italy as well." [63] In the *Moniteur* for January 10, 1803, appeared an article, probably the work of its editor, La Harpe, but, as was generally true of all such articles, doubt-

---

[60] Chuquet, II, 11; Tomiche, *Napoléon écrivain*, 20.

[61] MB, II, 275–276.

[62] *Correspondance de Napoléon I publiée par ordre de l'empereur Napoléon III*, 32 vols. (Paris, 1858–1869), III, 2223.

[63] Quoted in Herold, *The Mind of Napoleon*, 52–53.

less approved by Napoleon. It complained that the Revolution had wrongly rejected the teachings of Montesquieu for those of Rousseau. "Now that men and affairs are returning successively to their proper place, one can be certain that that which Rousseau will always have as an eloquent writer will be nothing beside that of Montesquieu as a political philosopher."[64] The stern necessities of public life seem to have made Napoleon more willing to approve the constitutional details of Montesquieu's argument than he was to accept the broad sweep of Rousseau's grand generalizations.

The impact of the other philosophes was unquestionably slight. Nothing indicates that Napoleon had read Diderot, had any enthusiasm for his *Encyclopédie*, or had even seen it. Notes from Buffon's *Histoire naturelle* deal with theories of the earth's origin, the nature and explanation of the tides, and the formation of the earth's surface. They conclude with a long account of various theories concerning reproduction and of the nature of infant development.[65] Napoleon briefly annotated Mirabeau's work on the *Lettres de Cachet*, but with more concern over the historical varieties of such procedures than with any clarion call against their injustice.[66] He did, however, point out in passing that if the edict of 1756 providing death for attacks on religion had been enforced, both Rousseau and Raynal would have suffered. In a long note on the *abbé* Duvernet's *Histoire de la Sorbonne* he observed that Montesquieu, Buffon, Raynal, Marmontel, and Mably had all been condemned and the Encyclopedists in general anathematized.[67] His account of Necker's report on the opening of the Estates General in May 1789 is little more than an attempt to summarize its statistics.[68]

The one essay that might give Napoleon some minor claim to be himself a philosophe is what has come to be known as the *Discours de Lyon*, composed in the autumn of 1791. In a fashion altogether typical of the times the *abbé* Raynal had offered a prize of 1,200 livres for the best essay on a subject to be set by the Academy of Lyon.[69] Over the years the project had languished, none of the various essays submitted being deemed worthy of a prize. The subject set in 1791, inescapably recalling the topics that had first brought fame to the young Rousseau, was to determine "the truths and sentiments most necessary to be instilled in men for their happiness." Napoleon's essay was the fifteenth and last but one to be submitted.

Napoleon evidently prepared himself by some rapid note-taking from a very unusual variety of sources—Ariosto's *Orlando Furioso*, Lieutaud's

---

64 Quoted in Healey, *Rousseau et Napoléon*, 65.

65 MB, I, 472–509.

66 *Ibid.*, 441–447.

67 *Ibid.*, II, 216–225.

68 *Ibid.*, 54–59.

69 Not, as Healey asserts, 12,000 livres, which would have been a most substantial sum.

Alcibiade, Bernardin de Saint-Pierre's *La Chaumière indienne,* William Coxe's *Lettres sur la Suisse,* Voltaire's *Essai sur les mœurs,* and Marmontel's *Les Incas.* He was concerned apparently not so much with the intellectual content of these works as with striking and unusual words and phrases which he could appropriate in order to dress up his own writing.[70] He also found time, as has been shown, to reread Rousseau's *Discours sur les origines de l'inégalité* and to write a few pages of strong disagreement. As a preliminary he also penned a brief sketch of his new argument.[71]

The completed *Discours* occupies forty pages in the printed version of Masson and Biagi.[72] It had an epigraph from Raynal, "There will be morality [*mœurs*] when governments are free," and began with a flowery invocation to him. The first part of the *Discours* considered man as an animal. He is born to be happy, and his first simple and essential needs are food, shelter, clothing, and a mate. Any thirst for riches must be replaced by "the consoling sentiment of happiness." Napoleon pointed out how Paoli had striven successfully to ensure these simple benefits for the people of Corsica. Man always has, however, more than animal needs, some of the others arising from what Napoleon called sentiment or feeling. This is explained as "that which unites the son with his mother, the citizen with *la patrie*." In an echo, perhaps, of the *Emile* he asked what constitutes the enjoyment of life and answered that we must look within our hearts and read what we find there. If one is indignant before injustice, "it is the indignation of feeling." On a still higher level comes reason, or intellect. This will enable us to master the passions, and the best means to attain this rationality is through the study of geometry and logic. Here the argument becomes uncertain, the inflated language diffuse rather than helpful, the conclusions something less than convincing. The artisan and even the peasant must make some simple use of mathematical science; even more should the governing classes be required to use the methods of mathematics and logic. One must, Napoleon wrote, use logic naturally to establish truth, as is the case in the *Dialogues* of Plato, the *Social Contract,* and the *Livre sur l'Entendement.* If this last is a reference to Locke's famous essay, it appears to be the only evidence of Napoleon's interest in it. He may well have been indebted for what he knew of Locke to Voltaire's *Lettres philosophiques.* "Let the legislator," Napoleon wrote, "after having assured to everyone by the civil law some portion of property, then assure him through the criminal law the independence of his life and the maintenance of his liberty; and then assure him by political laws the integrity of his rights and his dignity." [73]

The *Discours* boldly attacked the abuses affecting France. It was written

[70] See Tomiche, *Napoléon écrivain,* 105–111.
[71] MB, II, 288–291.
[72] *Ibid.,* 292–332.
[73] *Ibid.,* 315.

shortly after the royal flight to Varennes and at the time of the practical eclipse of the monarchy—a time when republicanism was in the ascendant.

> Let these principles be incessantly repeated to man. To resist oppression is his finest right, that which tyrants fear most. . . . After centuries the Frenchman, brutalized by his kings and their ministers, by the nobles with their prejudices, and by the priests with their impostures, has suddenly awakened and discovered the rights of man. Let these be the rule for the legislator.[74]

Thus to summarize the *Discours de Lyon* is no doubt to give too much clarity to a line of argument which at times was anything but clear. The judges were surely correct in pronouncing it "trop mal ordonné, trop disparate, trop décousu, et trop mal écrit," and were no doubt equally justified in denying it, along with the fifteen others, the prize.[75] Gourgaud's *Journal*, written at Saint Helena, preserves a curious minor episode concerning the *Discours de Lyon.* Under the Empire Talleyrand managed somehow to obtain a manuscript copy from Lyon and presented it to the Emperor, who asked him if he had read it. Talleyrand said he had not yet had time, whereupon Napoleon quickly threw it into the fire, adding the tongs for good measure. He did not, so he told Talleyrand, wish him to see a youthful work which could have made the Emperor seem ridiculous.[76]

Some further comments on the *Discours de Lyon* must be made. Evidence of Rousseau's early phraseology, if not of the early arguments, is still present, as well as evidence of some of the ideas of the *Contrat social.* There are echoes of Raynal in the references to the sufferings which "brigands" have inflicted on the natives of the New World and in the repeated attacks on the priesthood. The statement that law is general reason suggests Montesquieu's famous dictum that law in general is human reason and that political and civil law must apply this reason in special cases. Political liberty, Napoleon says, consists in obeying the law of the constitution. Along with much turgid romantic phraseology the essay has an occasional sharpness of style. Although Napoleon curiously warned against the danger of ambition, he also could write tellingly that "men of genius are meteors, destined to burn in order to enlighten their century." Healey observes that the essay gives some hints of the Napoleon of the Consulate and the Empire in urging that reason, force, and energy must be employed by the ruler to end injustice and to provide the institutions worthy of a new age.[77]

By 1791 Napoleon had reached the point when a career of action was

[74] *Ibid.,* 323.

[75] It can be noted, however, that Pierre Daunou, later one of the architects both of the Constitution of 1795 and that of 1799 and a founder of the Institute, was given honorable mention.

[76] See Healey, *Rousseau et Napoléon,* 56.

[77] *Ibid.,* 42–43.

taking precedence over all theorizing. He did not hesitate to take the civil oath required by the Constitution of 1791. His early ambition for a liberated Corsica had been replaced by his determination to see it as a part of the new France.[78] He had been active in the Jacobin club at Auxonne. He joined the Société des Amis de la Constitution at Valence in June 1791 and became its librarian. He frequented the Club des Amis de la Constitution at Grenoble during that autumn.[79] With the fall of the monarchy in 1792 he unhesitatingly became a republican of the Jacobin stamp. The literary evidence for his Jacobinism lies in a little work, *Le Souper de Beaucaire,* which he wrote at or near Avignon in July 1793, after his return from Corsica.[80] He had been involved in the military operations against the *fédérés* of Marseille who opposed the new Jacobin regime at Paris. The *Souper de Beaucaire* is in the form of a discussion like that of a Platonic dialogue between a Jacobin soldier on the one hand, and on the other two business men from Marseille, a worker from Nîmes, and one from Montpellier. These men doubt whether the troops sent by the Jacobin government will be able to reestablish order against the Marseillais. The answers of the soldier—in other words, Napoleon —are that the professional ability and the military force of the Jacobins will prevail over all else. Such strength will be decisive, particularly since the Brissotins have been discredited. Hence he urges his companions to abandon the role of counterrevolutionaries and accept the new constitution. In the end the soldier's arguments convince his companions.

The *Souper de Beaucaire*—a sixteen-page pamphlet—was ordered printed by the local Jacobin society of Avignon and a copy sent to the Convention at Paris. Napoleon was no longer the theorist of the *Discours de Lyon.* He had become the dedicated soldier, the Jacobin, the man of action. Chuquet calls him "a revolutionary and politician without illusions and without scruples"—one who attaches himself to the Jacobins not for reasons of ideology but because power is on their side.[81] Such indeed had been the outcome, and with it the youthful work of note-taking and pamphlet-writing reached its end.

[78] Corsica in point of fact was held by the English between 1794 and 1796, when the French reoccupied it.

[79] Garros, *Itinéraire de Napoléon,* 44, 45.

[80] MB, II, 479–497. For details about the composition of this work in the midst of Napoleon's soldierly duties see Chuquet, III, 153–168, and Garros, *Itinéraire de Napoléon,* 59–61.

[81] Chuquet, III, 166.

THE WRITINGS OF
ARTHUR M. WILSON

"Sensibility in France in the Eighteenth Century." *French Quarterly* XIII (1931), 35–46.

French Foreign Policy During the Administration of Cardinal Fleury, 1726–1743: A Study in Diplomacy and Commercial Development. Cambridge: Harvard University Press, 1936, xii, 433 pp.

"The Logwood Trade in the Seventeenth and Eighteenth Centuries." In *Essays in the History of Modern Europe,* edited by Donald C. McKay, pp. 1–15. New York: Harper Brothers, 1936.

"The 'Great Issues' Course at Dartmouth College." *The American Political Science Review* XLIII (1949), 91–94.

"A Bicentenary of the Enlightenment: Diderot in Prison, 1749." *Queen's Quarterly* LVI (1949–50), 522–33.

"Bicentenaire du Siècle des Lumières: Diderot en Prison 1749." Translated by Professor Bourdon, Lycée de Chaumont. *Les Cahiers Haut-Marnais* 1er Trimestre, No. 24 (1951), pp. 27–33.

"Une Partie inédite de la lettre de Diderot à Voltaire, le 11 juin 1749." *Revue d'Histoire Littéraire de la France* LI (1951), 257–60.

"An Unpublished Letter of Diderot, December 28, 1769." *Modern Language Notes* LXVII (1952), 439–43.

"The Great Issues Course at Dartmouth College: An Adventure in General Education." *Journal of Higher Education* XXV (1954), 229–38.

"Men of Letters and *Lettres de cachet* in the Administration of Cardinal Fleury." *American Historical Review* LX (1954–55), 55.

"Un Billet inédit de Diderot (1751)." *Revue d'Histoire Littéraire de la France* LV (1955), 56–57.

"The Age of the Enlightenment and the Contemporary World." A Review Article—*William and Mary Quarterly* XIV (1957), 89–97.

Diderot: The Testing Years, 1713–1759. New York: Oxford University Press, 1957, xii, 417 pp.

"Leningrad, 1957: Diderot and Voltaire Gleanings" *French Review* XXXI (1957–58), 351–63.

"The Enlightenment and Our World Today." A Wheaton College (Norton, Massachusetts) Lecture. May 1958.

"The Dowry of Diderot's Wife." *The French Review* XXXIII (1959–60), 286.

"Why Did the Political Theory of the Encyclopedists not Prevail? A Suggestion." *French Historical Studies* I (1960), 283–94.

"The Biographical Implications of Diderot's *Paradoxe sur le Comédien.*" *Diderot Studies* III (1961), 369–83.

"The Development and Scope of Diderot's Political Thought." *Studies on Voltaire and the Eighteenth Century* XXVII (1963), 1871–900.

"An Unpublished Letter of Diderot to Du Pont de Nemours (9 December 1775)." *Modern Language Review* LVIII (1963), 222–25.

"An Unpublished Letter from Diderot to Suard." *Studi Francesi* VIII (1964), 67–68.

"The Unpublished Portion of Grimm's Critique of *La Nouvelle Héloïse.*" *Modern Language Review* LIX (1964), 27–29.

"The Concept of *mœurs* in Diderot's Social and Political Thought." In *The Age of the Enlightenment: Studies Presented to Theodore Besterman,* pp. 188–99. Edinburgh: University of St. Andrews, 1967.

"The Philosophes in the Light of Present-day Theories of Modernization." *Studies on Voltaire and the Eighteenth Century* LVIII (1967), 1893–913.

With Mary T. Wilson. "Denis Diderot" (Nos. 4986–5362). In *A Critical Bibliography of French Literature,* Vol. IV, Supplement, *The Eighteenth Century,* edited by Richard A. Brooks, pp. 165–94. Syracuse, N.Y.: Syracuse University Press, 1968.

"Diderot en 1765–1766: Vie privée et bien public." Translated by Nelly Murstein. *Dix-huitième Siècle* III (1971), 297–316.

Diderot: Gli Anni Decisivi. Translated by Maria Lucioni. Milan: Feltrinelli, 1971, 427 pp.

Diderot. New York: Oxford University Press, 1972, xx, 918 pp.

CONTRIBUTORS

JOHN SLOAN DICKEY: President emeritus of Dartmouth College and Bicentennial Professor of Public Affairs

STEPHEN B. BAXTER: Professor of History, University of North Carolina

BLAKE T. HANNA: Linguistique et Langues Modernes, Université de Montreal, Montreal, Canada

ROLAND DESNÉ: Faculté des Lettres, Université de Reims, Reims, France

PETER GAY: Durfee Professor of History, Yale University

RICHARD KUHNS: Professor of Philosophy, Columbia University

JAMES L. CLIFFORD: William Peterfield Trent Professor of English emeritus, Columbia University

JACQUES PROUST: Faculté des Lettres et Sciences Humaines, Université de Montpellier, Montpellier, France

PAOLO CASINI: Istituto di Filosofia della Universita di Roma, Rome, Italy

ROLAND MORTIER: Faculté de Philosophie et Lettres, Université Libre de Bruxelles, Brussels, Belgium

ERNEST JOHN KNAPTON: Professor of History emeritus, Wheaton College

INDEX

Addison, Joseph, 48n
Albani, Alessandro, 145
Albemarle, earl of, 10
Alembert, Jean le Rond d', 79
Alexander the Great, 92
Ambrogi, P. A., 134, 136, 141, 143, 148, 151
Anet, Claude, 177
Anne (of England), 4, 5, 6, 8, 11
Archelaus, 125, 128
Archi, Bartolomeo, 147
Archimedes, 19
Archinto, Alberigo, 148
Ariosto, Ludovico, 102, 183
Aristippus, 125
Aristotle, 15, 123, 123n, 178
Arnaud, Baculard d', 155
Aron, Raymond, 71
Ashburnham, Lord, 167n
Asselin, Marguerite, 16
Augustus II (of Saxony), 145
Aulard, Alphonse, 176

Bagehot, Walter, 3, 11
Bailly, Jean Sylvain, 176
Barbeyrac, Jean, 123n
Baretti, Giuseppe, 99-109
Barnave, Antoine Pierre Joseph Marie, 176
Barrow, John, 172
Bayle, Pierre, 46, 52, 78, 83, 155
Beaumarchais, Pierre Augustin, Caron de, 155
Beaumont, Elie de, 113
Beccaria, Cesare Bonesana, Marchese di, 70

Bellessort, André, 48n
Benedict XIV (pope), 142n, 148, 151
Berkeley, George, 76, 77, 80
Bertrand, Louis, 157
Biagi, Guido, 167, 171, 184
Blackstone, Sir William, 113
Bodin, Jean, 3, 11
Boileau-Despréaux, Nicolas, 49
Bolingbroke, Henry St. John, Viscount, 52n
Bonaparte, Joseph, 172, 174, 176, 182
Bonaparte, Josephine, 179
Bonaparte, Lucien, 179
Bonno, G., 51, 54n
Bošković, Roger Joseph, 111, 112, 113
Bossuet, Jacques-Bénigne, 159
Boswell, James, 99, 100, 111, 114, 169
Bouchardon, Edme, 156
Boucher, François, 156
Boullée, Etienne Louis, 156, 160, 161, 162
Boyle, Sir Robert, 48
Brecht, Bertolt, 54
Brienne, Loménie de, 174
Broad, C. D., 75, 87
Bronson, Bertrand H., 162, 163
Broschi, Carlo (called Farinello), 149
Brucker, Johann Jakob, 120, 124, 126, 129
Brutus, Marcus Junius, 156, 175
Budgell, Eustace, 48n
Buffon, George Louis Leclerc, comte de, 183
Buonarroti, Filippo, 137, 140
Buondelmonti, abbé, 136
Burghley, William Cecil, baron, 11
Burke, Edmund, 100, 112
Bute, John Stuart, earl of, 10
Buttafuoco, Matteo, 176

Caire, Fernando, 108n
Calas, Jean, 68
Canolle, André-Joseph, 160n
Canova, Antonio, 156
Carbonnières, Ramond de, 155
Carlos of Bourbon, 135
Carmarthen, marquis of (Danby), 6
Carter, Jennifer, 6
Casanova, Giovanni Giacomo, 110, 111, 113
Catherine II (of Russia), 62, 69, 70
Cazamian, Louis, 159
Cerretesi, Giuseppe, 136
Chambers, Robert, 109, 113
Chamfort, Sébastien Roch Nicolas, 155
Charles I (of England) 5, 11
Charles II (of England) 4n, 5, 11
Charles VI (Emperor), 145
Charles Edward Stuart (The "Young Pretender"), 146
Chateaubriand, François René, vicomte de, 157
Châtelet, Madame du, 57
Chaumeix, Abraham-Joseph, 119, 128, 128n
Chénier, André Marie de, 155, 157, 161, 162
Chesterfield, Lord, 62, 140
Chiabrera, Gabriello, 149
Chubb, Thomas, 50n, 54n, 55
Chuquet, Arthur, 167, 169, 170, 182, 186
Cicero, 127n, 172
Cideville, de, 45n
Clark, Ruth, 47
Clemens XI (pope), 145
Clemens XII (pope), 135, 139, 148
Cocchi, Antonio, 133-138, 147-149
Collins, Anthony, 46, 49-52
Collison-Morley, Lacy, 108
Colman, George, 119
Colombier, Caroline du, 171
Colombier, madame du, 171
Compton, Sir William, 9
Condorcet, Marie Jean Antoine Nicolas de Caritat, marquis de, 155
Corneille, Pierre, 170
Cornelius, Nepos, 172
Corsi, Luca, 143n, 147, 149
Corsini, Neri, 135, 144
Cosimo III (of Tuscany), 134
Cotterell, Miss, 107
Coxe, William, 184

Crébillon, Prosper Jolyot de, 156
Croce, Benedetto, 149
Croker, Henry, 102-106
Cromwell, Oliver, 4, 5
Crudeli, Tommaso, 133-152

Dagoumer, Guillaume, 15
Dante Alighieri, 136
Dartmouth, Lord, 7
Daudé, 57
David, Jacques Louis, 156, 160, 162
Defoe, Daniel, 63, 64
Delille, abbé, 155, 157, 161
Demaizeaux, 57
Democritus, 125, 128
D'Éon, chevalier, 110
Descartes, René, 19, 37, 84, 85
Destouches, Philippe Néricault, 149
Devonshire, Lord 7
Diderot, Denis, 62, 63, 69, 70, 119-130, 149-162, 183
Diogenes, 122
Domairon, Louis, 170
Douglas, Dr., 111, 112
Du Bellay, Joachim, 158, 158n
Dupuy, père, 174
Duvernet, abbé, 183

Ehrman, John, 8
Elizabeth I (of England), 3
Engels, Friedrich, 61
Epicurus, 119
Eugene, Prince of Savoy, 145

Falkener, Everard, 46, 55
Fane, Charles, 146
Fesch, Joseph, 167n
Feugère, A., 174
Fisher, Kitty, 110
Flamsteed, John, 46
Fleury, André Hercule de, 54
Fleury, Joly de, 119
Fontenelle, Bernard Le Bovier de, 16, 52, 112
Formont, 44, 45
Forster, Robert, 63
Foscolo, Ugo, 159, 160
Francis, Grand Duke of Lorraine, 134, 135, 138, 140, 148
Franklin, Benjamin, 62, 70

Frederick II (of Prussia), 172
Frederick William I (of Prussia), 11

Gassendi, Pierre, 137, 150
Gay, Peter, 155n, 162
George I (of England), 4, 5, 8, 11
George II (of England), 3, 4, 4n, 106
George III (of England), 10, 11
George IV (of England), 5
Germanes, abbé, 173
Gian Gastone (of Tuscany), 134, 135
Gibbon, Edward, 62, 70
Girardin, Stanislas, 179
Goethe, Johann Wolfgang von, 171
Goldsmith, Oliver, 100
Greuze, Jean Baptiste, 156
Grimm, Friedrich Melchior von, 62
Grotius, Hugo, 127n

Hazen, Allen T., 107
Healey, F. G., 170, 179, 185
Heinsius, Antonie, 9, 10
Henry VII (of England), 7
Heraclitus, 120, 121, 121n
Hobbes, Thomas, 127n, 130
Holbach, baron d', 61, 70, 158
Holcke, comte de, 114
Homer, 45
Honour, Hugh, 162
Hopkins, Harry, 9
Horace, 119, 129
Houdon, Jean Antoine, 156
Houtteville, abbé, 46, 49
Huddesford, Dr., 109
Huggins, William, 102-107
Hume, David, 62, 69, 70, 75-95, 114
Husserl, Edmund, 85
Huygens, Christiaan, 37
Hyde, Mrs. Donald F., 102n

Ingres, Jean Auguste Dominique, 162

James I (of England), 4, 5, 11
James II (of England), 11
James III (the "Old Pretender"), 145, 146
Janelle, Pierre, 48n
Jefferson, Thomas, 62, 70
Jersey, Lord, 7
Johnson, Samuel, 62, 99-115
Jomini, Antoine Henri, 170

Jore, Claude-François, 45
Josselin, monsieur de, 171
Juvenal, 119

Kafka, Franz, 161
Kant, Immanuel, 62, 68, 69, 70, 86, 87
Kaufmann, Emil, 160n
Keill, John, 27, 37
Kennett, Basil, 48
King, William, 46
Knight, Cornelia, 112

Laclos, Choderlos de, 155
Lacroix, abbé Louis Antoine Nicolle de, 172, 180
Lafayette, marquis de, 176
La Fontaine, Jean de, 149
La Harpe, Jean-François de, 182
Lameth, Alexandre-Théodore-Victor, 176
Lanson, Gustave, 44, 46, 52n
Las Cases, Emmanuel, comte de, 168, 175n, 182
Laughton, Bennet, 99, 110
Lauri, Giovanni, 139
Ledoux, Claude Nicolas, 156, 161
Leeds, Duke of, (See Camarthen)
Leibniz, Gottfried Wilhelm von, 77, 126
Le Mounier, abbé, 119
Lennox, Charlotte, 101
Lequeu, 161
Lesser, Creuzé de, 157
Lessing, Gotthold Ephraim, 62, 69
Leszczynski, Stanislaus (Duke of Lorraine), 134
Letourneur, 155
Lévi-Strauss, Claude, 87
Lewis, L., 145, 146
Libri, Guillaume, 167n
Lichtenberg, Georg Christoph, 62
Lieutaud, 183
Livy, 172
Locke, John, 32, 49n, 50, 52, 54, 184
Louis XIV (of France), 155
Louis XV (of France), 156
Lucretius, 137, 150

Mably, Gabriel Bonnet de, 183
Machado and Pereira (firm), 5
Machiavelli, Niccolo, 150
Mahomet, 50

Malebranche, Nicolas de, 159
Mallet, P.-H., 157
Malone, Edmond, 108
Mandeville, Bernard, 55
Mann, Horace, 146, 146n, 148
Marchetti, Alessandro, 137
Maria Theresa (Hapsburg), 134
Marigny, abbé François Augier de, 172, 180
Markham, Felix, 169
Marlborough, Duke of, 47
Marmontel, Jean François, 183, 184
Martinelli, Vincenzio, 110
Martini zu Wasserberg, Karl Anton, Freiherr von, 70
Marx, Karl, 61, 130
Mary I (of England), 7
Masson, Frédéric, 167, 171, 178, 181, 184
Maty, Matthew, 110
Melon, Jean-François, 55, 56
Mercier, Louis-Sébastien, 155
Meslier, curé Jean, 53n
Metastasio, Pietro, 149
Methuen, John, 9, 10
Middlesex, earl of, 135
Milton, John, 159
Minerbetti, Andrea, 143, 144
Mirabeau, Honoré Gabriel Victor Riquetti, comte de, 176, 183
Montagu, Charles, 6
Montagu, Robert, 135
Montaigne, Michel Eyquem, seigneur de, 78, 172
Montesquieu, Charles Louis de Secondat, baron de, 150, 158, 172, 177, 178, 178n, 182, 183.
Moore, G. E., 64
Murphy, Arthur, 112

Napoleon, 167-186
Necker, Jacques, 174, 183
Newcastle, duke of, 146-148
Newton, Sir Isaac, 16, 32, 33, 37, 46, 47, 75-91, 93, 112, 160, 160n
Nicolai, Christoph Friedrich, 62
Nodier, Charles, 157
Nollet, abbé, 15-17
Notestein, Wallace, 4
Nottingham, Lord, 8

Ossian, 114, 157, 172

Paoli, Pasquale di, 101, 109, 169-176, 184
Parny, Evariste Désiré de Forge, 155
Pascal, Blaise, 43-57, 78, 159
Perier, Gilberte, 48
Pétion de Villeneuve, Jérôme, 176
Petrarch, 158
Petty, Sir William, 55
Pietro Leopoldo (of Tuscany), 152, 152n
Pigalle, Jean Baptiste, 156
Pindemonte, Cavaliere Ippolito, 159
Pitt, William (the Younger), 5
Plato, 172, 184
Plumb, J. H., 6
Plutarch, 162, 169, 172
Poggioli, Renato, 67
Polinière, Julien-Pierre, 16-38
Pomeau, René, 45n, 54, 57
Pope, Alexander, 159
Portland, Lord, 9, 10
Prichard, H. A., 75
Protagoras, 125
Psalmanazar, George, 100
Pufendorf, Samuel, Freiherr von, 127n, 130, 136
Pupiliani, Bernardino, 144

Racine, Jean Baptiste, 170
Raglan, Lord, 5
Raynal, abbé, 120, 172-185
Raynouard, François Just Marie, 157
Réaumur, René Antoine Ferchault de, 15
Reynolds, Sir Joshua, 100, 111, 112
Richardson, Samuel, 107
Richecourt, Emmanuel de, 134-151
Robert, Hubert, 158, 161
Robespierre, Maximilien, 176
Robinson, Sir Thomas, 105
Rochester, Lord, 6, 7, 11
Roederer, Pierre Louis, comte, 168, 179, 181
Rollin, Charles, 172
Ronquillo, Don Pedro, 8
Rosebery, Lord, 181
Rousseau, André, 52n
Rousseau, Jean-Jacques, 56, 62, 70, 127n, 155, 155n, 159, 161, 169, 173, 175-180, 183-185
Roustan, Antoine Jacques, 177, 178
Rucellai, Giulio, 134, 136n, 137, 140, 140n, 142

Sade, marquis de, 155
Sainte-Hyacinthe, Thémiseul de, 49n
Saint-Pierre, Bernardin de, 155, 173, 184
Sarpi, Paolo, 142, 142n
Schröder, E. 119
Seneca, 119, 162
Seznec, Jean, 119
Shackleton, Robert, 113ɪ
Shaftesbury, Lord, 46, 49, 52, 55
Shakespeare, William, 101, 114, 149, 157
Shrewsbury, Lord, 7, 10, 11
Sigorgne, Pierre, 16
Socrates, 121, 122, 125
Somers, Lord, 6, 9, 10
Sonnenfels, Joseph, Freiherr von, 70
Spinoza, Benedict, 83, 85
Staël, madame de, 157
Stoppani, 148
Stosch, Philip, baron von, 135n, 143-149
Sturz, Helfrich Peter, 113, 114
Sunderland, earl of, 10

Tacitus, 119, 172
Talleyrand, Charles Maurice de, 182, 185
Tanucci, Bernardo di, 137
Taton, René, 15
Terence, 119
Terrasson, abbé, 161
Thiériot, 44, 45
Tillotson, John, 9
Tindal, Matthew, 49n, 50
Toland, John, 49-52
Torrey, Norman, 50, 51
Tott, François, baron du, 172, 180
Tréogate, Loaisel de, 155
Trousson, René, 119

Van Tieghem, Paul, 155-158
Varignon, Pierre, 16
Vernon, 10
Verri, Alessandro, 70, 159
Vitrarius, 136
Voisenon, Claude-Henri de Fuzée, abbé de, 156
Volland, Sophie, 123
Volney, Constantin François de Chassebœuf, comte de, 155, 158, 176
Voltaire (François-Marie Arouet), 43-57, 62, 68-70, 156, 158, 159, 170, 181, 182, 184

Walker, Joseph, 48
Walpole, Horace, 3, 4n, 150
Walpole, Margaret, countess of Orford, 150, 151
Walpole, Sir Robert, 3, 54
"Walton, John," (See Stosch), 145, 146n, 147n
Warens, Madame de, 177
Warton, Joseph, 105
Warton, Thomas, 109
Washington, George, 5, 175
Weber, Max, 65
Whiston, William, 49n
Wieland, Christoph Martin, 70
William III (of England), 4-11
William IV (of England), 5
Wilson, Arthur M., 69n
Winckelmann, Johann Joachim, 156, 162
Wittgenstein, Ludwig, 91
Woolston, Thomas, 50
Wotton, William, 49n

Young, Edward, 158, 159